The Political Economy
of Science and Technology

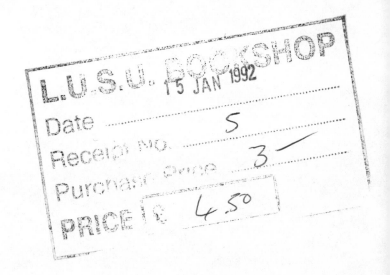

The Political Economy of Science and Technology

Norman Clark

Basil Blackwell

© Norman Clark, 1985

First published 1985

Basil Blackwell Ltd
108 Cowley Road, Oxford OX4 1JF, UK

Basil Blackwell Inc.
432 Park Avenue South, Suite 1505,
New York, NY 10016, USA

British Library Cataloguing in Publication Data

Clark, Norman
  The political economy of science and technology.
  1. Technological innovations—Economic aspects
  I. Title
  338'.06   HC79.T4

  ISBN 0-631-14293-2
  ISBN 0-631-14294-0 Pbk

Library of Congress Cataloging in Publication Data

Clark, Norman.
  The political economy of science and technology.

  Includes bibliographies and index.
  1. Technology and state. 2. Science and state.
  I. Title.
  T49.5.C53 1985   338.9'26   85-3874
  ISBN 0-631-14293-2
  ISBN 0-631-14294-0 (pbk.)

Typeset by Getset (BTS) Ltd, Eynsham, Oxford
Printed in Great Britain by The Camelot Press, Southampton

To my mother and father

Contents

List of Abbreviations

Advanced Gas-Cooled Reactor (AGR)

Agricultural Research Council (ARC)

Central Electricity Generating Board (CEGB)

Department of Education and Science (DES)

Department of Health and Social Security (DHSS)

Less Developed Country (LDC)

Medical Research Council (MRC)

Natural Environment Research Council (NERC)

Newly Industrialising Country (NIC)

Organisation of Petroleum Exporting Countries (OPEC)

Pressurised Water Reactor (PWR)

Science Research Council (SRC)

Social Science Research Council (SSRC)

Preface and acknowledgements

This book originated in a set of lectures given to the postgraduate students of the Science Policy Research Unit (SPRU) at the University of Sussex. For some time I, and colleagues, had been aware that there is a dearth of textbooks providing an introduction to the 'social studies of science', especially in the specific field of science, technology and public policy. What finally persuaded me to go ahead was a growing feeling that while economic analysis has a lot to offer in this context, the discipline itself has become ever more remote from the public gaze – on occasion reaching the level of an esoteric cult in which a narrow goal of mathematical rigour is pursued to the exclusion of reality and understanding, at least on the part of the uninitiated. Some redress was therefore called for.

Since the coverage is very broad, the book should be read as an introduction to a range of relevant literature, linked together by a number of broad themes which represent the ways I tend to view the subject. Each chapter is relatively self-contained and provides a short bibliography for those who wish to take its contents further. Since the science and technology policy literature has grown very rapidly indeed in recent years, there was some difficulty involved in the selection of suitable texts. In the end I settled for those I felt were most clearly written and which provided a point of entry, as it were, for the interested layperson. The list, however, is not by any means comprehensive.

Many people have helped me in the preparation of this text. I am particularly grateful to Christopher Freeman, who in addition to reading and commenting on an earlier draft, has been a constant source of encouragement and inspiration to all of us over the years, and to Charles Cooper who has also been in many ways a pioneer and who first suggested to me the format for the exposition of production theory presented in sections 4.3 and 4.4 of chapter 4. Martin Bell, Martin Fransman, Gordon Mackerron and Geoffrey Oldham provided valuable advice on an earlier draft. My thanks are due to them, as well as to the many other faculty and students at SPRU who kept me on the right lines at various stages.

Finally I am most grateful to Sally Marjoram who found time in the middle of running a busy teaching office to type and prepare the manuscript, to Steven Lowe who assisted in the preparation of the index, and to Brenda, Catriona and Zoë who tolerated my absence during many evenings.

Norman Clark
Science Policy Research Unit
University of Sussex

Chapter 1

SCIENCE AND TECHNOLOGY POLICY

1.1 Introduction

Systematic study in the 'social dimensions of science and technology' is unusually complex for two main reasons. *First*, the subject matter covered is highly heterogeneous, encompassing a wide range of interests from the Copernican revolution of the fifteenth and sixteenth centuries to problems of appropriate technology in developing countries in the 1980s. *Secondly*, those who have begun to concern themselves with this general area come from widely different disciplinary backgrounds, with differing appreciations of what constitutes legitimate scholarship, how problems may be defined and tackled, what is the most appropriate technical language for communicating ideas, and so on and so forth. The area is, therefore, essentially 'interdisciplinary' and from a pedagogic point of view at the very least, 'interdisciplinarity' is hard to handle. This book represents an attempt to achieve an element of coherence by focusing directly on problems of 'science and technology policy' and showing how economic analysis, broadly defined, can inform this discussion.[1]

Beginning with an overview of science policy as a legitimate field of interest, how it has arisen as such, how it may be defined and what its salient characteristics are, the book goes on to an historical discussion of the evolution of the modern economy. An account of pre-market forms of economic organisation, and the role of technology within them, precedes a discussion of the gradual transition to more complex forms of economic organisation in which technology and technical changes played a much more central role. Three features in particular will be emphasised. First, the fundamental importance of economic differentiation and functional specialisation are highlighted, particularly the evolution of capital goods production in the nineteenth century which provided the social context within which many important technical changes occurred. Secondly, emphasis will be placed on the unstable character of much of the 'new production' and it will be shown how technical progress lent an inherently dynamic character to economic systems. Finally, the changing relations between 'science' and 'production' are explored, with special attention paid to the evolution of institutionalised research and development (R & D) activities both inside and outside the productive sector.

The following two chapters are much more technical, unavoidably so since the use of economics to inform the analysis of science policy issues is often couched in terms of a range of concepts whose precise technical meaning is understood imperfectly, and sometimes unfortunately, not at all. However, a very important point to grasp is that the purpose of my treatment is to clarify the 'language' of economics. It should *not* be seen as a 'theoretical' account, at least not in any scientific sense. Chapter 3 provides a structural account of the modern 'macroeconomy'. The broad objective here is to provide a 'map' of a typical modern economy in terms of its constituent 'sectors' (including, for example, the 'government' and 'non-government' distinction) and to define the so-called 'science system' in relation to these. Chapter 4 concentrates upon the 'firm' as an economic unit which transforms resources into saleable commodities and services, using a 'technology' which is in some sense an 'embodiment' of scientific and other knowledge and which is therefore always liable to change in definable ways.

The fifth chapter is explicitly theoretical and is designed to set the stage for the subsequent discussion of direct policy issues. The starting point will be an exploration of the salient features of neo-classical economic analysis, contrasting this first with the older classical tradition and secondly with the Schumpetarian view of the nature of economic development. Schumpeter is fundamental, of course, *both* because his ideas placed technological changes in a central position (in contrast to neo-classical analysis which has always tended to regard technological changes as exogenous) *and* because many modern theoretical developments depend heavily upon his ideas. Indeed the book goes on in chapter 6 to describe the more important of these developments, particularly those associated with the 'product cycle', 'technological trajectories', theories of the firm which emphasise risk and uncertainty and theories of economic development which emphasise 'long waves' of economic activity. Finally, and again linked to Schumpeter in certain respects, there will be some discussion of the writings of Galbraith, particularly those associated with the 'bigness' of economic units and the rise of the modern corporation, but mention will also be made of his attack on the legitimacy of the micro/macro distinction in modern economic policy analysis. Both sets of ideas depend crucially on a certain (arguably deterministic) view of the nature of modern technology and of the social forms required to give it expression, but equally they are related to much of the earlier conceptual discussion.

Chapters 7 and 8 deal directly with science policy as it relates to the problems of less developed countries (LDCs). Chapter 7 sets the discussion in focus by surveying two broad conceptual traditions in development studies, 'modernisation' and 'structuralist', while chapter 8 surveys a range of 'issues' ranging from problems associated with the import of foreign technology to possibilities for science planning in poor countries. Finally, chapter 9 deals explicitly with selected areas which have some policy importance in the industrialised countries, including those concerned with institutional science, bureaucracy and the state; technological unemployment and related issues of social organisation; and the large-scale, complex nature of modern 'high technology' projects.

It should be noted that each of these topics/issues represents a field where much has been written. Inevitably, therefore, my coverage will be very much that of a summarised outline, and should be seen as providing a systematic introduction to further study. However, the discussion should also provide an indication that it is possible to be analytical about science policy questions and that much of the earlier theoretical discussion is relevant in this context.

1.2 The Genesis of Science and Technology Policy

Interest in science policy analysis is a comparatively recent phenomenon and one which has arisen from three separate but related forms of social demand, those emanating directly from the state, those related to scholarship and academic interest *and* those related to popular concerns over the pervasive (and often not beneficial) impact of science on the lives of ordinary people. The aim of this section is to present an outline of these with a view to providing an initial overview of the kinds of issues which typically arise.

1.2.1 The State

It is commonplace nowadays to argue that in some general sense technological changes have had a fundamental impact upon economic growth since the industrial revolution. However, the form this impact has taken and the social relationships involved are even now understood only very imperfectly. In particular, the influence of social expenditures upon science (through R & D, scientific institutions etc.) is problematic. There is no question but that there have been significant 'economic' breakthroughs as a result of systematic scientific research, but productivity advance has also occurred as a result of organisational changes, the migration of skilled manpower, induced changes, learning, luck and a variety of other social mechanisms and combinations of them.

Nevertheless, expenditures upon organised science have increased dramatically over the past 50 or so years and much of this has been funded by governments to be spent 'intramurally' through their own agencies/ministries etc. or 'extramurally' through private bodies, mainly industrial firms. Thus in 1978 the UK government, for example, planned to spend £3,510m on R & D, 61% through public bodies and 39% through industry.[2]

Clearly, such high and growing levels of expenditures have involved governments in a resource allocation problem. If massive sums of money are to be spent in 'harnessing science and technology to the national interest' then criteria are required which will permit the disposition of such sums on a rational, and it is to be hoped socially optimal, basis. Typical policy questions are:

— How far should governments fund industrial R & D?
— What mechanisms should they adopt to this end (e.g. direct subsidy, tax relief, provision of special facilities, public purchase)?
— What industrial sectors should be given priority?
— What areas of basic science research should be funded by governments, in what proportions and through which institutions?
— How should higher education and science policy be co-ordinated?
— How should spending ministries fund intramural research (i.e. through their own 'in-house' laboratories)?

These (and other) enormously complex policy questions may be grouped into three categories:

A.   Questions of resource allocation *per se* within and between categories of scientific expenditure (e.g. how much should nuclear physics be given in relation to radio astronomy?) however defined. Policy questions of this kind are intimately connected with more general policy imperatives concerning defence, nuclear energy, civilian efforts on the part of the state. Thus in the early post-war years R & D efforts in EEC countries went primarily into nuclear, space and aviation research rather than into industry or overseas development, thus reflecting more general government policy priorities. More recently there has been a shift to more direct 'economic' R & D particularly in view of problems of energy shortages and also as a result of growing competitive pressures from some developing countries (the so-called 'newly industrialising countries' or NICs), although the UK in particular continues to spend a very high proportion of public R & D funds on defence-related activities (55% in 1981/82, amounting to £1,726m out of a total of £3,316m).[3]

B.   A second category of questions concerns the growing science and technology content of the ordinary functions of government. We shall see in chapter 3 the precise extent to which modern governments provide goods and services to the public, funded by taxes and other sources of public revenue. Much of this provision represents a 'productive act' and hence requires the services of modern technology if it is to be done efficiently, but even where it does not (e.g. in the making of policy for intervention in the private sector) there is still a need for appropriate technical advice. In the UK, 'spending ministries' make use of their own government R & D establishments to fulfil this type of need and, naturally enough, there are all manner of concomitant policy questions about what kind of role such bodies should play, how they should allocate their resources, and so on.

C.   Finally, there are questions concerned with the 'administration' or 'government' of science, since evidently there is a need to explore the most suitable mechanisms for taking advice, for taking decisions and for monitoring the disbursements of funds. Indeed within the context of the UK there has been continuous debate on these matters since the second world war. One famous example is that of the 'customer–contractor' principle which was advocated by the Rothschild Report in the early 1970s and which raised all sorts of interesting science policy questions.[4] Basically the 'customer–contractor' principle was intended as a means of establishing a kind of 'market' for science and technology expenditures through which the 'customer', a government spending department, would identify research needs arising, or likely to arise, from its normal activities and request the 'contractor' (which would often be one of its own laboratories, but not necessarily so) to carry out the relevant research. The reform arose largely out of a feeling that the large and growing state science and technology infrastructure was tending to pursue autonomous research activities which tended not to be congruent with its formal responsibilities and hence represented a form of social inefficiency. The hope was that by establishing a form of 'market mechanism', government laboratories would be 'disciplined' into social relevance; or at least things would be moved in that direction.

Quite clearly the Rothschild reforms, and the type of thinking that underlay them, raise all sorts of interesting questions about the 'economic' content of science policy decisions. In particular they show how such decisions are 'economic' in the sense that they are usually concerned with questions of resource allocation under conditions of scarcity. These are important questions since the decision to allocate £X to function A_1 means that this £X will no longer be available to support functions $A_2 \ldots A_n$; i.e. function A_1 has an 'opportunity cost', namely that of *not* supporting other possible functions or projects.

One way of viewing things is to argue that the committal of resources to science and technology projects represents a form of social investment in the sense of 'adding to the available stock of capital' and as such, at least in principle, it can be handled analytically in much the same way as any other form of investment appraisal i.e. as a problem in constrained optimisation. Thus we may define science and technology policy as being concerned with making optimal decisions with regard to the allocation and mobilisation of resources devoted to science and technology. 'Optimality' may be defined in terms of the conventional socio-economic calculus and therefore in terms of spreading investible resources so as to maximise net social gains to the community. At the bottom *that* is the decision problem and correspondingly one may categorise a basic function of science policy research as that of unravelling the complexities of any given allocation problem so that the final 'decision' is as fully informed as possible.

What then are the chief factors which make the 'scientific' investment decision a particularly complex one? In the *first* place the estimation of costs and benefits is not easy since it involves the calculation of resource flows and prices well into the future (investment in science is often a long-term activity). Of course similar problems are faced with all planning activities. The decision to construct a steel plant according to a given set of specifications is also a long-term one and assumptions have to be made about future levels of market demands, materials inputs, prices and so on. What gives particular complexity to the scientific investment decision is a *second* factor, namely the uncertainty which attaches to research as an activity.

This is so even by definition especially as one moves away from the 'development' end of the research spectrum and into the realms of basic research. Most applied research projects cannot be assessed accurately in terms of their costs and likely future outcomes. And even if they could there would still remain the problem of placing a valuation on research outcomes which have yet to be realised in commercial terms. Put another way, the uncertainty is a double-edged one consisting first of *technological* uncertainty and secondly of *commercial* uncertainty. I shall try to describe how these problems might be handled in chapter 3.

A *third* problem is that in public scientific activity (and indeed in most research activity) it is not easy to separate ends and means in a clear and rigorous way. Thus in contrast to our steel plant, there is a necessary and continuous interchange between the 'outputs' (the results of any experiment or set of experiments) and 'inputs' (the design and execution of subsequent work). Very often the research process throws up new and unexpected results which open up new commercial possibilities and alter (sometimes radically) the nature of the initial problem. A related point is that the nature of much publicly financed activity is such that there are a number of possible steps before the ultimate services are provided, each decision point being amenable to various types/forms of research activity. Hence one of the problems of a Rothschild-like arrangement is that the 'contractor' often has to recommend to the 'customer' what kind of research ought to be done, or at the very least needs to be associated closely with the final policy decision. Clearly it may be seen that the pressures to scientific autonomy are still there and indeed one of the chief criticisms of the customer–contractor principle is that it has not changed the research/production interface that much, merely adding layers of bureaucracy to older, more autonomous arrangements.

A final problem is that many goals of contemporary science and technology are not directly concerned with economic output and to that extent (unlike our steel plant) investment in science and technology cannot be fitted into a conventional project appraisal analysis. For example, the allocation of research resources to defence, health or educational goals cannot be judged in productivity terms except in the rather narrow sense that these are given comparative value weights by some political authority.

For each of the above reasons (and others) the setting of science and technology policy questions as 'economic' problems pure and simple is to oversimplify such questions dramatically. Nevertheless, although the analytical tools that economics can provide help only to a limited extent, the decision problems still remain and I hope to show later that much of the theoretical and conceptual discussion which underlies science and technology policy analysis has an important 'economic' content on a variety of different levels.

1.2.2 Academic Interest

What I have tried to show above is that an important set of social demands for science and technology policy analysis has originated from the 'practical' needs of the state. A second set of interests can be categorised as that arising from the conceptual side – mainly the academic community which has tried over the last 20 or so years to give conceptual clarity to the impact of science on society in a rather different sense than was previously the case.

Traditionally the study 'of science' as a social/intellectual activity was very much dominated by history and philosophy and treated as sub-sets of these disciplines. Thus the history of science described the evolution of science as an intellectual activity through chronicling in detail its various discoveries and achievements, by describing the lives of famous scientists and by charting its professionalisation in terms of the evolution of its important institutions. Debates there were, as for example that between the 'internalists' and the 'externalists',[5] but overall the treatment was disciplinary and specialised and there was no important sense in which such 'academic' discussion was expected to inform questions of national *policy* towards science.

Similarly with the philosophy of science which moved from its original concern with the nature of matter (the study of natural philosophy) into more specialised concerns about the nature of scientific propositions and the rules governing their validity and acceptability – including those relating to experimental evidence. Again there was no (and still is not any) significant sense in which philosophers of science were expected to pronounce on science policy questions. Conversely, such questions were decided by direct recourse to the scientific community through its representative institutions (such as the Royal Society) or through its centres of professional activity (the universities, for example).

A number of developments were to change this state of affairs. First, as we have seen, the growing costs of science expenditures (including those on 'big science') and the resultant need for a more explicit 'science policy' on the part of government organs spilled over on to the academic community which found itself increasingly being asked to give advice on all sorts of policy issues, advice which, coming from 'specialists', could not in the nature of things be disinterested. Secondly, however, there occurred a number of intellectual developments which gave a significant impetus to the validity of treating the study 'of science' in an interdisciplinary way.

Very important amongst these was the publication of Thomas Kuhn's *The Structure of Scientific Revolutions* in 1962.[6] In this historical and empirical account of the development of science Kuhn confronted the 'profession' with a detailed critique of some widely held, if often rather implicit, views on the nature and progress of scientific knowledge. More specifically he argued that science as socio-intellectual process was not nearly as *rational* as its practitioners had made it out to be, and at times approximated to religion and politics in its overt characteristics. Thus Kuhn demonstrated that scientific research and development was not in practice an ever-increasing discovery of the 'truth' about nature through the progressive use of experiment and logical reason. Rather it was revolutionary and cyclical in character with long periods in which certain scientific traditions became established and were maintained often in the face of evidence which appeared to contradict their theoretical foundations. The famous Kuhn–Popper debate[7] was one in which Kuhn argued that scientists did not behave in ways that Popper felt they *ought* to (so as to maintain standards of good science) but in fact functioned as social groups often do, subject to fashion, political intrigue and other less then cerebral factors. Indeed at times Kuhn got close to maintaining that the *actual* development of science was, and is, as much a function of the sociology of the scientific community as it was of the experimental method. Certainly it did not obey simple rules of logic, whatever the philosophers might say.

Kuhn's work sparked off a spate of research into science as it is actually conducted, how it is professionalised and how the institutional behaviour of scientists influences matters of public policy. Since the scientific community could no longer be regarded as a homogeneous source of disinterested expertise, it was important to assess how it actually behaved if only so as to determine how far and to what extent the advice of its practitioners could be accepted. From our standpoint the important feature of a lot of this work is that it is interdisciplinary and policy-oriented in a sense that most of the earlier research never reached. This academic interest served to make science policy analysis respectable.

A second 'academic' development was that economists rediscovered 'technological change' and the act of doing so had certain significant repercussions. It is important to recognise that for nigh on 100 years the economics 'profession' has treated technology as a datum to its analytical procedures, although prior to this many of the 'classical economists' (Smith, Ricardo and Marx for example) took technological changes very seriously indeed. However, from around 1870 onwards economists became concerned mainly with questions about how scarce resources were allocated in the *short run* (i.e. when the stock of capital was invariant) and in the *long run* (i.e. when the stock of capital was allowed to vary in certain ways). Thus, in the main economists were interested in questions such as how markets behaved and how they could be classified, what determined the prices of resources and how prices related to economic efficiency, how income was distributed, how money (and monetary institutions) functioned, what determined foreign trade patterns and so on. The concerns were functionalist and analytical within well-prescribed boundaries. In so far as governments and government policy were included, prescription has always tended to concentrate upon a small range of monetary and fiscal instruments.

One very important canon of economic analysis has been that of 'comparative statics', namely that of comparing two 'states' of the particular system under investigation with a number of potentially relevant variables held constant and with one 'independent' entity allowed to vary. Often the two 'states' are held to represent 'social equilibria' which are stable in themselves, so that movement from one equilibrium to another is brought about by the shift of the independent variable. Many well-known economic propositions (such as those relating to the market price of a commodity under varying conditions of supply and demand) are built up using this sort of technique and indeed the method has a great deal of value as an analytical device i.e. in clarifying thought in a very complex area of enquiry.

However, there are certain things economic analysis does not do very well and one of these is to shed much light on the process of economic growth. The major reason for this is that it is designed to deal with a very small range of variables at discrete time intervals under restrictive assumptions about social behaviour *and* (most importantly) technical conditions. Indeed one major drawback of economic analysis is that it often has weak empirical power i.e. in the sense of producing non-trivial propositions which can be tested and thereby enrich our knowledge of the economic environment.

In the case of economic growth much of the earlier interest centred around charting how economic systems would grow through time in terms of their important sub-aggregates (consumption, investment, incomes, foreign trade etc.) and under restrictive conditions regarding technology (labour-saving, capital-saving, neutral). But such analyses told us little or nothing about the *causes* of growth. Nor were they intended to. As far as most economists were concerned growth simply took place and if it was determined by anything it was by the rate of investment i.e. by the rate of addition to the stock of capital within the economic system under consideration. Conveniently enough this made it possible for economists to treat technical conditions as *exogenous* − that is as a variable *not* determined by the system under study − and, by extension, something that need not concern professional economists.

This tradition was placed in question by a remarkable study carried out by Robert Solow in 1956.[8] Using conventional 'comparative static' techniques, Solow attempted to provide a statistical explanation of the causes of US manufacturing growth over the period 1911−56. He concluded that only 12.5% of the observed growth of labour productivity (output per worker) over this period could be 'explained' by increments in the stock of capital, the remaining 87.5% being a 'residual' or an unexplained 'technological change' or 'improvement in productivity'. What was significant about this study was that a major economic magnitude (the rate of growth) could not apparently be explained by the established economic variable. It was not so much the rate of investment that was important but rather the *productivity* of investment − and that remained unexplained.

Again, as with Kuhn's study, there followed a spate of investigations designed to test Solow's results, to specify the composition of the residual and to explore more specifically the factors affecting technological changes within the firm and the industry. Again much of this work has proved to be interdisciplinary and policy-oriented and although a great deal has been done we are still far from having a full understanding of this complex social process. It is the purpose of this book to go some way towards systematising what has been done and elaborating upon some of the consequent conceptual and policy issues.

1.2.3 More General Concerns

In addition, finally, to the state and academia it may be useful to categorise one other expression of social demand − that of popular concerns over the 'disbenefits' of modern science and technology, some of which have become more general political issues. Thus, for example, concerns over environmental pollution have concentrated around issues such as the control of automobile emissions. Similarly with the growing use, and abuse, of drugs in modern medicine, the apparent lack of popular control of major (and apparently irreversible) national project decisions such as those in power generation, *or* the seeming connection between modern technological changes and prospects for adult employment and income distribution.

Of course this 'Faustian' tension is not a new one. Bertrand Russell, writing in 1952,[9] noted that one very important consequence of 'modern science' and its 'impact on society' was the seemingly natural way that the conduct of science as a social endeavour becomes aligned to large-scale organisation, since only this way will the necessary co-ordinated mobilisation of resources on a sufficient scale take place. Similar views have been expressed by Schumpeter and Galbraith who have argued as we shall see, that the social exploitation of modern science and technology requires 'bigness' especially on the part of economic units. More recently Collingridge has explored the apparent irreversibility of many large-scale projects.[10]

We shall explore such analyses (and others) and related policy questions in chapter 9 but it may be worth noting that modern science and technology may have contributed substantially to social welfare but at the social cost of alienating the ordinary member of the public even further from a direct understanding of, and control over, the social forces of production. Since no one group is now able to comprehend the totality of modern production there may be a tendency to leave decision-making to 'experts' in conjunction with a bureaucratic machine which itself is only vaguely aware of the implications of its actions and which tends, often for the sake of convenience or ease of administration, to hide behind given policy paradigms. Paradoxically, therefore, while at a social level technological changes require a constantly radical approach, they bring with them the seeds of a rather pernicious authoritarianism with, in some cases, unfortunate consequences.

1.3 Policy Analysis

Up to this point I have tried to 'define' science and technology policy in terms of a notional set of institutional and popular 'demands'. I shall present later in the book a number of examples of the kinds of 'issues' which have contemporary policy relevance and the kinds of associated conceptual discussions which are often undertaken as part of the process of unravelling their complexities. However, at this stage it is necessary to delve a little bit into epistomology, and hence to clarify what exactly I mean by 'science policy analysis', how 'scientific' it is, what characteristics it has and to what extent empirical 'research' can inform such analysis. The main reason for exploring these points is that there is often doubt in students' minds on the precise standing of this sort of work and how it relates to policy-making. Although there is no clear cut view on such questions, it is possible to set them in perspective and in particular to 'lay a few ghosts' about the role of economic analysis.

1.3.1 Science Policy as Social Policy

To begin with I shall define science and technology policy analysis as being concerned with how and why social units commit scarce resources to science and technology, what sorts of problems arise in so doing and what sorts of improvements might be made.[11] Defined in this way it should be clear that the subject ultimately is concerned with *social* choices and the *social* context within which these choices have to be made. I emphasise this since it is sometimes suggested that the solutions to science policy questions are 'obvious' *or* that they can be decided by 'great men' (often senior scientists/ engineers who have made reputations within their own disciplines). What I hope this book will show is that such solutions are not all obvious and will almost always require interdisciplinary expertise for their articulation − and usually this will involve inputs from both the natural and the social sciences. Similarly whatever may be the potential contributions of senior scientists (and these are many) such people are often not trained to handle difficult questions of social choice. Indeed one of the problems that natural scientists often face is that they do not fully understand how the social sciences work.

One of the best places to start is with Brian Easlea's interesting discussion on the 'objectivity' of the social sciences.[12] Easlea argued that there was an essential distinction to be made between the natural and the social sciences in the sense that the latter could only be regarded as analogous to the 'applied' natural sciences and hence that the normal distinction between 'pure' and 'applied' work was not valid in such a context. He made the point in the following way. Natural scientists proceed by identifying relationships between states of nature, conceptualising these with reference to a body of accepted 'theoretical' knowledge and testing them using the experimental method. Thus they know that under specified contextual conditions the state, say T_1, will change to state, T_2, since that is what nature has shown to be true, or at least not yet false. If state T_2 is undesirable compared to another state, say T_2^1, then either the initial state T_1 *or* the contextual conditions must be altered in an appropriate way. To show how this can be done in specific instances is the function of the applied scientist or engineer.

Now the contrast with social science is interesting in the sense that there are no (or at least very few) non-trivial cases where we can say with confidence that given any state S_1 nature will lead automatically to state S_2. Conversely social scientists are *applied* in the sense in which natural scientists would normally use the term i.e. they identify social problems and recommend how things might be altered so as to deal with them. This activity is called policy analysis but it does not relate to 'theory' in any way that natural scientists would understand. Moreover, the altering of 'states of nature' (our S_1) is not something that policy analysts are allowed to get involved with since these are usually political decisions and therefore, by definition, come within the jurisdiction of different people and institutions.

The essence, then, of social science and by extension science policy research is that it is a diagnostic exercise. The trained social scientist is someone who has built up a certain understanding of a given part of the 'social universe', who identifies problems which he believes to be important (or who is commissioned to analyse problems that his sponsors regard to be important), who then tries to analyse the various social forces which have interacted to bring about these problems and to identify the major causal factors. He will then use the analysis to prescribe possible remedial policies and to suggest what the implications of these might be. However, since the world is a very complex place and since he will not in any case be responsible for policy execution, the social scientist ought not in general to be too categoric about the 'advice' given and should if possible anticipate the consequences of certain courses of policy action.

What then does this sort of activity imply? Clearly an important implication is that there is *no direct recourse to any unified 'theory'* which will instruct the analyst as to how to proceed. This is partly because of the inherent nature of social policy analysis as described above, but it is also due to the fact that most social problems are by definition *interdisciplinary*, and those that concern science and technology policy are very definitely so. Thus their analysis requires some elements of sociological understanding because, for example, it is necessary to understand certain features of the behaviour of the scientific community. They require similar expertise in political science because there are important power/institutional dimensions to science/technology policy decisions. Similarly, as we have seen, with economics. More often than not some detailed natural science or engineering knowledge is required because there is a need to know about the scientific activity in question or the nature of the productive activity under investigation. There is little point, for example, in studying the impact of the microprocessor if one is not willing to learn about what the device is, what forms it takes and how it is used as a building block in more complex systems.

The analyst is forced into drawing from a wide range of concepts and postulated relationships and herein, of course, lies a major difficulty since academic work is traditionally structured along disciplinary lines. Things have developed this way because it has proved the most efficient (in an 'academic' sense) method of extending the boundaries of knowledge (the research function) and to communicate a coherent body of ideas to students (the teaching function). The 'discipline' then determines the way that scholars think, the problems they regard as important, the 'language' with which they communicate, the research techniques they adopt and, ultimately, the criteria they use to judge the performance of their peers and to determine the 'ex ante' acceptability of research projects. These features then become enshrined in more general bureaucratic forms including budgetary procedures, levels of decision-making within academic institutions and grant-awarding bodies, and career structures for staff. Hence knowledge 'about the world' is pursued and diffused in ways which are not in *general* consonant with practical problems faced by people and institutions who have to make decisions on matters of public policy or, indeed, people who are concerned with economic production. In a very general sense, therefore, there is a problem of 'academic alienation' and the science policy analyst is often faced with the difficulty of having to know enough about the different disciplines so as to be able to use them in the evaluation of a given issue.

Aside from difficulties of a theoretical *or* an interdisciplinary kind, there are often severe problems with regard to the acquisition, processing and interpretation of data. Evidence is important, of course, simply because one needs it to substantiate (or not) the validity of the propositions one makes about the issue under investigation. One cannot say much, for example, about the structure of UK R & D without a good deal of information about how much has been spent upon it, who has spent it, how the money has been allocated through time, across industrial sectors, and so on. However, even if there is apparently available evidence, it still has to be handled with great care for a number of reasons.

First, there may be inaccuracies in the raw data themselves due to poor data collection procedures and the analyst needs therefore to reassure himself about his basic material. *Secondly*, there is almost always a lack of congruence between the raw data and what one wishes to use them for. For example, one well-known aspect of R & D statistics is that they are often not a good indicator of 'innovative activity' since firms often report under this heading routine engineering activities which cannot be classified as innovative. Hence if one requires a true measure of innovative activity one may have to reprocess the original information or supplement it in some way. Another well-known example of this relates to the use of national income measures to compare relative standards of living amongst countries.

Thirdly, there will be difficulties in how information is to be used. One does not collect data simply for the sake of it (those who do are sometimes accused of 'casual empiricism') but because there is need to establish some sort of relationship between variables that are significant for the purpose in hand. Usually this will mean that the evidence will need to be 'processed' in some way, often using established statistical techniques such as correlation/ regression analysis. Again there are all sorts of pitfalls in this area that require care.

Fourthly, there is a set of difficulties concerned with the *interpretation* of data. One way of looking at this is by viewing social analysis as taking place on a variety of different 'levels' of increasing generality. The higher the analytical level the more it approaches the policy question at issue but, paradoxically, the further it moves from its susceptibility to empirical research. Thus the debate between 'monetarist' and 'Keynesian' interpretations of macroeconomic instability is a very important one but is not apparently susceptible to empirical research (or at least its proponents do not seem to hold their positions because of empirical factors). Conversely it is usually possible to establish an empirical relationship between a small number of variables under given defined conditions, but this information may be only of marginal importance for wider policy questions.

A *fifth* set of problems concerns *prescription* since even if one can establish a set of propositions which relate to the issue under consideration, the jump from what *has happened* in the past to what *will happen* in the future (given any set of policy prescriptions) is a considerable one. And this is so for very obvious reasons. Contextual conditions change. Policy instruments may prove to be imperfect mechanisms for getting the desired policies to work in the intended way. Policies may have untoward side-effects which vitiate the intended results *or* which are undesirable in themselves *or* whose consequences require further policy measures, and so on. There is an infinite regress of things that can go wrong and the policy analyst (and maker) is always working in an imperfect environment. Indeed nothing could be further removed from the safe, well-articulated world of natural science where there is (relatively speaking) constant and productive dialogue between 'theory' and 'experiment'.

Finally, there is the fundamental, but inescapable, problem that social analysts have, like all human beings, their own values, prejudices and belief systems which they will bring to bear on the question in hand and which will introduce an element of subjectivity into their work. How great this element is will be a function of their capacity to abstract from any entrenched position which they might hold and/or their readiness to concede that such a position might be mistaken in the face of evidence. Notice that this is a much more debilitating problem in the social sciences than it is in the natural sciences since the complexity of the social order and the relative lack of recourse to the experimental method make it much easier to 're-interpret' the evidence in ways that are ideologically acceptable than is the case with research in the natural sciences. However, the more analysts do this the poorer the quality of their work and students especially should be aware of pitfalls of this kind.

It should now be clear that social policy analysis in general, and therefore science policy analysis in particular, is as much an 'art' as a 'science'. The practitioner must be prepared to be problem-focused and to accept the lack of direct theoretical guidance, to accept also the need to be interdisciplinary in approach, to have recourse to empirical evidence but to use it with great care, to be prescriptive but not categorically so and to try where possible to abstract from value positions when making judgements. These are very hard skills to develop but I hope later to show, using particular policy issues as 'cases', that it is possible to tackle science policy in a sensible and ordered way so as to promote at least chinks of light in what might otherwise be chaotic darkness.

1.4 The Role of Economic Analysis

What then can we say about the usefulness of economic analysis in this field? You will recall that one reason we have to pay attention to economic questions is because of the resource allocation implications of science policy questions. A second, and connected reason relates to concept formation. For purposes of analytical clarity it is essential to have an unambiguous grasp of the many social/institutional categories which are used in discussions of techno-economic changes and the role of science in these. Concepts such as 'Gross National Product' (GNP), 'unemployment', the 'capital goods sector', 'capital intensity', 'productivity' etc. abound in the literature and are widely used in both theoretical and empirical discussions. To the extent that their use is ambiguous the 'tightness' of both analysis and prescription is likely to be compromised.

Unfortunately, it is not feasible in a text book of this scope to provide a complete glossary of terms and how they are used. What I shall do in chapters 3 and 4 is to provide an account of two conventional 'types' of economic system and the categories and relations that are comprised within them. These are *first* − the 'macroeconomy' defined in terms of a simple social accounting framework and *secondly* − the conventional production function analysis which relates to the firm as a productive unit employing resources with a given technology and transforming these resources into saleable 'output' of goods and services.

The purpose of these treatments is mainly definitional although a number of analytical relationships will also be described. However, I should at this stage emphasise a number of points of reassurance to students who come from a disciplinary background in the natural sciences or the humanities and who sometimes misunderstand the nature and purpose of this sort of discussion. In particular, it is essential to grasp that the method of exposition is very much that of telling a 'story' or a 'fable' in which analysts 'abstract from reality' in a number of important respects. Thus they will confine their analysis to a very small number of social variables and explore the likely relationships between these variables *holding everything else constant*. Once they have explored the logic of their position in terms of what they know about 'human and technical conditions' they will then be in a position to 'relax assumptions', starting with the strongest and so on down the line of reality.

Empirical testing of the resulting propositions is a major problem since the more you relax the assumptions the less amenable to statistical analysis many propositions are, mainly because they tend to become much more ambiguous. Conversely strong statements may not be testable simply because the assumptions made are unrealistic. The result is the well-known hiatus between conceptual work in economics (often heavily mathematical, relatively obscure and with little empirical value) and empirical work using relatively simple techniques to assess crude relationships — two 'styles' of activity which do not reinforce each other symbiotically in ways common to the natural sciences. In fact it is probably best to regard economic analysis not so much as a branch of 'science' (to which it does not conform closely) but rather as a branch of 'philosophy' where the use of simple logical procedures can serve to highlight the important relationships involved. If you like, the economic analysis represents a series of intellectual 'pegs' on which to hang some sort of ordered appreciation of a very complex environment, but it is only ever a tool, to be used with great care along with many others.

Looked at in this light, economic analysis can be quite useful. Indeed, as we have said and as will be seen, it is essential in so far as much of the related theoretical literature on science and technology policy rests upon it and depends upon it in a number of respects. For example, it is difficult to discuss the influence of technological changes on employment without tracing through some of the 'compensating' price and income effects of any given change on the economic system as a whole. Similarly much of the recent literature on innovation can only be fully understood within the context of the behaviour of firms in competitive relationships with other firms. Unfortunately, to say this is only to scratch the surface of social relations which are still only very imperfectly understood, not least because their evaluation requires also the complementary skills of other disciplines. How to weld these together productively is a problem of a different order altogether.

1.5 Some Concluding Remarks

Let me recap finally on the points that I have been making by way of introduction.

1   Science and technology policy analysis is a 'new' academic area, relatively speaking. It may be defined very broadly in terms of how and why social units commit resources to science and technology, what sorts of problems arise in so doing and what sorts of improvements might be made.

2   Much of the reason for its development depends upon demands on the part of the state for 'expert assistance' in the making and monitoring of

policy, although two other relevant factors are the evolution of inter-disciplinary academic interest and more general popular concerns.

3   Science and technology policy should be regarded as a form of social policy and therefore its analysis is akin to that of the social sciences rather than to that of the natural sciences.

4   This means that analysis is problem-focused and interdisciplinary in the sense that no one academic discipline by itself can provide the necessary conceptual background. In particular, the examination of any issue will often require complementary input from the natural sciences.

5   The gathering, processing and interpretation of empirical evidence is an essential part of science and technology policy analysis. However, satisfactory handling of empirical evidence is a subtle and difficult task involving an appreciation of the strengths and weaknesses of data in any given context as well as the ability on the part of the analyst to abstract from value positions.

6   The role of economic analysis is central to much of science and technology policy analysis partly because at bottom the issues involve the allocation of scarce resources, partly because much relevant theoretical discussion uses economic conceptualisation and partly because the analytic technique, if correctly employed, provides a useful method of sorting out the complexities of any given set of issues.

7   In this context, however, it is probably best to regard 'economics' as a branch of philosophy rather than as akin to the natural sciences. Also economics should not be regarded as the only relevant discipline in the analysis of any given issue.

Bibliography

Probably the most important general text is still that of C. Freeman, *The Economics of Industrial Innovation*. The edition that I shall refer to is the Penguin edition (1974), although Frances Pinter (1982) has now brought out a considerably revised and updated second edition. A summary sketch of related issues is provided by K. Pavitt and M. Worboys, *Science, Technology and the Modern Industrial State* (London, Butterworth, SISCON, 1977) which contains also a useful annotated bibliography.

On the social studies of science more generally, see I. Spiegel-Rösing and D. Price (eds), *Science, Technology and Society* (London, Sage, 1977) which contains a wide range of papers and also deals with issues covering different country experience.

A very useful text on British science policy is P. Gummett, *Scientists in Whitehall* (Manchester, Manchester University Press, 1980), while a number of current British issues are reviewed in R. Williams, 'British Technology Policy', *Government and Opposition*, Winter 1983/84, pp. 30–51. On public policy more generally, see R. Nelson, *The Moon and the Ghetto: An Essay on Public Policy Analysis* (New York, W. W. Norton, 1977).

Useful collections of articles on innovation and industrial policy are contained in K. Pavitt (ed.), *Technical Innovation and British Economic Performance* (London, Macmillan, 1980) and C. Carter (ed.), *Industrial Policy and Innovation* (London, Heinemann, 1981). Finally two very important collections of his papers on economics and technology are N. Rosenberg, *Perspectives on Technology* (Cambridge, Cambridge University Press, 1976), *Inside the Black Box: Technology and Economics* (Cambridge, Cambridge University Press, 1982).

Notes

1 Hence science and technology policy issues, their definition and analysis, should be regarded as a subset of a wider range of intellectual concerns. For simplicity I shall use the term 'science policy' as a shorthand for 'science *and* technology policy' except in cases where this is clearly inappropriate. One further point should be stressed. Throughout the text there is a strong emphasis on *public* policy with respect to science and technology. This should not be taken to mean that there are not important science policy issues faced also by the corporate sector, nor that much of my discussion is irrelevant outside government. However, for purposes of exposition it was easier to write the text from a public policy point of view.

2 See, for example, Williams, 'British Technology Policy'.

3 House of Lords Select Committee on Science and Technology, *Engineering Research and Development* (London, HMSO, 22 February 1983, Vol. I), p. 23.

4 For a discussion on the Rothschild experiment see Gummett, *Scientists in Whitehall* chapters V and VI. The original source is Lord Rothschild, 'The Organisation and Management of Government R & D', in *A Framework for Government Research and Development*, (London, HMSO, Cmnd. 4814, 1971).

5 See R. MacLeod, 'Changing Perspectives in the Social History of Science', in *Science, Technology and Society*, Spiegel-Rösing and Price pp. 149–95.

6 T. S. Kuhn, *The Structure of Scientific Revolutions* (London, Chicago University Press, 1970, 2nd edn).

7 Discussed for example in I. Lakatos, 'Falsification and the Methodology of Scientific Research Programmes', in I. Lakatos and A. Musgrave (eds), *Criticism and the Growth of Knowledge* (Cambridge, Cambridge University Press, 1970). There are a number of interesting and readable papers in this volume.

8 R. Solow, 'Technical Change and the Aggregate Production Function', *Review of Economics and Statistics*, August 1957, pp. 312–20.

9 B. Russell, *The Impact of Science on Society* (London, Allen and Unwin, 1952), chapter 2.

10 References to these and other relevant sources may be seen later in the text.

11 This very general definition should be contrasted with that of Gummett which is related more to politics and administration, and is articulated differently. See Gummett, *Scientists in Whitehall*, pp. 1–7.

12 B. R. Easlea, *Liberation and the Aims of Science* (London, Chatto and Windus, 1973). See chapter 6 which contains also a discussion about the role of 'values' in social analysis.

Chapter 2

ECONOMIC ORGANISATION AND TECHNOLOGICAL CHANGE

2.1 Introduction

This chapter deals with the ways in which science and technology relate (and have related) to different forms of economic organisation. My main reason for exploring these points is concerned with providing some degree of *comparative perspective*. There is sometimes a tendency to imagine that the potential and problems of 'modern' science can only be discussed within the context of one's own society, or one like it, whereas of course our own culture and social structure is by no means the only one that has existed or indeed could exist. And it is changing constantly in ways that even we do not immediately recognise. Unless this point is clearly grasped students' analytical perspectives are bound to be blinkered and they will have difficulty coming to terms with the subject.

A second reason is concerned with *history* since the impact of science on society is very much bound up with social change and economic development. I intend to demonstrate that the integrated and productive role that science and technology now play in our society is in fact the consequence of a long period of evolution. And the study of that evolution can yield important insights into the complex web of interrelationships between technical conditions and the social order which we are now experiencing. Such insights are then capable of providing the conceptual framework within which we may examine contemporary circumstances in a more fruitful way.

More particularly, I should like to get across four basic propositions. *First*, the industrial revolution experienced initially by Great Britain during the late eighteenth and early part of the nineteenth centuries, and then later on by other European countries (the so-called 'latecomers') represented a necessary and fundamental *watershed* in the evolution of these relations. Before the industrial revolution, although there were (often crucial) inventions and innovations, technological change was never an integral characteristic of economic systems. Afterwards, technological change became endogenous in a number of important respects. In particular (and this is my *second* point) changing technology has imparted an *instability* and a *dynamism* to social systems which is historically unique. In a number of important ways scientific 'progress' has become 'built into' modern society so that the notion of an unchanging social order, natural to earlier epochs, is for all practical purposes no longer relevant. Conversely, the problem for most modern societies is how can people cope both individually and institutionally with continuous and rapid technological change.

A *third* proposition is that the *systematic* application of *scientific knowledge* to the process of economic production only became common relatively late in the day. In the earlier phases of industrialisation the technical basis for production was provided by such factors as practical experience and craft knowledge, linked to important innovations but developed and passed on through the skills embodied in people. The 'R & D laboratory' attached to the firm or the publicly-financed 'research institution' with an industrial remit only began to appear towards the close of the nineteenth century and after the social process of industrialisation had proceeded some distance. Earlier on, 'science' appeared to learn from 'technology' rather than vice versa, although a number of writers now argue that science was an important factor in the industrial revolution when viewed in a cultural or attitudinal sense.

My *final* proposition is that the technological changes which accompanied the industrial revolution produced a social order which became highly *specialised* and *integrated* to a marked degree. Henceforth, the interrelatedness of economic production was such that no one set of activities could alter without this having implications for all other activities. Moreover, growing technological complexity brought along with it the need for *greater control* and *increased size* of productive units. Nowadays one of the paradoxes of modern science-based industrialisation is that its very success in an apparently economic sense carries within it the seeds of its own bureaucratic stultification. How to reconcile these two aspects in particular contexts has become a major issue in contemporary science policy discussion.

Because economic growth and development are necessarily related to our discussion, section 2.2 attempts to define these concepts perfectly generally i.e. independently of the form of economic organisation under discussion. Section 2.3 explores briefly three 'pre-industrial' classes of society and shows how technological changes were essentially peripheral to them. Section 2.4 looks more closely at the transition from feudalism to capitalism paying particular attention to some of the factors which may have been instrumental in bringing about this fundamental transformation in the social order. Section 2.5 explores the notion of the division of labour which is so central to the analysis of industrialisation while section 2.6 looks more closely at a particularly significant aspect of this division, the growth of a specialist and dynamic capital goods sector within which many important technological changes occurred during the nineteenth century.

2.2 Economic Growth and Development

The notion of 'economic growth' is one that has exercised the minds of people greatly over the centuries, if only because it relates to society's growing (or declining) capacity to provide the material basis for human and social existence. Nowadays it is primarily thought of as a problem facing the so-called 'underdeveloped countries' (considered in chapters 7 and 8) although despite their relative affluence when viewed historically, many of the world's richer countries still do not feel that economic growth has proceeded far enough. But what exactly do we mean by the notion? How does it relate to living standards? How may it be measured and how can it be distinguished from its counterpart notion 'economic development'? Above all, what brings it about and how do 'science' and 'technology' relate to it in a causal sense? Questions of this kind are important since very often social expenditures on 'science' are justified in terms of prospective economic returns. They are also important because they raise, implicitly, more funda-mental issues about the relative importance of material welfare as a social goal, about the social costs involved in achieving such a goal and how these costs change through time.

I shall define economic growth as the rate of change of the capacity of any economic system to produce goods and services for the consumption and investment requirements of its citizens. In terms of the macroeconomic concepts to be discussed in chapter 3, therefore, it relates to the rate of change of the rate of production of a community over a given time period (usually a calendar year) and may be *measured* in terms of the rate of increase (or decrease) of some measure of national product (GNP for example). Strictly speaking, of course, such a measure provides only an estimate since the economic system under consideration may not be producing up to its capacity potential. Where this is the case, the system is sometimes described as operating under 'x$-$inefficiency' and the discussion about why this is happening is treated as a short-run problem of resource allocation. More generally, as was pointed out in chapter 1, economists tend to treat economic growth, in a formal sense, as the classification of different 'paths of growth' obtaining under specified conditions of technological change (labour saving, capital saving, neutral), changes of a narrow range of inputs (capital and labour) and changes in a community's consumption and savings habits. In a causal sense, therefore, the analysis of economic growth has become very limited indeed.

However, not only has it become an offshoot of a fairly narrow type of macroeconomic analysis, implicitly also (and sometimes explicitly) the study of economic growth has become associated primarily with a particular form of economic organisation (or system) namely that of a fully developed exchange economy of the kind we now see amongst the industrialised societies of Western Europe and North America. Since our purpose is to examine economic growth from a much wider standpoint, it should be clear that the formal analysis of economic growth has little value and may be safely ignored. Sometimes, the analysis of growth from this rather broader perspective is called the study of *economic development*. Although this does not possess the analytical precision of formal growth theory, it has greater generality. In particular it allows for the introduction of political and institutional factors and hence can deal with a much wider range of questions.

Thus we are interested in questions such as how does growth take place in different types of economic system? What are the institutional characteristics of such systems? What social classes or groups possess economic/political power and what relationship has such a power structure to the process of social transformation? Under what conditions should we expect one form of economic system to be transformed into another? Notice that we are still discussing economic growth, albeit in a much more complex 'causal' sense, a context sometimes called that of political economy. And, by extension, the phrase 'political economy of science and technology' denotes the study of how 'science' and 'technology' as social institutions have influenced the rate and direction of economic development and social transformation, and what sorts of problems have arisen as a result.

At its most general, then, economic development occurs where the productive potential of any community increases thereby raising the quantity of goods and services available. This can occur in three basic ways:

(i)   The improved organisation/management of existing facilities.
(ii)   The mobilisation of new resources.
(iii) Capitalisation of the productive process.

Usually when we speak of technological changes we are considering the third of these but generally all three are going on simultaneously. Concentrating upon the third of these categories, development then proceeds as a function of the accumulation of capital, defining 'capital' as the stock of manmade materials, plant, equipment and buildings (often 'embodying' new technology) available to the community at any point in time.

Similarly the rate of accumulation achievable is a function of the rate at which the community 'saves' i.e. abstains from current consumption in order to reallocate resources into investment. Furtado[1] has attempted to define this social process of accumulation perfectly generally (i.e. independently of the form of economic organisation appertaining) as requiring two types of social mechanism — an *appropriation* mechanism which enables society to mobilise and concentrate resources (or 'economic surplus') and a *translation* mechanism which permits the community to convert this surplus into the accumulation of productive capital. Historically, appropriation has been carried on by minority groups (e.g. social classes or military castes) who have succeeded in appropriating (or expropriating) by such means as slavery, taxation, plunder and the manipulation of prices. The point that Furtado intends to make is that in most ancient societies most of this surplus was used 'unproductively' in the building of monuments, conduct of wars and the support of the luxury consumption needs of aristocratic or priestly castes. Very seldom were such minority groups an effective 'translation mechanism' in the sense of having both the incentive and the means to accumulate capital. As we shall see it was only with the growth of a powerful commercial bourgeoisie towards the end of the Middle Ages that we begin to see the emergence of such a mechanism.

2.3 Pre-Market Economic Systems

It is now possible to use this very broad model of economic development to explain the relative lack of technical dynamism of most societies before the industrial revolution. We shall follow Heilbroner[2] in defining an 'economic system' in terms of how a society organises itself in order to solve its 'economic problem' i.e. in order to produce enough material goods to ensure its own survival and distribute the fruits of this production in a way which is seen to be socially legitimate and which at the same time ensures that more production can take place in the future.

Broadly speaking there are three forms of economic organisation which can fulfil this function:

(i)   *Traditional* where both production and distribution are 'based on procedures devised in the distant past, rigidified by a long process of historic trial and error, and maintained by heavy sanctions of law, custom, and beliefs'.[3]

(ii)   *Command* where economic decisions are made by an absolute authority (say a monarch *or* a small oligarchy).

(iii) *Market* where economic decisions are made through 'market forces' i.e. through the interplay of the individual demand and supply decisions of buyers and sellers, mediated and co-ordinated by a system of prices.

In practice social systems are a mixture of all three forms of economic organisation, but what characterises modern industrial capitalism is the *pervasive market* where the division of labour and exchange of goods and services have reached a high level of complexity. Conversely, in the case of pre-industrial economic systems, although there was of course 'exchange' and although markets did exist, overall resource allocation was not decided by anything corresponding to a market mechanism. Thus in what is generally classed as the most primitive type of economic system, the *hunter/gatherer society* there was no settled production at all because of the nomadic mode of existence. Indeed, Sahlins[4] points out that in such a society 'commodities', beyond what is absolutely necessary for acquiring and cooking food, become of negative value. Life is a continuous trade-off between 'work' (to gain the means of subsistence) and 'leisure' (to enjoy it). Under these circumstances 'markets' can have no economic function, while 'exchange' takes on ritualistic aspects which fulfil a number of social goals ranging from the propitiation of gods to the ensuring of peaceful relations between potentially hostile tribes. Similarly, since economic scarcity has little meaning in the sense that we understand it, not only would it be organisationally impossible to accumulate capital, the activity itself would be pointless.

While there are still some hunter/gatherer societies in existence today (although they are finding it increasingly difficult to resist the encroachments of 'civilisation') the same is not true of that other well-known economic system of ancient times, the *slave economy* built upon a foundation of settled peasant-based subsistence agriculture. In this case the economics of command were very strong for, by and large, ownership of land was vested in a ruling class or oligarchy who either employed peasants as slaves on their large estates or let small parcels of land to peasants as tenants in return for a share (usually substantial) of the resultant produce. Again 'markets' were peripheral to such economic systems, since the main preoccupation of the majority of peasants was that of staying alive.

> Hence the peasant, who was the bone and muscle of the economies of antiquity, was in himself a prime example of the nonmarket aspect of these economies. Although some cultivators freely sold a portion of their own crop in the city marketplaces, the great majority of agricultural producers scarcely entered the market at all. For many of these producers — especially when they were slaves — this was, accordingly, an almost cashless world, where a few coppers a year, carefully hoarded and spent only for emergencies, constituted the only link with a world of market transactions.
>
> Thus whereas the peasant's legal and social status varied widely in different areas and eras of antiquity, in a broad view the tenor of his economic life was singularly constant. Of the web of transactions, the drive for profits of the modern farmer, he knew little or nothing. Generally poor, tax-ridden and oppressed, prey to nature's caprices and to the exploitation of war and peace, bound to the soil by law and custom, the peasant of antiquity — as the peasant today who continues to provide the agricultural underpinnings to the civilisations of the East and South — was dominated by the economic rule of tradition. His main stimulus for change was command — or, rather, obedience. Labour, patience, and the incredible endurance of the human being were his contributions to civilisation.[5]

In fact the magnificent cities of ancient civilisation were 'centres' of aristocratic consumption which depended heavily also upon massive slave labour to support this existence. The well-known city states of ancient Greece were 'democracies' only for a minority of highly privileged people, and since 'wealth was ... a surplus to be seized by conquest or squeezed from the underlying agricultural population, it was not yet a natural adjunct of a system of continuously increasing production in which some part of an expanding total social output might accrue to many classes of society'.[6] Again it is evident that under such circumstances, technological changes could only ever play a very marginal social role.

Similar points could be made about the third well-known type of pre-market system, *feudalism*, a characteristic of much of European society during the late Middle Ages. Here a large proportion of populations were engaged in 'unfree' subsistence agriculture, tied to the *manorial estate* to which they paid dues mainly in kind or in labour in their lord's fields and workshops. The ruling landed classes were thus able to maintain comparatively high income and plentiful leisure time which was spent on religious, courtly and military pursuits. Again within the manorial estate itself there was very little incentive or means to accumulate capital and the technical conditions of society remained virtually stagnant. Indeed there is evidence that many Eastern civilisations had by the fifteenth and sixteenth centuries, advanced further economically, culturally and scientifically.[7]

Hence, however heterogeneous and differentiated those ancient and early societies were in terms of their social, political and cultural characteristics, *from an economic point of view* they demonstrated important points of similarity which distinguish them sharply from most modern societies. In particular they were largely static in technological terms, markets were peripheral adjuncts to the social order, towns were important cultural centres but had little economic importance compared to our modern urban centres, and the accumulation of wealth was causally associated with the power of minority groups rather than the other way around. In short while Furtado's appropriation mechanism was omni-present, there was nothing which could remotely be classified as a translation mechanism. Economic development was conspicuous by its absence. The social order remained comparatively static, often for long periods.

2.4 The Transition to Capitalism

How and why then, did the pre-industrial period come to an end? This is an enormously complex question and not one that a book of this kind is competent to explore with any thoroughness. However, what is generally agreed is that the feudal system contained within itself the seeds of its own destruction and that progressively towards the latter part of the Middle Ages, economic forces were unleashed which ultimately brought about the downfall of the old feudal order and the power structure upon which it was based, paving the way for the industrial revolution and the market systems of contemporary industrial societies.

It is useful to return to a feature of the early Middle Ages which we have not so far mentioned but which is an important starting point for our discussion. The fall of Rome marked the beginning of a period of economic dissolution for Europe, since what had been an environment conducive to the widespread conduct of inter-regional trade was progressively destroyed by repeated invasions from Asiatic and Slavic tribes. Gradually the Roman roads, wonderful arteries of communication, fell into disrepair, and the security associated with the Roman administrative and military apparatus disappeared along with the towns which had grown up as adjuncts to the Roman encampments and which had acted as economic sectors of some little importance.

By the tenth and eleventh centuries, argues Furtado, although the general level of technique was rather higher than in Roman times (thereby permitting societies to exist under feudal relations as opposed to those associated with slavery), Western Europe had disintegrated into a series of disaggregated social 'fiefdoms' organised primarily for defence and economic self-sufficiency. Economic surplus was appropriated by the baronial 'warlords', communications were poor and trade almost vanished. Furtado argues that such an 'involuted' system could never have been shifted out of its rut of static economic equilibrium through anything approximating to political integration, but only through some kind of external stimulus — which is precisely what happened.

> It commenced as the historian Henri Pirenne has perspicaciously remarked, as a consequence of the radical change which the upsurge of Islam brought about in Byzantine trade routes. As a result of the Moslem invasions, Byzantium, the immense commercial metropolis, found itself suddenly cut off from its sources of supply along almost the entire southern and eastern Mediterranean seaboards, and the Byzantines turned with much zeal towards the coasts of Italy. Those contacts, as is well known, propitiated the emergence of powerful mercantile economies along the Italian coast. The propagation in the ensuing centuries of further currents of trade all over the European continent has been extensively studied. Along the European coast a network of commercial entrep&o4'ts sprang up and, through the great inland waterways, the whole continent was, as it were, contaminated by the traders' activities.[8]

Thus trade sprang up as an 'exogenous phenomenon in the feudal world' leading eventually to a process of 'agglutination' by which isolated communities became linked together economically, thereby creating the conditions for further economic development. Profits were ploughed back into further ventures involving longer journeys of transportation, the building of bigger ships and the opening up of more distant markets. What had begun as a process of geographical integration continued as one of geographical expansion and colonisation in the interests of trade.

But what were the important features of these developments? Furtado argues that it required above all the growth of a new economic class – the *mercantile bourgeoisie* which had the motivation, and increasingly the means, to 'translate' economic surplus into capital accumulation and economic growth. The roots of this dynamic class lay probably in the itinerant merchants who in earlier periods endured incredible hardships and dangers, and travelled long distances in the pursuit of their trading activities. Heilbroner points out that although such merchants had very low social status and no 'natural place' in medieval society, nevertheless the *fairs* at which they exhibited their wares represented an 'occasion' which few would have missed.[9] Moreover, they were the source of a range of consumption goods which would not otherwise have been available to the landed aristocracies of the period, and hence acted as a means of consumption stimulation and diversification.

The more successful of these merchants became eventually a new trading bourgeoisie, an elite who lived in the *towns* which arose as adjuncts to trade usually under the walls of a manorial castle or fortress for security reasons but which were eventually to encapsulate these strongholds much as a pearl does with a grain of sand. Within these medieval townships grew also the beginnings of industrial production – the 'craft' activities which provided the artifactual needs of the manor in terms of textiles, fabrics, tools, jewellery, construction materials and a range of further commodities which were within the technological compass of the time. However, the activities of these early productive units were heavily controlled through a system of 'guilds', the guild being a sort of producers' union for each craft which laid down very strict rules for the conduct of production and sale, right from the recruitment and training of labour, through the establishment of wages and conditions of work to the determination of prices and quality of the final product, and even the social conduct of its members.

Thus the medieval manufacturing workshop was not a 'profit centre' as is the case with the modern business enterprise.

> Rather [its purpose] was to preserve a certain orderly way of life – a way which envisaged a decent income for its master craftsmen but which was certainly not intended to ally any of them to a big businessman or a monopolist. On the contrary, guilds were specifically designed to ward off any such outcome of an uninhibited struggle among their members . . . [competition] was strictly limited and profits were held to prescribed levels. Advertising was forbidden, and even technical progress in advance of one's fellow guildmen was considered disloyal.[10]

Hence although in a sense such artisanal activities were embryos of the factories of the industrial revolution, they were not, and could not have been, an important engine of social change – a 'translation mechanism' in Furtado's terminology. That role was reserved for the commercial class whose profit-seeking activities were never controlled in a similar way and whose members, especially the 'business houses' of the larger towns, grew increasingly wealthy and powerful as we move into the fifteenth and sixteenth centuries, becoming in many cases a threat to the established order.

Of course, it would be foolish to ascribe the breakdown of the feudal system solely to the emergence of a new dynamic social class and the growth of the towns since there were many other factors widely held to be of great importance. For example, one factor often mentioned is the progressive *monetisation* of the medieval economy, fed initially by the Crusades and latterly by the silver mines of the Spanish colonies of South America. Clearly the success of trade required a universally acceptable coinage as a store of wealth and a medium of exchange, and the monetisation of manorial dues spread economic power much more widely. Routh stresses the *Black Death* (1348–9) which decimated the populations of Europe, and the *overthrow of the Mongol Empire* which disrupted trades routes to the East.[11] The *Crusades* themselves are often mentioned as having had a profound cultural influence on the relatively backward peoples who embarked upon them. Tawney[12] and Weber[13] emphasise the *Reformation*, especially the teachings of the Protestant reformer John Calvin (1509–64), which socially legitimated the wealth-seeking and wealth-using activities of the new business world in opposition to the older Roman Catholic injunctions against usury but rather tolerant of luxury consumption. And, of course, the early *enclosures* of the 'common land' in the interests of sheep raising and wool production, are held to have had widepread economic repercussions, both in raising the technical basis for agricultural production as well as in the creation of a new class of 'free' landless labourers with none of its forebear's feudal rights and forced for its very survival to seek work wherever it could and under whatever conditions.[14]

Nevertheless, from our relatively narrow standpoint it is difficult to do better than Furtado's analysis.

Prior to the Industrial Revolution, economic development was mainly a process of agglutination of small economic units and of geographical division of labour. The dynamic agency of development consisted of the commercial class. By promoting the agglutination of economic units into larger markets, it created more complex forms of division of labour and made possible geographical specialisation. The fruits of the resultant increase in productivity were largely absorbed by the ruling groups presiding over the communities engaged in promoting trade, and this made substantial concentrations of financial capital possible. However, since there was little or no articulation between the commercial and the productive groups, accumulation of profit in the hands of traders had little or no effect on production techniques. From the point of view of the traders of those days, the most lucrative investment lay in opening up new labour fronts or financing the destruction of competitors. Only in very special cases were they concerned with production methods.[15]

The final stage of Furtado's analysis, then, is his explanation of the conversion of extensive growth to that of 'involuted' capitalistic growth which laid the basis for industrialisation in the nineteenth and twentieth centuries. This occurred because of physical and economic limits to expansion through trade. Gradually mercantile ventures grew bigger and more risky involving greater distances and, most importantly, greater costs. The Ottoman invasions began to close off the 'economic frontier' of Southern and Eastern Europe, and competitive pressures amongst traders became much fiercer. This led to protectionism on the part of European nation states in an attempt to boost the fortunes of their own business houses. It also led to a direct search for methods of cost reduction primarily in three directions:

1   **The development of the factory system** which enabled master craftsmen and merchants to exercise much greater control over the production process. Especially within the textiles industry the concentration of productive activities within the one centre enabled much greater systematisation and rationalisation through such means as the division of labour, control of stock and the use of simple tools.

2   **Reduction in wage levels.** Despite the opposition of the guilds, wages declined progressively between the fifteenth and the eighteenth centuries, helped as we have seen by the enclosures.

3   **Progressive improvements in production technique.** Since, however, both the factory system and reductions in wage levels represented social changes which were inherently limited in their effectiveness from the standpoint of cost reduction, the first because it represented a 'once-and-for-all' change in production organisation and the second because the subsistence wage put a lower limit to wage reductions, ultimately these pressures began to move businessmen into thinking more systematically about production technology itself. And it is this feature of the industrial revolution which is so important from our point of view since it represented a *shift* in the 'translation mechanism' of a fundamental kind. Once industrialisation had begun, the act of seeking wealth need no longer be confined to the expansion of trade. Instead growth through the capitalisation of the productive process was a feasible and increasingly, a powerful possibility. And it is in the exploration of this 'development in depth' that we can begin to grasp the sheer economic power of this new type of economic system, industrial capitalism, which has so transformed the world in so short a time.

Thus from the point of view of the technological and economic historian, the transition from one type of economic system (feudalism) to another (capitalism) was one full of significance. For the first time technological changes were capable of playing a fundamental role in social change. The fact that they did so warrants a closer examination of the industrialisation process as it evolved throughout the nineteenth century.

2.5 Economic Differentiation — The Division of Labour

It is difficult to understate the dramatic changes that took place during the period which we classify roughly as that of the 'industrial revolution'. In a matter of a century Great Britain (and later other European countries) was transformed from a largely agricultural society based on subsistence farming supplemented by some cottage scale handicraft industry, into a major industrial power. Population moved substantially from the countryside into the new industrial towns, industrial output grew exponentially, mass internal transportation was developed, initially through the building of canals and latterly through the railway system. Colonisation and international trade were given a big boost through the development of the steamship. And, as we have seen, the factory system became the dominant mode of industrial production, taking over from the older 'putting-out' tradition common in the textiles industry.

In addition, the content of industrial output changed. To begin with the growth of cotton textiles dominated the scene, along with coal and iron production. However, as the nineteenth century progressed economic production expanded and became differentiated into a range of 'new' industries. Particularly important was the growth of the chemicals industry (initially in relation to washing and bleaching in the textiles industry, later diversifying into bulk consumer goods such as soap and glass and 'bulk' chemicals such as sulphuric acid) and the sector which we now associate with capital goods production, mechanical engineering — the range of industries associated with the fashioning of metal into machines which themselves enabled more difficult tasks to be performed on metals, producing a whole range of the components and machinery necessary to underpin an increasingly differentiated and complex industrial sector.

But what was it about this new industrial system which gave it such dramatic economic power? What were the sources of these quite remarkable growth rates in labour productivity, which had never been known before? And what had developments in 'science' to do with it? In recent years a number of writers have begun to explore these matters in some detail, and although there are differences in emphasis all agree that a fundamental factor was the *division of labour* which this new form of economic organisation permitted. The resultant *specialisation of function* was not only inherently more efficient, in an economic sense, compared to the older 'craft-based' mode, it was also inherently *dynamic* and ultimately, it is argued, paved the way for the systematic application of scientific knowledge to the productive process enshrined in the modern R & D laboratory.

2.5.1 Adam Smith

But this analysis is by no means a product of modern intellectual thought. Right from the outset of the industrial transformation of Britain, thinkers and scholars were endeavouring to understand the changes which were occurring, to put them into some kind of context and to approve (or disapprove) them. The most famous (and most relevant from our point of view) was the Scottish philosopher Adam Smith, Professor of Moral Philosophy at the University of Glasgow who is now recognised as one of the first great economists and whose book *The Wealth of Nations*, published in 1776, is still a standard reference work in the history of economic ideas.

As the title of his book suggests, Smith's main preoccupation was to understand what brought about economic growth, but like many of the early 'political economists' of the 'classical school' his was no disinterested quest. On the contrary, Smith was a philosopher of the enlightenment and argued very strongly in favour of a particular political viewpoint − that of a nascent industrial class.

> Smith saw manufacturers ... as the carriers of progress and he urged that they be afforded more space in which to manoeuvre. Much of his practical message was that institutional restrictions (whether legislated by governments or rooted in parochial traditions) were unhealthy. They cramped the rate at which a new and more productive industrial era could mature.[16]

In this sense, Smith was an economic radical arguing against the numerous petty (and some not so petty) restrictions on trade and production associated with the earlier mercantilist era and, by extension, asserting that enormous energies would thereby be released to the ultimate benefit of all.

On a more technical level, however, his starting point was 'the extent of the market' and the resultant 'division of labour' which this made possible.[17] Thus in his famous pin-making example Smith argued that the more the manufacturer was able to 'resolve the handicraft into its constituent operations' the more economic/efficient would the resultant operation become. There were three broad mechanisms through which this would happen − (a) the savings of time involved in artisans passing from one task to another; (b) improvements in dexterity as workmen became adept at particular tasks through continuous practice; (c) the invention of machines which would 'facilitate and abridge labour, and enable one man to do the work of many'. But it is the third which is important in the long term, and arises itself from three further sources:

- through workmen engaged on one task beginning to see possibilities for improvement through the use of machines and tools
- through the ingenuity of machine makers themselves

—   through a group of people whom Smith called 'philosophers' or 'men of science' who themselves became subdivided into specialised 'classes and tribes'.

Cooper[18] argues that each of these 'sources' of innovation arose themselves as result of antecendent changes in economic organisation: namely the *first* by means of division of labour within the enterprise itself, the *second* through an embryonic division of labour into capital and consumer goods production, and the *third* through the scientific revolution itself, about which more below.

Hence, division of labour in this sense was the basic means through which possibilities for economic progress could occur, although there was another sense in which Smith used the term. This was to connote economic differentiation between different lines of productive activity. Clearly the greater the extent of the market, the greater would be not only possibilities for rationalisation within the enterprise itself but also the possibilities for the exchange of goods and services in the economy as a whole, and indeed internationally. Not only would pin makers make pins more sensibly, they would begin to specialise in the production of different types of pins with further improvements in economic efficiency. All that was required for the system, or the 'invisible hand', to work was the absence of bureaucratic restrictions. Actually, yet a third variant on this theme was Smith's insistence that there were two classes of employment which he described as 'productive' and 'unproductive'. The former gave rise to tangible commodities and hence could realise an 'economic surplus' which could be used for the accumulation of capital (Smith probably treated this as a 'wages fund'), while the latter were synonymous with services of various kinds, including the functions of government. He included also in this category '. . . some both of the gravest and most important, and some of the most frivolous professions: churchmen, lawyers, physicians, men of letters of all kinds; players, buffoons, musicians, opera singers, opera dancers, etc.'[19] Clearly he did not regard such activities as contributing to economic growth, however socially valuable they might seem to be.

2.5.2 Karl Marx

Writing nearly a century later, and with the benefit of hindsight, Marx took issue with aspects of Smith's analysis. He too had a broad political message to get across and in order to do so was attempting to get to grips with the underlying logic of capitalist development, one important feature of which was the role of scientific knowledge in bringing about improvements in labour productivity. In a recent book Rosenberg[20] argues that Marx's view of the relations between 'science' and 'production' was not that of a naive economic determinist believing simply that growth in scientific knowledge is merely a response to industrial demands, although this was a strand in his thinking. He argued also that the systematic application of scientific principles to economic production was only feasible after industrial capitalism had reached a certain stage — that stage corresponding to an industrial system which was fully mechanised and where the separation of the worker from his product was complete.

In order to demonstrate this proposition, Marx began by drawing attention to an important limitation to Smith's analysis, namely the failure to distinguish between 'manufacturing' and 'mechanised' modes of production. In fact, argued Marx, it was more accurate to distinguish three production modes:

(a)   Handicraft Production
(b)   Manufacturing Production
(c)   Mechanised Production

and while (b) represented 'the resolution of the handicraft into its constituent operations', and led therefore to some improvements in labour productivity, it shared with (a) an essential feature which was that both modes were constrained by the physical and mental capacities of the artisan himself. A second constraining factor was that neither mode was amenable to the use of mass unskilled labour.

Both limitations are, however, swept away once the 'manufacturing' mode has been replaced by the 'mechanised' mode. Cooper puts it as follows:

> The grouping and organisation of detailed labour skills which is the guiding principle of the manufacturing system, is replaced by the grouping and organisation of machines. The technical determinants of the process are no longer the possibilities offered by the division of labour; they are the possibilities of increasing the specialisation and perfection of the machine with its tools. This latter process . . . is subject to far less stringent limitations than was the perfection of the 'instruments of labour' under the manufacturing system — where the physical and mental capabilities of the craftsman set strict limits to the kind of technical advance that can be achieved.[21]

The mechanisation of production, particularly within the capital goods sector and the accompanying differentiation of engineering skills are indicators, according to Cooper, of a profound form of *organisational change* which antedated the systematic application of science to production. Only when the separation of the worker from his product had reached this institutional stage, could man's understanding and control over nature be the limiting factor in economic progress. Possibilities were now present which were never feasible before.

Rosenberg argues in a similar fashion:

> So long as the worker continues to occupy strategic places in the productive process, that process is limited by all of his human frailties. And, of course, the

individual capitalist is, in many ways, continually pressing the worker against those limits. But the point which Marx is making here is of much broader significance: The application of science to the productive process involves dealing with impersonal laws of nature and freeing itself from the dependence upon the organic. It involves calculations concerning the behavior of natural phenomena. It involves the exploitation of reliable physical relationships which have been established by scientific disciplines. It involves a degree of predictability of a purely objective sort, from which the uncertainties and subjectivities of human behavior have been systematically excluded. Science, in short, can only incorporate its findings in impersonal machinery. It cannot be incorporated in human beings with their individual volitions, idiosyncracies, and refractory temperaments. The manufacturing period shared with the earlier handicraft system the essential feature that it was a tool-using economy where the tools were subject to human manipulation and guidance. It is this element of human control, the continued reliance upon the limited range of activities of the human hand, and not the nature of the power source, Marx insists, which is decisive in distinguishing a machine from a tool.[22]

But that is not all. It is not just mechanisation that is necessary, since if machines continue to be made by craftsmen, production is still up against the same constraints. And well into the nineteenth century most capital goods production was essentially artisanal since, as Cooper points out, for example, all the original textiles entrepreneurs readily found millwrights, ironsmiths and other tradesmen who could build their devices for them. The vital step, therefore, was that of building 'machines to make machines'. Once the worker had become 'separated from his product in this way' the division of labour had taken a fundamental and irreversible step.

The improvements in the machinery-producing sector constitute a quantum leap in the technological arsenal at man's disposal. They make it possible to escape the physical limitations of a tool-using culture. They do this, ironically as Marx points out, by providing machines which reproduce the actions of a hand-operated tool, but do so on a 'cyclopean scale'.[23]

Finally, of course, once an economic sector had evolved which was big enough to support the continued production and reproduction of capital goods, the possibilities arose for producing cheaper and better machines – for 'cheapening the elements of constant capital', as Marx would put it. This could arise through progressive specialisation and technological changes within the machinery-producing sector itself, a point to which I shall return.

2.5.3 Recap and Evaluation

What then can we say about this type of analysis of the development of early capitalism? The first point, I think, is that it provides a useful, if rough, backcloth against which to view a number of important features of this development. Thus, during the early part of the industrial revolution working people were gradually shifted from a rural setting into the factories of the new industrial towns where they were employed as mass unskilled labour often at wages not very much above subsistence levels, and held down by the sheer volume of labour available and the 'combination laws' which prevented any form of collective action on the part of workers to raise wage levels. Furtado[24] argues that in the early stages of the industrialisation process, the resultant income distribution in favour of profits had a positive effect on the rate of economic growth because of high rates of investment. Landes[25] too shows how for the successful industrial capitalist, often coming from a relatively humble background, truly enormous sums of money could be gained.

For Furtado[26] the final impetus pushing economies like Britain into a pattern of 'internalised' growth in which technical change played a key role, was the absorption of the rural labour reserve which reduced the elasticity of labour supply to the industrial sector. With given technique wages rose, leading to a declining rate of profit, which in turn reduced the rate of investment. The resultant excess supply of capital goods was absorbed partly through capital export and partly through competition via technical change in the capital goods sector. Prices of equipment then fell in relation to prices of manufactured consumer goods resulting in a relative fall in the demand for labour. The net effect was a progressively increased degree of mechanisation throughout the whole system, with technical change in the capital goods sector acting as the driving force.

A second, and related, point is the insight that our analysis gives us on the attack on the 'craft activity' which industrialisation brought about. In his classic analysis *The Making of the English Working Class* E. P. Thompson[27] shows graphically how many skilled trades, and the ways of life and human dignity associated with them, were systematically destroyed by the march of industrial progress, leaving a legacy of class bitterness which still survives in Britain to this day. A particularly extreme view of the role of the worker in industrial production was taken by one Frederick W. Taylor (1856–1915), the father of 'scientific management' who lived in the closing decades of the nineteenth century and who believed that in a world where the need for craft skills was disappearing, one could apply rigorous principles of 'job evaluation' and 'time-and-motion study' to the highly differentiated and machine-paced tasks which the unskilled labourer performed. Moreover, Taylor argued that it was important that this *should* be done since otherwise the 'division of labour' would never realise its full potential in terms of industrial output. Needless to say, Taylor had a great deal of trouble in persuading management and workers of the value and practicality of his ideas, although Guest concludes:

> Few men in the history of American technology have had greater impact on the organization of work than . . . Taylor . . . What Eli Whitney and others did to

lay the groundwork of mass production in the 1800's, later perfected in the continuous-flow technology of Henry Ford in the 20th century, Frederick Taylor applied to the motions of men at work. Today's large fraternity of industrial engineers, systems and methods experts, work-standards specialists, and a whole host of management experts in a very real sense owe their jobs and allegiance to Taylor. While many would credit America's great industrial leap forward in the twentieth century in large measure to the work of this man, others − especially in the trade union movement − would condemn Taylor for 'making man just another machine'.[28]

Nowadays, this issue is still an important ingredient arising out of the impact of technological changes on industrial activity. Some writers, like Braverman,[29] take a hostile view, arguing that:

(a)   Managements are motivated by a psychological desire to *control* the labour force as much as by the need to run their businesses profitably.
(b)   The 'labour process' is ultimately alienative in the sense that workers become mindless wage slaves, not comprehending the productive process as a whole.
(c)   'De-skilling' of work is an increasingly pervasive phenomenon, and that whatever the production imperative may be in an economic sense, much more attention should be paid to the skill content and security of people's jobs.

The contrary view is that there is little evidence of secular de-skilling for the labour force as a whole, though there are many 'cycles' of de-skilling with respect to particular occupations. There are also corresponding benefits from rapid industrial and technical change which Braverman tends to play down, such as cheaper commodities and a shorter working week. In any case the harking back to the golden age of the craftsman is probably unrealistic given present trends in international trade. Very recently, however, some evidence suggests that in periods of very rapid technological change the set of ideas associated with the division of labour may produce misleading prescriptions for science and technology policy.[30] I shall return to some of these issues below.

A *third* point I should like to emphasise at this stage concerns the role of 'science' in the process of economic production as it evolved throughout the nineteenth century. As we have seen Marx was quite clear on this point. It was only possible to apply scientific knowledge *systematically* to productive activities after the division of industrial labour had reached a given (complex) stage of economic and technical differentiation. Conversely so long as the 'craft' activity predominated, industrial development was bound to be a rather messy, practical affair with entrepreneurial success being determined as much by the drive, ruthless ambition and technical flair of the early 'masters' as by any more systematic form of 'knowledge'. Indeed it is likely that in some areas 'science' probably learned from 'technology'.

Reviewing some of the literature on this issue, Pavitt and Warboys appear to concur with the 'majority view' that there was '… little or no interaction between science and technical change in the industrial revolution in most industries' in any practical sense, although equally 'there is no denying that during (this early period) there was considerable interest in science, a growing number of scientific societies and that these were often associated with technical ambition.'[31] However, this apparent interest was due rather to the 'cultural' and 'ideological' significance of science which, following the scientific revolution, acted so as to combine 'rationality and mastery over nature' and hence to give a measure of social legitimacy to the profit-seeking activities of the new industrial bourgeoisie.

Certainly as industrialisation proceeded into the late nineteenth and twentieth centuries, the direct role of organised science became increasingly important in economic production. Freeman in particular stresses the 'professionalisation of industrial R & D' which gradually took over as the major source of invention and innovation in a number of industrial sectors. Thus in the earlier stages of industrialisation, innovations (in textiles, metal-working and railways, for example) were based upon

> the practical experience of engineers and craftsmen … Technical progress was rapid but the techniques were such that experience and mechanical ingenuity enabled many improvements to be made as a result of direct observation and small-scale experiment. Most of the patents in this period were taken out by 'mechanics' or 'engineers', who did their own 'development' work alongside production or privately.[32]

Conversely, 'what is distinctive about modern industrial R & D is its scale, its scientific content and the extent of its professional specialisation'.[33] This specialisation in turn has become associated primarily with the increasingly scientific character of technology, its growing complexity and the growing division of labour within the engineering profession itself (cf. Adam Smith's 'philosophers'). Factors such as this began to place a premium on the specialised R & D laboratory which could house under 'one roof' the appropriate range of skills, devices, information services, pilot plant equipment etc. and which became increasingly necessary in competitive industrial production. Beginning with the German chemicals and electrical industries in the late nineteenth centuries Freeman shows how systematic exploitation of scientific knowledge has become a critically important source of economic growth and how an understanding of the important characteristics of these relations is a necessary condition for adequate science policy-making nowadays.[34]

A *final* point to stress, and one which was not apparently given much consideration by Marx, for example, is the increasing *instability* and *dynamism* brought about by the progressive division of labour which we have been discussing. For example, Cooper[35] points out that once technological changes became an important ingredient of economic production they began to create disproportionalities within and between industrial sectors. Thus within cotton textiles innovations in spinning led to bottlenecks in weaving thread into cloth, thereby creating the need for technological changes in the weaving sector. In turn the much greater volumes of unfinished cloth gave rise to bottlenecks further downstream in bleaching and dyeing which helped to pave the way for the alkali and related industries which came along later.

Henceforth, industrial society could no longer be anything other than potentially anarchic, in an economic sense, if only because of the vastly increased number of specialised centres of productive activity, each at all times both a possible source of technological change as well as having to react to such changes in 'customer' and 'supplier' and 'competitor' firms. Murray[36] has argued that it is precisely this feature of industrial capitalism which has helped to breed the tendency towards greater size in economic units and what he terms 'corporate inequality'. Economies of scale are determined by three 'principles', those of (1) specialisation; (2) communication and control; and (3) insurance.

Specialisation occurs for Smithian reasons, although Murray argues it in terms of 'time economy' i.e. the savings of time required to perform tasks. However, time-savings in order to be realised need greater initial investments and progressively, as industrialisation proceeded throughout the nineteenth century, these investments became larger. In effect the ability to realise economic benefits through specialisation required greater integration of the total industrial process in question, which placed a premium on larger units of production. However, the other side of the coin was that of *communication* and *control* since greater indivisibilities may place managerial constraints on economic performance. Thus time-savings are predicated upon good co-ordination between the differentiated phases of production, including co-ordination and processing of information, and Murray argues that there is increasing evidence that technological changes in the middle of the twentieth century (particularly in electronic capital goods) have had the effect of relaxing managerial constraints on greater size of production units. Indeed he argues that communications (and responses) are often better and swifter within a vertically integrated firm rather than through 'arms-length' transactions between separate firms.

The third principle, *insurance*, again placed a premium on 'bigness' since larger firms could spread risks more easily and cheaply. In this way the uncertainties which arose as a result of the organic integration of technological changes within the productive process could at least be mitigated in terms of potential economic loss, but we shall see later on how this tension between size and social productivity has become very much a live issue as we approach the closing decade of the twentieth century.

2.6 Capital Goods Production

A particularly important way in which economic producton became specialised after the industrial revolution was, as we have seen, the development of a sector devoted to the production of *capital goods* and it is worth spending a little time on this aspect of industrialisation if only because, as we have seen, much of the dynamic of economic growth actually occurred within this sector. One writer in particular has, in recent years, done a great deal to improve our understanding of the precise mechanics of this process, through a series of historical studies of industrial production in the USA during the nineteenth century.[37]

Nathan Rosenberg's hypothesis may be put very simply — what gave the tremendous push to the development of early US capitalism was the changing character of capital goods manufacture, in particular the growing concentration on the production of producer-durables — machinery, equipment, tools and other fixtures which became the necessary building blocks in the later manufacture of 'final goods' to the consumer. This represented a very specific form of the division of labour which contained within itself important characteristics of dynamic change and nowhere could this be seen more clearly than in the growth of machine tool production itself.

Machine tools occupied a strategic role both because their production became a locus of important technological changes and because they were used in a wide range of downstream sectors (as well as in the production of machine tools themselves). Rosenberg maintains that three features of the growth of machine tool manufacture were of central importance.

- Technological convergence.
- Vertical disintegration.
- Sequential innovation.

Taken together they revolutionized the rate and direction of industrial change in the nineteenth century. They can also be seen as key characteristics of the innovation process today.

2.6.1 Technological Convergence

We have seen that the industrialisation process may be regarded as one of increasing specialisation and differentiation of economic production both horizontally (the production of new goods and services) and vertically (the capitalisation of the productive process). However, what is often ignored is the fact that many of the 'new' industries used broadly similar productive processes, involving a metal using technology with decentralised sources of power. Hence, for example, what was common to the manufacture of sewing machines, bicycles, boilers, ships, railways, motor cars and armaments was that they all required power-driven machinery to perform a (relatively small) range of operations on metals − turning, boring, cutting, milling, grinding and polishing.

Moreover, the productive operations of these machines faced similar *technical* problems in areas such as power transmission (gearing, belting, shafting), friction reduction, measurement and control, and metallurgy (concerning, for example, the ability of metals to withstand heat and stress). Hence a heterogeneous collection of industries from the point of view of the final consumer, was homogeneous in terms of the technology embodied in the machinery required for production. Rosenberg defines this property as one of *technological convergence* and argues that it had important consequences both for the development of new techniques and for their diffusion, once developed.

2.6.2 Vertical Disintegration

The process by which specialist machine-tool firms became established was one of progressive vertical disintegration as firms 'spun-off' from 'mother firms'. At the outset a growing industry often has to undertake the full range of productive operations including the design and development of necessary capital goods. As the industry develops in size and experience, however, many tasks and functions can be subcontracted to specialists.

> If one considers the full life of industries, the dominance of vertical disintegration is surely to be expected. Young industries are often strangers to the established economic system. They require new kinds of qualities of materials and hence make their own; they must overcome technical problems in the use of their products and cannot wait for potential users to overcome them; they must persuade customers to abandon other commodities and find no specialised merchants to undertake this task. These young industries must design their specialised equipment and often manufacture it, and they must undertake to recruit (historically, often to import) skilled labor. When the industry has attained a certain size and prospects, many of these tasks are sufficiently important to be turned over to specialists.[38]

Rosenberg's point is that vertical disintegration became significant at that stage in US industrialisation precisely because of the simultaneous growth of a large number of industries which were technologically convergent.

> With technological convergence, however, milling and grinding became important operations in a large number of metal-using industries, thus permitting a degree of specialisation at 'higher' stages of production which would not otherwise have been possible. Since, as Adam Smith, Allyn Young, and

George Stigler have taught us, 'the division of labor is limited by the extent of the market', the unique degree of specialization developed in the American machinery-producing sector owed as much to technological convergence as it did to the expansion in the demand for individual final products.[39]

2.6.3 Sequential Innovation

Finally, the importance of this form of specialisation must also be seen in a dynamic sense since in effect the machine-tool sector became a centre of continuous learning and technological improvements through technical imbalances and through applications engineering with customer industries. Notice that this subtle but fundamental feature represents a different aspect of technological dynamism from the *economic* imbalances discussed above. What Rosenberg is at pains to emphasise is that any technological change in the construction or application of a complex capital good like a machine tool, immediately creates the conditions for further change in a virtually endless series of *technical* shifts which owe more to the engineering appreciation of the skilled mechanic than to the economic pressures of the market place.

Two examples are the introduction of the forming tool for the outside of bicycle hubs and the use of high-speed steel in cutting tools. The first of these created a

disequilibrium between the operations carried on for the outside and the inside of the hub. Since the forming tool worked more rapidly on the outside of the hub than the old-fashioned drills worked on the inside, the fullest gains from the use of the forming tool required a speeding up of drilling operations. This imbalance was corrected by the oil-tube drill which, in speeding up drilling operations, brought about a closer synchronisation between the two operations.[40]

In the case of high-speed steel the removal of metal at high speeds placed much greater stress on other components of machine tools thus generating substantial redesign in structural, transmission and control elements.

In this manner, then, capital goods production in general, and machine-tool production in particular, became the main avenue through which technological changes were introduced into the nascent industrial economy, and the insights which Rosenberg has given us have equal relevance today. One case of contemporary importance might be that of information technology, where the advent of the microprocessor shows clear similarities in terms of all three of the features we have been considering. Thus the specific example of computer aided design shows us how an innovation initially developed within the electronics capital goods sector has now been shown to have applications in a wide variety of other industries with dramatic impacts on employment patterns, prices and industrial structure. Another example might be that of the development of appropriate technologies for developing countries. Rosenberg himself argues that only through the creation of their own autonomous capacity for the manufacture of capital goods will poor countries acquire technologies suitable for their own purposes,[41] and we shall see in chapter 8 and that the question of the development of 'technological capabilities' is now a key issue for the planning of science and technology in many parts of the third world today.

However, students are urged to treat these theoretical ideas with care and discrimination since they have not been fully articulated as yet. It is not always the case, for example, that vertical disintegration results in, or takes place because of, the greater possibilities for innovation at higher stages of production. Freeman[42] has shown in the case of chemical process plant that the separation of specialist plant producers from the chemicals companies themselves occurred for reasons of a more organisational or narrowly economic type, often connected with difficulties in coping with business cycle fluctuations or the sheer extent of necessary managerial control. Conversely, *innovation* takes place much more at the stage of actual production of the product. Chemicals firms do the bulk of the R & D, employ their own designs and act as technologically sophisticated buyers (from plant manufacturers) who innovate as part of a competitive strategy in sophisticated world markets.

2.7 Summary and Some Concluding Remarks

In this chapter I have tried to build up a picture to show how the way science and technology impinges on society is very much a function of economic organisation. Before the industrial revolution the nature of the social order was such that technological changes could never play an important role. Indeed the 'economic problem' as we understand it today was perceived quite differently in most pre-industrial civilisation. Similarly scientific activity, in the modern sense of the disinterested pursuit of knowledge gained through the experimental method and sanctioned by the authority of a homogeneous set of professional institutions, was virtually unknown at least in Western civilisation. In a very real sense such societies were not receptive to science and technology. For that to happen a differentiated 'market' society had to evolve.

The industrial revolution for good or ill heralded just such a society − an exchange economy based upon the division of labour in which freedom existed for capitalist production. This 'new' form of economic organisation not only evolved with the aid of technological changes (many other factors were just as important in this very complex story) but produced also the setting within which science and technology became mechanisms for constant instability and dynamism. From being an essentially *exogenous* phenomenon, technological changes and science itself began to become socially *endogenous* for the first time in recorded history.

The implications of these new and evolving relations were (and are) dramatic. Economic productivity increased substantially and permanently but at the 'price' of radical social change on a variety of planes. I have emphasised the significance of capital accumulation, the development of capital goods production, economic differentiation and the pressures towards greater size of productive units, the gradual (but later) integration of organised scientific research into economic production, and the social and economic instability which resulted. Other factors could have been mentioned, such as the importance of colonies and foreign trade, but I have concentrated on a narrower range simply because I believe that it is through an examination and articulation of these ideas that we can best lay the foundations for the systematic analysis of science policy issues in the late twentieth century. Nevertheless, it should be re-emphasised that we are some way from such a conceptual goal. In chapter 5 we shall examine how historically some economists have tried to progress in this respect and in particular I shall explore briefly how different 'traditions' of economic thought have attempted to explain the phenomenon of technological change. In the subsequent chapter I shall bring the discussion up to date by reviewing a range of contemporary theory of relevance to this general theme.

Bibliography

There are a variety of texts which provide a good introduction to the historical development of present day economic society. I have used R. L. Heilbroner, *The Making of Economic Society* (Englewood Cliffs N J, Prentice-Hall, 1968 2nd edn) and C. Furtado, *Development and Underdevelopment* (Cambridge, Cambridge University Press, 1971) chapters 1−3 as my main texts (there is an updated edition of Heilbroner now available) but students might also consider G. Routh, *Economics: An Alternative Text* (London, Macmillan, 1984) especially chapters 1−5 and C. Furtado, *Accumulation and Development: The Logic of Industrial Civilisation* (Oxford, Martin Robertson, 1983) − both very stimulating reads. Rather more complex but a valuable general source is M. Dobb, *Studies in the Development of Capitalism* (London, Macmillan, 1976).

Other economic history texts having strong reference to technological change and/or dealing mainly with later periods are E. J. Hobsbawm, *Industry and Empire* (Harmondsworth, Penguin, 1969), D. S. Landes, *The Unbound Prometheus*, (Cambridge, Cambridge UP, 1976) and P. Mantoux, *The Industrial Revolution in the Eighteenth Century* (New York, University Paperbacks, 1964). Students might refer further to some of the texts cited at the end of chapter 1, especially both volumes of Rosenberg, Freeman (chapter 1), and Spiegel-Rösing and Price where the article by MacLeod on the social history of science contains an extensive bibliography much of which has relevance to the evolving relations between science and industry. See also P. Mathias (ed.), *Science and Society 1600–1900* (Cambridge, Cambridge University Press, 1972) and Pavitt and Worboys, *Science, Technology and the Modern Industrial State*, pp. 4–23. The latter provides an annotated bibliography covering the nineteenth century.

Finally there are a number of texts written from the standpoint of the developing countries, but which contain material of more general relevance e.g. R. E. Baldwin, *Economic Development and Growth* (New York, John Wiley, 1966).

Notes

1 Furtado, *Development and Underdevelopment*, chapter 3
2 Heilbroner, *The Making of Economic Society*, chapter 1
3 Heilbroner, *The Making of Economic Society*, p. 9.
4 M. Sahlins, *Stone Age Economics* (London, Tavistock, 1976), see chapter 1. See also Routh, *Economics: An Alternative Text*, chapter 2.
5 Heilbroner, *The Making of Economic Society*, p. 22, 23.
6 Heilbroner, *The Making of Economic Society*, p. 26.
7 This point is discussed in Rosenberg, *Inside the Black Box*, p. 12 who cites the work of Joseph Needham, *Science and Civilisation in China* (Cambridge, Cambridge University Press, 1954).
8 Furtado, *Development and Underdevelopment*, p. 93
9 Heilbroner, *The Making of Economic Society*, p. 46, 47.

10 Heilbroner, *The Making of Economic Society*, p. 35.

11 Routh, *Economics: An Alternative Text*, pp. 25–8.

12 R. H. Tawney, *Religion and the Rise of Capitalism* (Harmondsworth, Penguin, 1961).

13 M. Weber, *The Protestant Ethic and the Spirit of Capitalism* (London, Allen and Unwin, 1930).

14 For a discussion of this point see Dobb, *Studies in the Development of Capitalism*, chapter 2.

15 Furtado, *Development and Underdevelopment*, p. 116.

16 W. J. Barber, *A History of Economic Thought* (Harmondsworth, Penguin, 1967), pp. 23, 24.

17 There are a number of useful discussions of Smith's treatment of the division of labour. See for example, C. M. Cooper, 'Science, Technology and Development', *Economic and Social Review*, Vol. 2, No. 2, January 1971, pp. 165–189; S. Hollander, *The Economics of Adam Smith* (London, Heinemann, 1973), chapter 7.

18 Cooper, 'Science, Technology and Development', p. 170.

19 A. Smith, *The Wealth of Nations*, Edwin Cannon ed. (Methuen, London, 1961), Vol. I, p. 352. Quoted in Barber, p. 29.

20 Rosenberg, *Inside the Black Box*, chapter 2. See also Rosenberg, *Perspectives on Technology*, chapter 7.

21 Cooper, 'Science, Technology and Development', p. 173.

22 Rosenberg, *Perspectives on Technology*, pp. 131, 132.

23 Rosenberg, *Perspectives on Technology*, p. 135.

24 Furtado, *Development and Underdevelopment*, pp. 115–127.

25 Landes, *The Unbound Prometheus*, chapter 2.

26 Furtado, *Development and Underdevelopment*, pp. 119–120.

27 E. P. Thompson, *The Making of the English Working Class* (Harmondsworth, Penguin, 1968), see chapters 6–9.

28 R. H. Guest, 'The Rationalisation of Management', in M. Kranzberg and C. W. Purcell (eds), *Technology in Western Civilisation* (New York, Oxford University Press, 1967), Vol. II, p. 52.

29 H. Braverman, *Labor and Monopoly Capital* (New York, Monthly Review Press, 1974) is the main source for this theme. On the related theme of technological determinism and industrial development see D. Noble, *America By Design* (New York, Oxford University Press, 1977) and some of the recent writings of H. Rosenbrock, e.g. 'The Future of Control', *Automatica*, Vol. 13, 1977, pp. 389–92.

30 See R. J. Schonberger, *Japanese Manufacturing Techniques* (London, Collier Macmillan, 1982), chapter 2.

31 Pavitt and Worboys, *Science, Technology and the Modern Industrial State*, p. 7.

32 Freeman, *The Economics of Industrial Innovation*, p. 24.

33 Freeman, *The Economics of Industrial Innovation*, p. 24.

34 Freeman, *The Economics of Industrial Innovation*, Part I.

35 Cooper, 'Science, Technology and Development', p. 179.

36 R. Murray, 'Underdevelopment, International Firms and the International Division of Labour' in Society for International Development, *Towards a New World Economy* (Rotterdam University Press, 1972), see p. 165 *et seq.*

37 Rosenberg, *Perspectives on Technology*, especially chapters 1, 2, 3 and 10.

38 Rosenberg, *Perspectives on Technology*, pp. 16, 17.

39 Rosenberg, *Perspectives on Technology*, p. 17.

40 Rosenberg, *Perspectives on Technology*, p. 29.
41 Rosenberg, *Perspectives on Technology*, chapter 8.
42 C. Freeman, 'Chemical Process Plant: Innovation and the World Market', *National Institute Economic Review*, No. 45, August 1968, pp. 29–57.

Chapter 3

THE MACROECONOMY – ACCOUNTING FOR SCIENCE AND TECHNOLOGY

3.1 Introduction

This chapter is concerned with the macroeconomic system. My main aim here is *first* to introduce students to the ways in which economic systems are normally 'accounted for' in terms of important aggregates and sub-aggregates and *secondly* to show how social expenditures upon science and technology may also be accounted for although they do not relate in any simple fashion to the conventions which underlie social accounting.

It is important for students to try to engage with these matters for several reasons. First, a set of national accounts provides a 'map' of the economic system in terms of the various sectors which make it up. Understanding how the various pieces fit together considerably improves the overall grasp of the structure of a modern economy, at least up to a given level of approximation. Secondly, many of the categories utilised have precise technical meanings which it is best to be clear about at the outset since they are used widely in the literature, often not altogether unambiguously. Thirdly, the types of categories used and the ways they are accounted for, reflect in large part more theoretical conventions within economic analysis which in turn bear a close relationship with the preoccupations of standard economic policy-making. Since policy questions relating to science and technology have usually to be settled within the broader context of macroeconomic policy it is best to be clear about the empirical basis for the latter.

The chapter is divided into two broad parts. In the first part I shall describe how a set of national accounts is conventionally built up, starting from an oversimplified two-sector economy consisting of just households and productive units and gradually broadening out to include government, foreign trade, savings and investment, and industrial diversity. Inter-sectoral relations are described in terms of flows of goods and services per unit of time (usually a year), and the services involved include those of factors of production (such as labour, capital and so on). As will be seen with the microeconomic discussion in chapter 4 an important convention underlying much of this treatment is that productive activity may be divided into two distinct categories, 'inputs' and 'outputs', the transformation of the one into the other taking place within the productive sector, while the distribution of the 'outputs' takes place outside the productive sector. More generally resource flows into and out of any sector may be described in terms of double-entry bookkeeping, in such a manner that the quantitative importance of inter-sectoral relations may be established fairly readily.

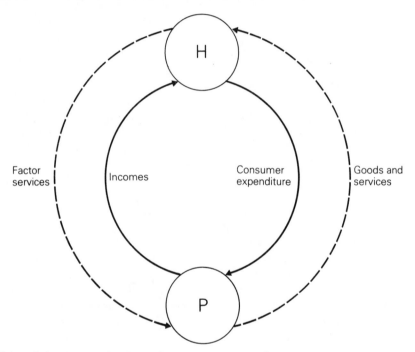

Figure 3.1   The circular flow of incomes and expenditure

In the second part I shall try to perform a similar type of exercise for the structure of science and technology, although not in a formal accounting sense. The delineation will be in terms of how resources are allocated to science and technology in the context of important organisational categories within the public and private sectors. Although there are great difficulties in attaching statistics to scientific activity, and although the inaccuracies are probably more significant than is the case with economic accounting, nevertheless it is argued that such is the importance of scientific and technological activity in the modern world that efforts in this direction are certainly necessary. Most of the discussion in both sections relates to the British economic system.

3.2 Social Accounting

3.2.1 The Circular Flow of Income

Let us start then by imagining a simple two-sector economy consisting of a productive sector, P, which produces consumer goods and sufficient capital goods to replace equipment used up in the course of a year, *and* a household sector, H, which supplies factor services to P, the income from which is used entirely to consume the goods and services produced by P. The relations between the two sectors may then be described in terms of two 'flows', namely a real flow of resources (anti-clockwise in figure 3.1) and a financial flow (clockwise in figure 3.1).

There is no government or foreign trade in this simple economy while the need to replace depreciated equipment can be treated as occurring within the productive sector, P.

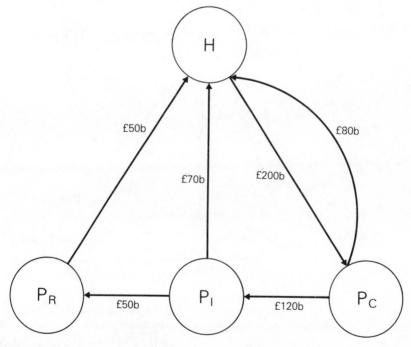

Figure 3.2 Intersectoral relations
(1) − raw materials/intermediates/consumer goods

We may now elaborate the model slightly by expanding the P sector into three constituent sub-sectors as follows:

P_R – producing raw materials;
P_I – producing intermediate goods;
P_e – producing 'final' (or consumer) goods.

Let us also lend a touch of realism by enumerating the system in money terms, as shown in figure 3.2.

Production is carried out in three successive stages with each stage 'adding value' to the preceding one. The 'national product' may be measured either in terms of the production of final goods (= £200b in value) or in terms of the incomes accruing to the H sector (£50b + £70b + £80b = £200b), thus illustrating an important convention in social accounting – the equivalence between national product and national income. More specifically:

National Income = £200b = £50b + £70b + £80b = total value-added summed over each production stage = total national output of consumer goods (£200 b) = consumer expenditures.

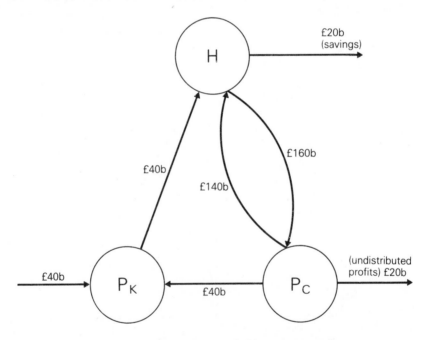

Figure 3.3 Intersectoral relations (2) – capital/consumer goods

Without altering the essence of the argument we may split the P sector in another way so as to differentiate the production of capital goods from that of

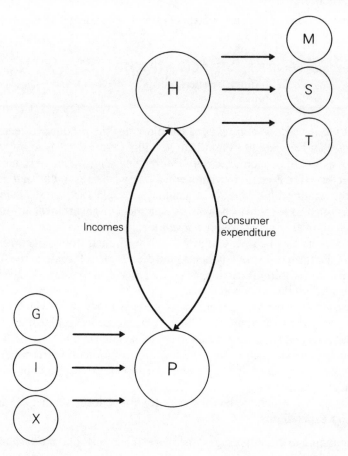

Figure 3.4   The generalised circular flow of income and expenditure

consumer goods, and hence to illustrate the fact that the economy does not simply produce and consume, but also *saves* and *invests*. Savings are defined in terms of abstinence from consumption on the part of the household sector. Investment is defined in terms of the expenditure upon new capital goods by the productive sector, thereby enabling it to produce more in subsequent periods. In figure 3.3 the consumer goods producing sector, P_C, produces £160b worth of consumer goods which are sold to the household sector. It then pays out £140b for factor services to H withholding savings in the form of £20b of undistributed profits. These, along with £20b of direct household savings are then borrowed by the capital goods producing sector, P_K in order to produce £40b worth of capital (or investment) goods which are subsequently sold to P_C. Hence, again national product may be estimated from both 'sides' of the circular flow of income, namely:

Total Expenditure = Consumer Expenditure + Investment Expenditure
$$= \pounds160b + \pounds40b$$
$$= \pounds200b$$
Total Incomes = £40b (P_K->H) + £140b (P_C->H)
+ £20b (undistributed profits)
$$= \pounds200b$$

All that we have done is to expand (or blow up) the productive sector in a different way compared to that illustrated in figure 3.2 so as to highlight a different aspect of economic activity. More generally, we may expand either the H sector or the P sector in whatever way we wish so as to illustrate various economic relationships. The act of national (or social) accounting is to do so in ways which have relevance to the management of government affairs.

The analytical schema which conventionally underlie such a system of social accounts may be seen in figure 3.4. The circular flow of incomes from P to H in the form of factor payments, and then back to P again in the form of consumer expenditures, is no longer viewed as a closed system. Instead there are 'leakages' of three general types:
—   **Imports**: household expenditures upon *imports* (M), which have no productive counterpart since they are produced by foreigners.
—   **Savings** (S), which are withheld by households in one form or another, but usually as assets through monetary institutions (such as commercial banks, building societies) or as claims upon productive units (through stocks and shares).
—   **Taxes** (T), which are levied by the government so as to help finance its own expenditures.

Corresponding to these 'leakages' there are 'injections' into the system again of three major forms:
—   **Exports** (X), goods produced by the productive sector (and hence providing incomes for H) but which are bought by foreigners.
—   **Investment** (I), expenditures by the productive sector on capital goods and other 'long-lived' assets.
—   **Government expenditures** (G) on behalf of consumers.

In general any incomes which are not passed on in the circular flow are classified as *withdrawals* while expenditures which are introduced into the circular flow other than from the household sector are classified as *injections*. However, we generally concentrate upon the six categories mentioned above since these have particular importance in the management of the modern economy. Where, for example, imports remain consistently above exports, foreign exchange reserves will fall or at least foreigners will have increased debt claims on the economy in question. Sometimes also pressures of this kind lead to a currency depreciation as more people wish to sell the local currency than wish to buy it. Where the international price of the currency is normally fixed or 'pegged' in terms of other currencies, the act of reducing its international price is called a 'devaluation'. A contentious issue amongst economists for many years relates to how effective such currency devaluations are in the stabilisation of economic systems which get themselves into debt, as is the case with a number of less developed countries today.

Table 3.1

Incomes		Expenditures	
Incomes from Employment (wages and salaries)	146	Consumption	152
		Government Consumption	55
Incomes from Self Employment	18	Gross Investment	39
		Inventory Increases	− 3
Gross Profits (Private Companies)	31	Domestic Expenditure	243
		Exports	68
Gross Profits (Public Companies)	8	Final Expenditure	311
		Less Imports	− 61
Rent	15	Gross Domestic Product at Market Prices	250
Consumption of Non-Trading Capital	2	Less Indirect Taxes	− 42
Domestic Income	220	Plus Subsidies	+ 6
Less Inventory Appreciation	− 6	Gross Domestic Product at Factor Cost	214
Gross Domestic Product	214		
Residual Error	− 1	*Less* Depreciation	− 31
Net Property Income from Abroad	1	Net National Product	183
Gross National Product at Factor Cost	214		
Less Depreciation	−31		
National Income	183		

*In some cases figures (in £ b.) do not match because of rounding errors
Source: Annual Abstract of Statistics, London, HMSO, 1984 p.249.

3.2.2 The Production Account

Table 3.1 provides a national income and product account for the UK in 1981 in £billion. From this table you will see that not allowing for wear and tear of capital used up in the course of the year, the UK produced some £214b worth of goods and services over the course of 1981 measured at 'factor cost', that is having 'netted out' expenditure taxes and subsidies which affect the valuation of the national product on the expenditure side but which do not reflect any real productive input. This *Gross National Product* (or GNP as it is customarily called) may also be measured by adding up categories of incomes, as in the left hand column, and making a number of adjustments to account for statistical error and to allow for inflationary increases in unsold inventories of goods. The category 'net property income from abroad' is an important one since it differentiates Gross *Domestic* Product (GDP), the output of a given geographical area, from Gross *National* Product (GNP), the output produced by residents of that area. The distinction, though not significant in this case for the UK, becomes more important in poor countries where a sizeable fraction of assets are owned by foreigners. In such countries the GDP, the apparent produce of the country, is often much greater than the GNP, the income accruing to the country's residents.

The main reason for distinguishing government consumption from domestic or household consumption is that they are each determined by different forces. Whereas the latter is influenced mainly by incomes and tastes the former is more directly the outcome of the political process. Usually government consumption may be sub-divided into two categories. One is government purchases from the productive sector on behalf of consumers, as with the distribution of free school milk for children. In this case the government acts as a surrogate customer for sections of the population as a whole and there is a statistical counterpart in terms of value-added within the productive sector itself. The second category is where the government in effect becomes its own productive sector and purchases from itself, as with the provision of education, for example, where in theory at least the government purchases various types of professional services and other inputs, which are then combined to provide a service to schoolchildren. You will see from table 3.1 that public authority investment is separated from government consumption and included along with private company investment in this summary of the national accounts.

The data which go to make up social accounts are culled from a variety of sources. For example, income data may be obtained from Tax Offices and the published statements of registered companies. Expenditure data are often obtained from periodic expenditure surveys, while data on output are provided by periodic censuses of production. Finally data on foreign trade come from Customs and Excise offices. In most countries there is a particular agency, or bureau, charged with the function of collecting and processing data in a form useful to policy-makers and the public more generally. In the UK this function is discharged by the Central Statistical Office which publishes periodically a wide variety of useful digests.

3.2.3 Important Conventions

Generally speaking there are a number of conventions which underlie the establishment of a system of national accounts and it is necessary to be clear about the more significant of these at least. One very important one is that a distinction is made between truly productive activities and *transfer payments*. The distinction is that the former are to be seen as flows of money which have some counterpart in real productive activity whereas the latter represent simply a transfer of resources between people or institutions, like for example the provision of sickness benefit. Transfer payments are not included as part of the measurement of GNP. There are, however, ambiguities about what constitutes a productive activity. Thus people who look after the home and raise children (mainly women) are held by convention to be non-productive and their labour time is not included in GNP estimates, despite the conclusion of most commentators that even imputing very low wages indeed to such activities would increase substantially the GNP's of most countries. Similarly a parent giving money to a child for performing a household chore would not normally expect this sum to be included in the GNP.

In general the conventions which govern the establishment of national product estimates are governed by three factors:

(a) **Convenience** – how easy it is to collect reliable data.
(b) **Quantitative importance** – how significant is the function in question to the economy as a whole.
(c) **Ideological** – what functions are held to be productive in the eyes of the government.

A well-known example of the latter convention relates to the difference between Soviet and Western practice in the computation of services. In the West, activities such as 'entertainment' or 'social services' are treated as productive activities which require effort and cost. In the USSR, however, an activity is only regarded as 'productive' if it is concerned with material output. All other activities are treated as 'non-productive' and paid for out of the economic surplus provided by the material goods sector, an interesting throw-back to the views of some of the classical political economists (like Adam Smith) as we saw in the last chapter. It should be noted that there is nothing inherently good or bad about such conventions, since they merely reflect ideological positions about what is, or is not, 'productive'. It does mean, however, that in the interpretation of official data one has to be very clear about the underlying conventions. For example, in the case we have just been discussing it is very difficult to come to unambiguous conclusions about the comparative economic production of, say, the USA and the USSR, for obvious reasons.

A second convention of importance is that all transactions involving *intermediate goods* are excluded from the computation of national product. This is because to include them would be to account for them more than once, as for example in the well-known case of flour and bread, where to add sales of bread to sales of flour to the bakeries over the time period in question, would be to count the output of flour twice. Again, while examples like this one are fairly clear cut, the decision as to what is and what is not an intermediate good raises similar problems of definition to those of transfer payments. Should not transportation to work, for example, be counted as an intermediate good (or in this case, service) since without its provision output would be drastically curtailed? What about the purchase of clothes, for similar reasons?

The normal convention is not to include such items as intermediate goods, partly because they also fulfil other 'final consumption' demands and partly no doubt because to do so would be to complicate enormously the lives of many hard-pressed statisticians. But this discussion does raise a more fundamental point about social accounting which should perhaps be stressed, and that concerns its philosophical basis. Essentially, systems of national accounts tend to place implicit valuations on certain areas of social activity which are sometimes not fully understood by those who use the resultant data. The fact, for example, that 'work' may be a positive 'good' for people, and that loss of work is more than just loss of income, cannot easily be accounted for in conventional terms since there is no 'market' available to assign values to such 'psychic' incomes. Similarly, as we have seen, there are huge areas of 'productive activity' where the resultant 'output' simply cannot be measured – as with education, defence and much scientific research. For this reason many areas of public expenditure are measured *at cost*, by adding up the inputs, and not by a valuation of outputs, an important implication of which is that it is rather more difficult in such cases to identify statistically gains in productivity. Hence, although a set of social accounts does provide a useful picture of broad economic interrelationships their interpretation should be conducted with great care.

A third convention is that *consumer durables*, i.e. goods which are 'consumed' in practice over a significant period, like cars and washing machines, are treated in accounting terms as being used up entirely during the year of purchase. One practical reason for this is the extreme complexity involved in assessing the stream of services accruing from a consumer durable over its real life. A second reason is that such a convention makes it possible to divide output neatly into two categories, consumption and investment, thereby providing a ready, if approximate, guide to the extent the economy in question is laying by resources for the future. The greater the share of investment in total output the faster in general will be the rate of economic growth, defined in terms of the rate of change of the economy's capacity to produce economic output. Of course in reality, commodities demonstrate a spectrum of longevity from instantaneous obsolescence (ice cream) to very great age (St Paul's Cathedral) but provided this is kept in mind, the convention is quite useful. One concession to realism on the part of social statisticians is the common practice of treating dwellings as investment items. In order to compute the services of dwellings, householders who own their houses are treated as productive units renting the houses back to themselves at a price determined by a number of fixed rules about maintenance, depreciation, and so on.

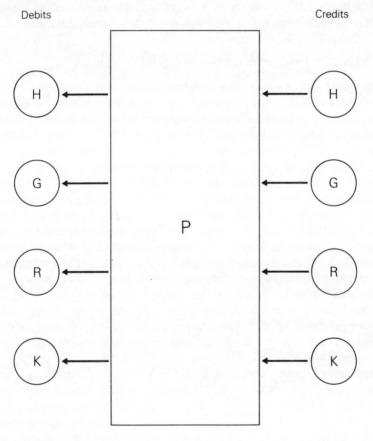

R = the 'foreign' sector
K = the 'capital' sector

Figure 3.5 A generalised social account

Finally, there is a set of conventions regarding the treatment of investment items which ought to be mentioned for the sake of completion. Inventory accumulation, in the form of increases in unsold stocks of goods and work-in-progress, is accounted for separately from 'fixed' investment (e.g. plant and machinery) since the economic implications of each category are clearly quite different. Secondly, any differential on foreign trade account (exports less imports) is treated as an investment item, since the associated 'debt' provides interest payments either from or to other countries. Finally, all systems of national accounts make an attempt to compute the depreciation of capital stock over the course of the year under consideration since a true measure of national product (i.e. *net* national product) must clearly take this into account. Unfortunately it is rather difficult to compute reliable estimates of this statistic for a variety of reasons, and so social analysts prefer in practice often to work with gross estimates of national output.

3.2.4 National Income as a Set of Social Accounts

Quite a neat way of viewing an economic system is as an interlocking set of social accounts, drawn up much as conventional current account balance sheets are for any business i.e. with outgoings (or debits) on the one side and incomes (or credits) on the other. Thus for the productive sector, P, a stylised account would look something like figure 3.5. P pays out incomes to households (for use of factor services), tax payments to the government, payments for imports and savings in the form of undistributed profits. It receives income from household consumption, exports, government expenditures and investment. Since an important principle of double-entry bookkeeping is that all accounts should be made to balance, the necessary adjustment is made to the savings and investment entries, which are treated as payments to and incomes from a 'capital' sector. Similarly import and export entries are treated as payments to, and incomes from, a 'foreign' sector with the productive sector treated as buying imports on behalf of consumers. Viewed in this way it may readily be seen that the set of national accounts outlined in table 3.1 is in fact an enumerated double-entry account for the UK productive sector, the one difference being that imports have been transferred to the credit side with a negative sign.

More generally any economic sector may be accounted for in a similar fashion. The extent to which this is done, as well as the complexity of the enumeration, in terms of the number of different creditors and debtors, depends of course on the adequacy of the available data. The greater the number of different categories enumerated the more information a set of social accounts provides about the economic system under consideration, but conversely there is a resultant danger of more frequent and greater inaccuracies. Where the data are good enough a useful summary method of presenting social accounts is the input/output table. Table 3.2 provides a stylised input/output table for a mythical economy. You will see that in addition to the four non-productive sectors (i.e. households, H, 'capital', K, government, G, and the foreign sector, R), the productive sector itself has been blown up into three constituent sectors (I_1, I_2, I_3) which conduct transactions amongst each other.

Table 3.2

Debits Credits	I_1	I_2	I_3	H	K	G	R	Total
I_1		40	10	20		10	40	120
I_2	20		30	40	35	15	15	155
I_3	10	15		30	5	10	30	100
H	30	55	30			5		120
K	15	15	10	10		25		75
G	20	20	5	20				65
R	25	10	15		35			85
Total	120	155	100	120	75	65	85	

Source: This table is a modified version of a similar table provided by W. Beckerman, *An Introduction to National Income Analysis*, London, Weidenfeld and Nicolson, 1976, 2nd edn., p. 117, figure 6.2.

The columns represent 'debits' or flows of resources out of the sector concerned while the rows represent 'credits' or flows of resources into the sector concerned. For example, table 3.1 shows the household sector paying out £40b to industry I_2 and the 'capital' sector receiving £10b in the form of household savings. Also any sectoral account may be read off immediately. For example, staying with the household sector for the moment, the sectoral account is demonstrated in table 3.3.

Table 3.3 Account for the Household Sector (£ b.)

Income		Expenditures	
Incomes from Factor Services (e.g. wages, salaries, interest etc.)	115	Consumption	90
		Savings	10
Government Transfer Payments	5	Taxes	20
	120		120

Finally the table may be viewed as consisting of four quadrants each illustrating a different facet of inter-sectoral relationships. The north-west quadrant describes transactions involving intermediate goods within the productive sector while the north-east quadrant describes sales of the productive sector *to* 'final demand' in terms of consumption, investment, government expenditures and exports. The south-west quadrant describes 'value-added' or 'incomes' to the suppliers of factor services. Finally the south-east quadrant represents transfer payments between sectors i.e. where there is no direct counterpart in terms of productive activity.

3.3 Accounting for Science and Technology – the 'Science System'

So far in this chapter I have tried to convey a picture of how economists and statisticians conventionally describe the economic system and the interrelationships among its various parts. In this section I shall perform a similar type of exercise for what has come to be called the 'science system' (or 'scientific infrastructure') of a modern industrialised economy. I shall do this by showing how it is possible to be quantitative, again up to a given level of approximation, about the science system and its important sub-aggregates, although it should be noted that 'accounting for science' is a much more recent practice compared to social accounting, and the conventions and assumptions underlying it not nearly so well worked out. Students wishing to look more closely at these matters are advised to consult the relevant texts cited in the bibliography.

There are several reasons why it is important to be quantitative about scientific efforts. First of all it provides something of a constraint on received wisdom. If you do not at least attempt to measure the relevant variables, argument tends to become very much a matter of opinion and decision-making on science policy issues a matter of power politics. Thus for example, it may be politically expedient to cut back on research conducted by universities, but if it can be shown that university research in general produces significant social benefits then such an act of retrenchment will be seen to involve clear social costs. More generally measurement increases the information available to decision-makers and, hopefully, helps to produce better decisions, both at the level of government and for industry. A second, and related, factor is that measurement of scientific aggregates improves understanding of the science system much in the same way as social accounting does for the economic system as a whole.

A third reason concerns the use of measurement in identifying and testing relationships which have an important bearing upon science policy decision-making. As pointed out in the first chapter the increasingly large sums of money being spent on science and technology give rise to important questions about 'pay-off'. What is the rate of return to R & D? Does it vary across industries and if so, how? Can we perform similar sorts of calculations on basic science expenditure? How easily can we go from *ex post* to *ex ante* *prognosis* for the future.

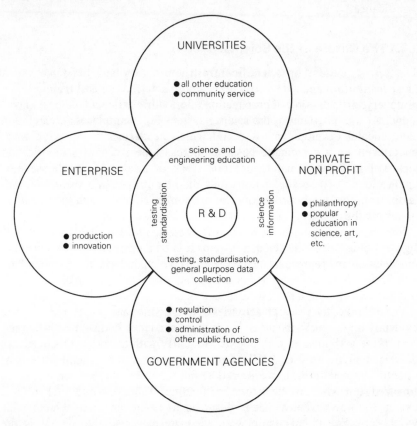

Figure 3.6   The science system

An important contemporary example relates to how quickly industrial activity will recover from recession. An influential traditional view has been that in the downswing of the business cycle, although *investment* falls dramatically, R & D and scientific expenditures in general remain fairly constant. Under such circumstances there is no problem about any economic system 'falling behind' technologically and hence losing out in terms of international competitiveness, since the general level of technological competence is rising continuously − the 'technological shelf' is being systematically 're-stocked' with the newest equipment vintages, processes, systems etc. More recently, however, this view has been questioned by those who argue both that R & D activity does indeed fall during recessions and that falling behind in this respect can adversely affect recovery. It is within this context that the work of Mensch,[1] Freeman and others,[2] which attempts statistical measurement of innovation in relation to cyclical trends, has great significance.

3.3.1 The Nature of the Science System

The 'science system' or 'scientific infrastructure' may be defined in terms of those institutions and social structures whose activities consist mainly in the discovery, articulation and propagation of scientific and technological knowledge. At the heartland of the science system Freeman places research and experimental development (R & D) which he defines as 'creative work undertaken on a systematic basis to increase the stock of scientific and technical knowledge and to use this stock of knowledge to devise new applications'.[3] These applications may then be utilised in a variety of contexts, from the purely productive, or economic, right through to the educational and the cultural.

Somewhat analogous to the circular flow of income described in figure 3.4, figure 3.6 describes the science system. It is taken from Freeman's original presentation and represents the conventions which underlie the way in which R & D activities relate to the science system as a whole, since clearly much scientific work cannot be described as R & D.

For example, the research activities of universities and polytechnics, while evidently important to the *other* functions of academic bodies, represent only part of the activities of such bodies. Similarly with the other broad sectors described in figure 3.6. While figure 3.6 outlines the general pattern of scientific expenditures, however, it does not show how these expenditures are financed, nor what are the sources of funding. Table 3.4, again taken from Freeman, shows what a matrix designed to bring out these relationships would look like if only there were adequate data available. Omitting the 'private non-profit' sector the rows illustrate certain important categories of scientific expenditure while the columns represent both the sectors of performance as well as the sectoral sources of funds, and it may be seen, for example, that in this hypothetical system around 53% of government scientific activity is accounted for by R & D expenditures. It may also be seen that while the productive sector carried out 60% of total R & D, only half of this figure is financed from within its own resources.

Of course this table is only a hypothetical one but it is not unrealistic. For example, recent evidence for the UK shows that while the productive sector performed some two-thirds of total R & D, around 60% of this figure was financed from within its own resources and around 30% from government.[4]

Table 3.4 Hypothetical Matrix of Expenditures for Scientific and Technological Services by Sectors of Performance and Sources of Funds in Million US Dollars

Scientific and technological services	Sectors of performance					Sectors of source of funds				
	Productive Enterprise		General government	Higher education	Total	Productive enterprise (enterprise level)	General government and branch level of productive enterprise sector	Higher education	Abroad	Total
	Enterprise Level	Branch Level								
Research and experimental development	400	200	300	100	1000	300	680	0	20	1000
Education and training of high-level manpower	5	0	5	150	160	15	140	0	5	160
Scientific library and information services	10	20	20	5	55	25	25	0	5	55
Testing, standarisation and quality control	90	50	115	5	260	135	125	0	0	260
Museums, zoological and botanical gardens	0	0	20	0	20	5	15	0	0	20
Geological, geophysical, meterological and technical survey work, incl. mapping	180	20	40	0	240	175	50	0	15	240
General purpose social and economic data collection	20	5	15	0	40	25	15	0	0	40
Technical and scientific advisory and consultancy services, incl. patent, licensing and know-how activities	150	10	25	5	190	130	15	0	45	190
Design and engineering services	220	220	20	5	445	380	55	0	10	445
TOTAL	1055 1580	525	560	270	2410	1190	1120	0	100	2410

Source: C. Freeman, *The Economics of Industrial Innovation* (Harmondsworth, Penguin, 1974), pp. 328-9.

Again, as with the input/output table shown in tables 3.2 and 3.3, it is possible to 'blow up' any box so as to illustrate specific resource flows, always provided of course adequate resources are available for the entries. A particularly contentious issue relates to the disposition of R & D expenditures, especially those which are financed by government and hence are directly subject to public policy. For the UK, Williams[5] has pointed out that the pattern of R & D expenditure funded by central government has continued to be biased overwhelmingly (around 60% of the total) in favour of defence, aerospace and nuclear energy to an extent unmatched by any other OECD country except the USA. A typical table showing the relationships between sources and objectives of R & D funding in the UK would look something like the (partially hypothetical) table 3.5 for 1978.

Table 3.5   Sources of R & D Expenditures and Expenditure Objectives for the UK in 1978 (£ million)

Source of Funds Objectives	Government	Industry	Other	Total
Defence	1040	(0)	(0)	1040
Other Industry	103	(1400)	(0)	1503
Other	542	(109)	(316)	967
Total	1685	1509	316	3510

Source: House of Lords Select Committee on Science and Technology, *Engineering Research and Development*, London, HMSO, 1983

Since we do not have data on the disposition of objectives regarding the R & D expenditures of industry and other (mainly higher education) the figures in brackets represent 'guesstimates' of the true situation. More generally, any entry in the table 3.5 may be 'blown up' and enumerated always provided adequate data exist.

A number of points, however, should be borne in mind regarding this form of 'science and technology accounting', which differentiate it from the broader 'economic accounting' described in the first half of this chapter. To begin with the tabular entries themselves, while analogous, do not strictly concern relations between 'inputs' and 'outputs' in quite the same sense or to quite the same degree. Hence scientific accounting should be thought of more in terms of the ways in which resources are allocated over different categories of scientific expenditures rather than in 'input/output' terms. The main reason for this is that scientific and technological expenditures, including those related directly to R & D, are measured 'at cost' i.e. as 'inputs' into scientific activity. The 'output' in terms of new ideas, knowledge, blueprints, processes, machines etc., are much more difficult to quantify unambiguously as we shall see later.

However, some preliminary work has been carried out, initially by Schmookler[6] and later more fully by Scherer[7] into intersectoral *flows* of technology, where an attempt has been made to compute in financial terms the technological relations amongst economic sectors using an input/output table technique for the US economy. Essentially what Scherer did was to split the economic system into 41 'origin' sectors and 53 'user' sectors, and to compute the flows of technology between them in the following way. For each of the 41 'origin' sectors R & D data were available divided into 'product oriented' and 'process-oriented' categories. The latter were allocated to the matrix diagonal and hence were treated as being 'used' within the originating sector. The former were then allocated amongst the 53 'user' sectors by means of a complicated technique which involved using patent data (enumerated by product type) as a proxy for inventive 'output'. Some more recent work along similar lines is currently being carried out by Pavitt and his colleagues at the Science Policy Research Unit of the University of Sussex.[8] We are still, however, some way off being able to link statistically scientific activity to socio-economic performance in any accurate or comprehensive manner.

Another point to bear in mind is that unlike conventional social accounting, scientific expenditures have to be divided between (a) sector of source of funds and (b) sector of performance. This becomes particularly important because of the commonly high proportion of scientific expenditures financed by government in most advanced economies (40% – 60% in most OECD countries) much of which is not actually spent directly in state-controlled institutions, although the state may still have some jurisdiction over how the funds are spent. In the case of the UK, for example, the 1979/80 data show that £1,695m out of a total of £2,609m central government expenditure (roughly two-thirds) was spent outside its own institutions, mainly in private industry and universities.[9] Finally it should be noted that there are very great difficulties involved in providing accurate estimates of expenditures upon science and technology, and, more importantly, in subdividing such estimates into operationally useful categories. We shall review in chapter 4 Freeman's distinction between genuinely 'innovative' and 'non-innovative' R & D expenditures, and it should be emphasised that it is not easy to be sure that relevant data supplied by government, industry and other bodies are saying precisely what they are supposed to. A similar point might be made about the splitting of R & D into 'defence related' and 'other industry related' objectives, since whatever the source of funding might wish, it is often difficult in practice to ascertain what the real objective of the R & D might be.

3.3.1 Measuring the Output of Science and Technology

Up to this stage we have concentrated on R & D expenditures as a major category in science accounting. We have done so for the very good reason that whatever the inaccuracies in R & D data may be, they do represent a homogeneous and relatively available source of information on the disposition of scientific and technological activity. However, they are also 'input' data i.e. they measure resource allocation *at cost*, and so cannot be used as measures of scientific 'output' except under very restrictive, and probably unrealistic, assumptions about research productivity. Hence, I should like finally to turn to the question of how we may appraise and evaluate the 'output' of scientific expenditures, and in particular to summarise the main measures which are conventionally used. Since this is only a brief introductory discussion students are strongly encouraged to consult some of the more detailed treatments cited in the bibliography, especially Freeman's Appendix to the *Economics of Industrial Innovation* which is a clear and comprehensive summary of a more detailed piece of work undertaken earlier for the OECD.[10]

The main reason why it is hard to assess the 'output' of scientific and technological activity, at least in socio-economic terms, is because such 'output' realises its value mainly within the context of later productive activity. This disjunction makes it impossible to place an unambiguous 'value' on the scientific output itself, whatever its form, since the 'value' of the final (economic) product is the result of a combination of many inputs of which scientific research is only one. The problem becomes greater the more fundamental the nature of the research in question.

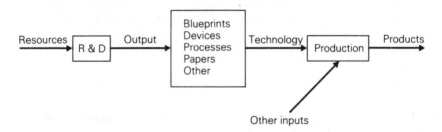

Figure 3.7

In the 'limiting case' of purely fundamental research, its 'value' may be described as largely cultural and devoid of any socio-economic significance, at least in the short term. Nor should it be forgotten that a good deal of scientific research, undertaken for socio-economic ends, does not end up producing 'outputs' which are suitable for socio-economic use.

Two further characteristics about the 'market for knowledge' which have relevance to this discussion are first the *uncertainty* which attaches to any research activity and secondly, the *inappropriability* of at least a proportion of the scientific output which does eventually result. The first means that firms will often commit resources to innovation in the full knowledge that they might not receive any return at all. The second relates to what economists classify as a 'public good' − a commodity which on being produced cannot be readily 'appropriated' by the producer and which to that extent cannot command a demand price. Again both these factors render attempts to measure the output of scientific expenditures a very hazardous operation, and students are warned to treat such data with very great care.

3.3.2 Social Cost/Benefit Analysis (SCBA)

Conceptually the most complete evaluative technique is that of SCBA, used normally in the appraisal of large investment projects (such as the construction of dams) where the decision choice depends upon the costs and benefits likely to accrue, and where there are limited investment funds available. It is also used to evaluate past projects so as to help determine the extent to which the project in question has paid off. For purposes of illustration, let us assume a project with a 'life' of 20 years over which period the initial investment costs get amortized. Assume also that the expected costs and benefits associated with the project be respectively C_0, C_1, C_2, C_3 ... C_{20} and B_0, B_1, B_2, B_3 ... B_{20} where the subscript numerals represent the year. Then at a first approximation the project's value, V, may be given by:

$$V = (B_0\text{-}C_0) + (B_1\text{-}C_1) + (B_2\text{-}C_2) + (B_3\text{-}C_3) + 5\,5\,5\,5 + (B_{20}\text{-}C_{20})$$

We may bring this crude figure to a *current* value by using a rate of interest, r, to 'discount' each annual flow of net income back to the present as follows;

$$\text{Net Present Value } (NPV) = B_0\text{-}C_0 + \frac{B_1\text{-}C_1}{1+r} + \frac{B_2\text{-}C_2}{(1+r)^2} + \cdots + \frac{B_{20}\text{-}C_{20}}{(1+r)^{20}}$$

which may be written as:

$$NPV = \sum_{i=0}^{20} \frac{B_i\text{-}C_i}{(1+r)^i}$$

Provided the data underlying this calculation for current and projected future resource flows turn out to be correct, and provided that the prices used to evaluate these resource flows reflect the true social costs of the resources in question, then the resultant monetary value gives an indication of the social value of the project under consideration. If this is positive, then other things being equal the investment should take place. More generally SCBA may be used to rank competing projects in terms of social value where scarcity of investible resources requires that choices have to be made.

Unfortunately, SCBA suffers from a whole series of drawbacks as a decision-making tool even with respect to straightforward investment projects. These concern factors such as the non-measurability of certain important inputs and outputs, complementarities between projects and the choice of the discount rate.[11] In general, therefore, it is used as only *one* input in the decision-making process. Where we consider its use in the appraisal of scientific expenditures i.e. with respect to R & D projects, for example – these drawbacks are compounded by the much greater uncertainty which attaches to scientific investigation *both* in terms of technology *and* in terms of commercial viability. And since we are considering 'uncertainty' (which cannot be handled through the use of the statistics of probability) as opposed to 'risk' (which can), the general view of most commentators is that SCBA cannot be safely used as a selection device with regard to research policy.

There have been a number of attempts to use SCBA in evaluating *past* research, possibly the most famous being Griliches's calculation on the rate of return to investment in hybrid corn (referred to further in chapter 6).[12] The problem here, however, is that viewed as a technique for measuring the *output* of scientific expenditures, SCBA is so complex and time-consuming a task that in practice it is only feasible to use it occasionally. Hence, although in principle SCBA might appear to be the most complete technique for evaluating scientific output, in practice it is a very imperfect one and as a result is used only very occasionally.

3.3.3 Patents

These are now widely used as a measure of inventive/innovative output, especially where it is possible to aggregate the resultant data for analytical purposes, in the way that Scherer did in the construction of the scientific input/output table. The advantages of patents are that statistics are readily available from patent offices in a well-annotated form, and that they are available internationally. There are, however, a number of disadvantages:

(i)   They provide quantitative indices but have no economic value attached to them.

(ii) They tend to reflect 'inventive' rather than 'innovative' output, and so are only an appropriate measure in certain circumstances.

(iii)   International comparisons using patent data are hazardous because of variations in patent law between countries.

(iv)   There are variations in patentability amongst different classes of invention.

(v)   Sometimes inventors do not patent since to do so would draw the attention of potential imitators, who might well be able to circumvent patent legislation. This is especially the case where subsequent innovation costs are likely to be high and where the invention in question is only a part of a larger technological system.

(vi)   Patenting activity varies through time.

Despite these limitations, however, patent statistics have been widely used in a number of important studies of invention and innovation. One hopes that, with improved methods of recording, registration and processing they will continue to provide an important form of quantitative evidence.

3.3.4 Counts of Innovations

An alternative to the enumeration of patents is the enumeration of innovations. You will recall that an innovation may be defined as the first 'commercial introduction' of a new product or process, and from time to time researchers such as Mensch[13] have attempted to count the number of significant innovations emanating from particular industries or sectors over a given time period, using data from trade journals supplemented by interviews with knowledgeable people. The main advantage of this approach is that it provides an indicator which more truly reflects the actual *economic outputs* of R & D activity whilst at the same time making allowance for differential value of innovations. The main disadvantage is that there are few existing series of innovations so that the researcher normally has to construct his or her own − and that is usually a long and painstaking task.

3.3.5 Licences

A measure of technological output frequently used in the assessment of international flows of technology is the 'licence', defined as the right on the part of one firm to make commercial use of a proprietary technology belonging to another, subject to certain agreed conditions (e.g. prohibition of re-license to a third party). The payment, or 'royalty' for the licence is often reckoned as a percentage charge on subsequent sales (less imports of intermediate inputs supplied by the licensor), although lump sum charges are sometimes made either in lieu or as an additional fee. Again the licence has the advantage that it represents technological value in so far as this is reflected in direct economic output. A second advantage is that international statistics on licence payments are readily available, since they are collected and processed as part of the normal operation of foreign exchange control. An important disadvantage is that licence fees are not the only form in which suppliers of technology receive payment (profits from joint-venture arrangements and returns from the sales of intermediate goods are examples of other important types of financial payment).[14] Hence the use of aggregate licence data as a financial measure of flows of technology needs to be carried out with caution.

3.3.6 Scientific and Technical Papers

Returning now to the problem of evaluating 'scientific output' which is some way from realising itself in socio-economic terms, the most common 'currency' is that of the scientific paper, developed as an analytical measure mainly by Derek de Solla Price in the 1960s. The chief justification for adopting a count of scientific papers as a measure of the output of science (especially basic science) is that this is the principal means through which research scientists communicate to their peers, and to the outside world, the results of their endeavours. Moreover, it is a measure which must pass through a 'quality control' procedure; namely the scrutiny of a system of referees before being accepted for publication in an 'established' journal. It is for these reasons that Freeman concludes that a count of scientific papers is 'the only method which lends itself readily to large-scale statistical application'.[15]

Nevertheless it too has its drawbacks. Scientists often have other things to do with their time (like teaching students), there is quite a lot of variation across scientific fields as regards susceptibility to publication and in some cases (as with 'secret' defence work) it is often impossible to publish at all. Moreover there are problems involved in how you establish the comparative value of a publication, since journals vary in the quality of their contents and since one very penetrating paper may be seen by scientists to be 'worth' more than several worthy but rather pedestrian pieces. One important method of dealing with the problem of quality discrimination is that of *citation*, of counting the number of times, over a given period, that a particular paper is cited by other authors, either in its original field or in other fields. This is a relatively new analytical tool since it is only recently that adequate data on citation have been capable of being readily developed, and clearly we shall have to wait to see how useful it is likely to be, although already it has produced some interesting results. Nevertheless Irvine and Martin, for example, argue that citation indices are still only imperfect measures of quality. Published work, they maintain, possesses three broad characteristics.

(i)   Quality − how good the paper is according to the established 'canons' of scientific enquiry.

(ii) Importance – what the paper's potential influence is on the advance of knowledge.

(iii) Impact – actual influence the paper has had within its own scientific field.

And citation counts tend only to measure the third of these. More generally Irvine and Martin suggest, along with Freeman, that combinations of different measures be used so as to reach some sort of convergent estimate of scientific output and in recent years, as we shall see later, they have attempted to use this technique to compare scientific institutions within specific disciplines.[16]

3.3.7 Other Measures of Scientific Output

Two further measures which are commonly used are *first* straightforward counts of major discoveries, and *secondly*, peer evaluation, i.e. asking peer groups to rank the quality of research shown by specific institutions, publications or disciplines. Each of these measures, of course, has drawbacks similar to those we have already discussed in the context of other measures. It is perhaps advisable, however, to strike a note of general caution at this stage, which is very simply that modern scientific research has an inbuilt tendency to proliferation in terms of the spawning of new and more esoteric disciplines, and sub-disciplines, as more scientists are trained and as more complicated machines and other forms of apparatus are developed. Looked at in this light the products of scientific endeavour, measured in terms of papers or whatever, may simply reflect growing public expenditures upon science and very little else.

It is with this in mind that students are advised always to remember that the fundamental economic question, namely the allocation of scarce resources to any scientific activity, is an act which involves social costs. That is, it is carried out at the expense of other activities which *might* have had access to these resources and which *might* have produced results which were socially more beneficial. And however difficult such a question is to resolve, it is the obligation of any science policy analyst always to have it in view if only because *not* to do so amounts to a form of self-censorship which may preclude adequate investigation. An example of a more fundamental question of this kind relates to research into the causes of cancer, much of it funded by state resources (the balance mainly through charities) and controlled by a medical establishment which concentrates its activities on microbiological and genetic research of great complexity and great expense, in many of our leading universities, teaching hospitals and research institutions.

Now, the important larger questions to ask are; is this the right way to allocate research funds amongst all the different possible methods of 'dealing with' this major disease? Are there other avenues which are currently very much under-funded (like psychogenic research or research into chemical additives, for example)? What evidence is there that the current pattern of cancer research has had any appreciable effect on the rate of cure? Should more money be allocated to preventative medicine? Are there powerful vested interests which insist that research funds be channelled in particular directions, regardless of consequences? And so on. Questions of this much more fundamental kind will not in general be answered by counts of scientific papers, and yet they are of very great social importance. Students are advised not to forget about them.

3.4 Some Concluding Remarks

This chapter has had two major aims − first to show how it is possible to 'account' for the broad economic interrelationships which characterise modern economic systems and secondly to suggest an analogous accounting framework for science and technology. It is clear that this latter function is still at a very rudimentary level, mainly because of the quality and appropriateness of data needed to do the job, but also because it is difficult in any event to apply numerical values to the inputs and outputs of scientific and technological activity. This does not mean that attempts to measure should not be made. Indeed a great deal of valuable work is currently being done to put together better and more systematic indicators for science and technology. It does mean, however, that students should treat statistical analyses in this field with care, and wherever possible pay close attention to the more qualitative aspects of the topic under investigation.

Bibliography

There are of course very many texts dealing with national income and social accounting many of which will provide students with the necessary introductory knowledge. I have used W. Beckerman, *An Introduction to National Income Analysis* (London, Weidenfeld and Nicolson, 1980) chapters 1–6, and B. van Arkadie and C. Frank, *Economic Accounting and Development Planning* (London, Oxford University Press, 1966). The latter is particularly useful to students from developing countries and because it goes into the ideas and conventions underlying the drawing-up of business and social accounts. More general introductory texts such as R. G. Lipsey, *Positive Economics* (London, Weidenfeld and Nicolson, 1979) 5th edn, Part 7, are also worth looking at.

On accounting for science and technology indicators there is no one source which covers all aspects thoroughly. The best is still C. Freeman, *The Economics of Industrial Innovation* (Harmondsworth, Penguin, 1974), pp. 313–31 but reference might also be made to H. Stead, 'The Costs of Technological Innovation', *Research Policy*, Vol. 5, No. 1, 1976, pp. 2–10; UN National Science Board, *Science Indicators, 1982* (Washington, 1983); Select Committee on Science and Technology, *Engineering Research and Development* (House of Lords, HMSO, 1983); OECD, *Resources Devoted to R & D* (Paris, OECD, 1984); K. Pavitt, 'R & D, Patenting and Innovative Activities: A Statistical Exploration', *Research Policy*, Vol. 11, No. 1, January 1982, pp. 33–52; L. Soete and S. Wyatt, 'The Use of Foreign Patenting as an Internationally Comparable Science and Technology Output Indicator', *Scientometrics*, Vol. 5, No. 1, 1983, pp. 31–54. On Basic Science, see J. Irvine and B. Martin, *Foresight in Science: Picking the Winners* (London, Frances Pinter, 1984), and 'What Direction for Basic Scientific Research?', in M. Gibbons, P. Gummett and B. M. Udgaonkar (eds), *Science and Technology in the 1980s and Beyond* (Harlow, Longmans, 1984).

Notes

1 See, for example, C. Freeman, J. Clark and L. Soete, *Unemployment and Technical Innovation*, (London, Frances Pinter, 1982) where much of this work is reviewed and discussed.
2 See, for example, C. Freeman, (ed.), *Long Waves in the World Economy* (London, Butterworth, 1980) and H. Giersch (ed.), *Emerging Technologies: Consequences for Economic Growth and Structural Change* (Tubingen, JCB Mohr (Paul Siebeck) (1982)).
3 C. Freeman, *The Economics of Industrial Innovation*, p. 313.
4 House of Lords Select Committee on Science and Technology, *Engineering Research and Development*, HMSO 22/2/83. See Vol. I, p. 13
5 Williams, 'British Technology Policy', pp. 35 *et seq.*
6 J. Schmookler, *Invention and Economic Growth* (Cambridge, Mass., Harvard University Press, 1966).

7 F. Scherer, 'Inter-Industry Technology Flows in the United States', *Research Policy*, Vol. 11, No. 4, pp. 227–46.

8 See, for example, K. Pavitt, 'Sectoral Patterns of Technical Change: Towards a Taxonomy and a Theory', *Research Policy* (forthcoming).

9 House of Lords, *Engineering Research and Development*, p. 87, Appendix 6.

10 Freeman, *The Economics of Industrial Innovation*. The original source is OECD, *The Measurement of Scientific and Technical Activities* (OECD, DAS/SPR/70.40. (mimeo), 1970).

11 The higher the discount rate the greater the relative value of the earlier resource flows. Since costs tend to be incurred early in the life of projects, therefore, a high discount rate will tend to bias estimates of the NPV downwards.

12 Z. Griliches, 'Research Costs and Social Returns: Hybrid Corn and Related Innovations', *Journal of Political Economy*, October 1958, pp. 419–31.

13 See, for example, G. Mensch, *Stalemate in Technology: Innovations Overcome the Depression* (New York, Ballinger, 1979).

14 For a discussion of the various channels through which 'Technology payments' are made and received see C. V. Vaitsos, *Intercountry Income Distribution and Transnational Enterprises* (Oxford, Clarendon Press, 1974).

15 Freeman, *The Economics of Industrial Innovation*, p. 341.

16 J. Irvine and B. Martin, 'Assessing Basic Research: Some Partial Indicators of Scientific Progress in Radio Astronomy', *Research Policy*, Vol. 12, No. 2, 1983, pp. 61–90. See also references above in bibliography.

Chapter 4

THE MICROECONOMY

4.1 Introduction

I argued in the first chapter that much of the discussion about the 'impact of science on society' concerns economic activity. This is so in two senses. *First*, we are concerned with economic growth as a potentially liberating force and we know that technological changes have played a very important historical role in enabling rapid rates of economic growth to take place. Scientific activity has also been closely associated with technological changes, although the relationship is a very complex one. *Secondly*, many of the issues of science and technology policy which have contemporary significance, usually have an important economic dimension, i.e. they are concerned with questions of resource allocation and economic production. For example, we are interested in such questions as, Why do firms spend money on R & D, why do some firms spend more than others and what factors influence the rate and direction of inventive activity? Hence, although science and technology policy issues have very important political, social and moral aspects, discussion about them is often conducted in a rather technical manner using 'jargon' which may not be familiar to those without a background in economic analysis.

The discussion of the production function, its properties and its uses, should be seen therefore as an explanation of technical language which is often used to describe the ways in which technological changes take place, rather than as a description of theoretical tools as such. In fact as things stand at present, formal production theory has very little practical value and there is no sense in which important policy issues can be resolved directly with reference to it. Nevertheless, it can help to clarify logical thinking in an extremely complex field of enquiry. In order to simplify exposition I have used elementary mathematics. It should be emphasised that this is only a device. The important thing is for students to grasp the underlying ideas.

The following section covers a range of definitions regarding social units of production. From there the discussion goes on to portray productive activity in technological terms and in so doing defines a range of relevant properties/concepts widely used in production analysis. There is also an introduction into the discussion of socio-economic behaviour and an illustration of how production activity can be described in terms of 'costs'. In this section too the notion of returns to scale will be introduced. Finally a range of concepts associated with invention/innovation are described and defined. For those wishing to go into more detail on many of these points there are a number of good teaching texts which may be consulted some of which are cited in the bibliography at the end of the chapter.

4.2 Social Units of Production

The basic unit of economic activity is the *firm* (or *enterprise* or *company*) which is usually to be seen in one of three forms of business organisation, namely a single proprietorship, a partnership or a joint-stock company. Lipsey mentions two other categories which are becoming increasingly common. These are the nationalised industries controlled and managed by the state, and the government's *own* provision of services, such as education, health, defence etc. which are provided '*free*' to the public in so far as a large proportion of the cost is a general levy on the public through the fiscal system. The consumer does not pay at the point of 'consumption' of the 'public good' although its provision, of course, is still a productive act.

The important point to grasp is that the 'firm' is a legal and financial entity and the different forms it takes reflect differences in ownership, methods of financing and legal liabilities (particularly regarding debts). It is thus an entity in 'economic' rather than 'geographic' space. In the latter context, conversely, we speak of the *plant* (or *factory*) as a geographically located unit of production. Very often a 'firm' consists of several 'plants'. An extreme case of the multiplant firm is the multinational company with productive operations taking place in a variety of countries and co-ordinated centrally by a headquarters office. Sometimes the word 'firm' is used where the context is really that of the 'plant'.[1] This is particularly the case when the discussion is about technology and technological change.

The type of commodity that the firm produces is commonly defined as belonging to an *industry*. Thus a firm producing canned foodstuffs belongs to the 'food processing' industry while one producing ph meters and other laboratory devices belongs to the 'scientific instruments' industry. Industries can be defined more or less narrowly depending upon the purpose in hand but clearly the more specified the industrial groupings used the more likely it is that any given firm will be producing in more than one industry. Where a firm enlarges or shifts its production into new areas either within its original industry or into another industry, it is said to be *diversifing horizontally* or becoming more *horizontally integrated*. Firms diversify their activities in this way for all sorts of reasons connected with the competitive conditions under which they are operating and the resources/skills to which they have access. Sometimes, for example, reasons of long-term corporate security are paramount, as when oil companies become involved in coal technology as a 'hedge' against future depletion of petroleum supplies. In other cases the technology and machinery employed may have potential applicability in the production of a different range of commodities, and indeed there may be strong pressures on a firm to diversify if demands for existing products are weak and/or if existing capital stock is under-utilised. The low 'marginal costs' involved in the utilisation of existing machinery for diversified production are an example of 'economies of growth' — extra output can be achieved more cheaply than if a firm had to invest in new plant/machinery from scratch. The notion of 'technological convergence' developed by Nathan Rosenberg has much in common with those ideas, as we have seen in chapter 2. Similarly with the notion of 'learning' to be discussed in chapter 8.

Nowadays most economic production takes place in discrete *stages* each part of which involves its own specialised technology often taking place in separate factories. For example, the production of textiles may be viewed as consisting of the following major processes:

Spinning(thread)→₁ weaving(cloth)→₁ dyeing→₁ finishing→₁ retailing

A firm which carries out all or most of these stages (*or* operations) is called a *vertically integrated* firm and the process through which stages of production are 'subcontracted' or 'spun off' to separate firms is called *vertical disintegration*. A well-cited example of the large vertically integrated corporation is the international oil company where all the different stages from exploration, production, refining through to marketing, are controlled by one large firm such as Exxon or Shell. An example of vertical disintegration is where a firm making electronics instruments subcontracts component production to an independent specialist firm.

Again there are many reasons why the degree of vertical integration might alter. For example, a firm might wish to integrate 'backwards' so as to reduce the profit element in its purchases of inputs from suppliers or because a process innovation requires direct technological links with prior stages. Conversely new firms might spin off from larger 'mother' companies because of lower management costs. And machinery suppliers exporting to developing countries might try to acquire the assets of their customers so as to establish a monopolistic market position. In general the organisation of industrial production is in a constant state of flux as input and output combinations change in response to technological changes and market conditions.

4.3 Technical Relations

4.3.1 The Production Function

Because economic production is such a complex affair, its analysis requires that we simplify the picture fairly dramatically. It is common to define 'production' as that part of economic activity which involves the conversion of 'inputs' (finance, labour, machines, raw materials etc.) into 'outputs' (commodities, services) using a 'technology' which describes the way in which the conversion is done. Sometimes this process is described in terms of a perfectly general functional relationship:

$$F_1[Q_1, Q_2 \bullet \bullet \bullet Q_n] = F_2[T; X_1, X_2 \bullet \bullet \bullet X_m] \qquad (4.1)$$

where there are n outputs $Q_1 \bullet \bullet \bullet Q_n$
m inputs $X_1 \bullet \bullet \bullet X_m$

and a technology T.

Since (4.1) is still complicated we usually simplify the function to:

$$Q = Q(K, L) \qquad (4.2)$$

where Q is the only output, K and L represent physical inputs of capital and labour respectively and the technology T is simply understood. The function is assumed to be continuous and the variables are each homogenous. The particular form of abstraction adopted is no accident since much of the theoretical discussion of technical changes concerns relations between these three variables. A further distinct advantage of a three-dimensional formulation is that we can summarise the production function graphically and hence describe its important properties. The assumptions of continuity and homogeneity are rather heroic, but can be justified in terms of clarity of exposition.

Thus for a given output value (Q_0) the production function may be that shown in figure 4.1.

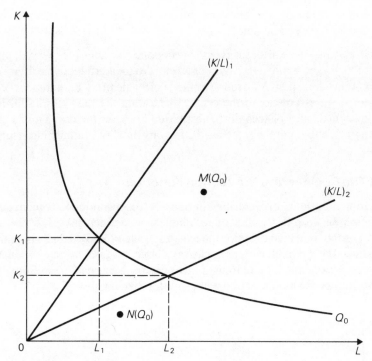

Figure 4.1   The production function

4.3.2 Properties of the Production Function

(i)   The production function refers to economic activity but is a purely *technical* relationship (this follows from the homogeneity assumption).

(ii)   Its variables (Q,K,L) refer to *flows* of resources per unit of time.

(iii)   It defines *alternative techniques* for a given output. Hence technique is defined in terms of specific combinations of inputs (*or* factors of production) for a given Q. Sometimes, we find a definition in terms of K/L ratios in which case the 'technique' can be constant over different output values. However, this is normally only used in relation to (iv) below.

(iv)   As the K/L ratio rises the technique is said to become more 'capital intensive' and vice versa. Notice, however, that the factor intensity of a technique is a purely relative concept. It has no cardinal value.

(v)   The production function defines the range of 'efficient' techniques in the given 'state of knowledge'. Thus point $M(Q_0)$ is 'inferior' or 'technically inefficient' in that no economically rational producer would choose it (very simply because for the same output it utilises more of at least one factor and not less of any other factor compared to another available technique). Similarly point $N(Q_o)$ cannot be chosen because it has not yet been invented.

(vi)   It can refer to different types of economic system (household, firm, industry, economy etc.). Where it refers to total productive activity of a country it is often referred to as the 'aggregate production function'.

(vii)   Its shape is convex to the origin illustrating the 'law' of diminishing marginal rates of technical substitution between factors. This is analogous to, but not the same as, the famous 'law' of diminishing returns.

4.3.3 The Engineering Production Function

The production function described in figure 4.1 is a continuous one in that it comprises an infinite number of techniques, as defined in 4.3.2. (iii) and 4.3.2. (v) above, which describe the existing 'state of knowledge'. In reality, of course, the number of techniques available for use in any productive operation is very much more limited. This can be illustrated in the form of an engineering production function with, say, four techniques, $T_1 \ldots T_4$,

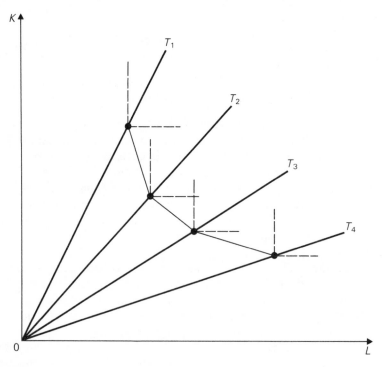

Figure 4.2   The engineering production function

which illustrates the actual technical choices available to a manufacturer at any point in time and which might approximate to an empirical measurement of the production function using statistical techniques. However, it should be noted that this form of the production function no longer possesses property 4.3.2.(v), above, since it does not include techniques which are *feasible* in the given state of knowledge, but not yet innovated.

4.3.4 The Elasticity of Factor Substitution

One important property of the production function is held to be its 'elasticity', namely the extent to which a wide range of techniques are available across the K/L spectrum. An 'elastic' production function

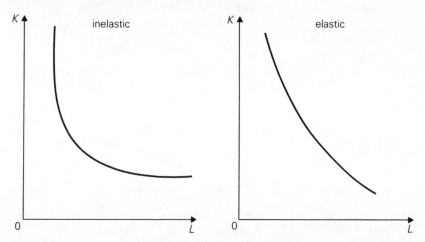

Figure 4.3(i) Inelastic production function **(ii)** Elastic production function

is defined as one for which the proportionate substitution of one input for another, resulting from changing input or factor prices, is high. Conversely, in the case of an 'inelastic' function. More formally the elasticity of factor substitution, 6, may be defined as:

$$\sigma = \frac{\Delta\left(\dfrac{K}{L}\right)\Big/\dfrac{K}{L}}{\Delta\left(\dfrac{W}{r}\right)\Big/\dfrac{W}{r}}$$

(4.3)

where Δ =change
W/r=relative price of L and K

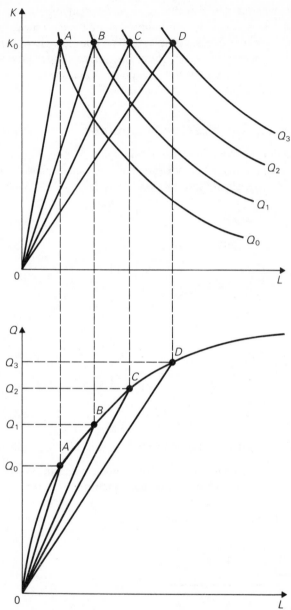

Figure 4.4 The production surface

Very often 'classes' of production functions are defined in relation to a given value of σ and used as a point of departure for formal mathematical operations (e.g. the Cobb-Douglas function where $\sigma = 1$). However, analysis of this type rarely has much significance for issues of science and technology policy. In a more general sense the elasticity of substitution may have importance where policies advocating changing input prices are suggested. (For example, so as to encourage more labour-intensive production techniques in countries facing severe problems of under-employment and unequal income distribution.)[2]

4.3.5 The Production Surface

The production function is a three-dimensional function. As represented in figure 4.1 above, the isoquants can be thought of as 'cuts' from a three-dimensional production surface for various values of output Q. In a similar fashion we can take a cut across the LQ plane for given values of capital K as in figure 4.4.

Notice that the points A, B, C, D, represent exactly the same points on the production surface in both cases, but now that various 'techniques' are described by the rays OA, OB, OC, OD. Notice also that the shape of the function now illustrates the 'law of diminishing returns' to labour holding other inputs (in this case capital) constant. Apart from these points the properties of the LQ production function are precisely analogous to those portrayed on the KL plane. Finally, of course, the production function may be described as a relationship between K and Q, holding L constant.

4.3.6 Technological Change

Technological change can now be defined fairly simply as an improvement in the 'state of knowledge' or as a shift in the production function. The spectrum of technological possibilities improves which means:

(i)   more output can be produced with the same resources *and/or*
(ii)   the same output can be produced with fewer resources.

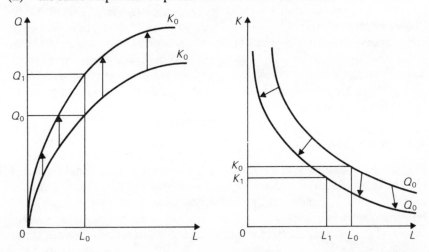

Figure 4.5(i)   Technological change (i)   **Figure 4.5(ii)**   Technological change (ii)

In his famous attempt to isolate the causal role of technological changes in US manufacturing output growth over the first part of this century Solow (1957)[3] used a production function formulation very akin to that described in figure 4.5(i), but using the 'engineering' production function described in (4.3).

4.3.7 Bias and Technological Change

Very often technological changes are described in terms of their biases. Three types are usually distinguished — labour saving, capital saving, neutral — and they are defined in terms of what happens to the K/L ratio as a result of shifts in the production function where relative input prices are held constant.

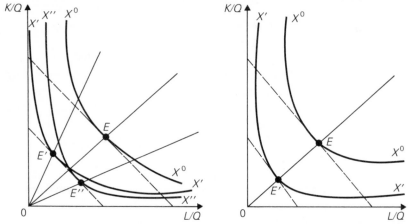

Figure 4.6(i) Biased technological change   **(ii)** Neutral technological change

Figure 4.6(i) illustrates the cases of labour-saving technological change $(E \rightarrow E')$ and capital-saving technological change $(E \rightarrow E'')$. Figure 4.6(ii) illustrates neutral technological change. Relative factor prices are held constant so as to isolate the purely technical (as opposed to economic) features of the shift. We shall see below that movements in the relative price of labour and capital will normally influence the technique actually chosen. More generally we are interested in the question of 'bias' because it has practical and historical significance.

4.3.8 Productivity

This is usually discussed in two senses. The most complete definition is that of total factor productivity which is defined as the ratio of the value of output Q to the value of *all* inputs. This gives the best measure of how 'productively' resources are used. However, for a variety of reasons, including ease of statistical operations, analysis is often carried on in terms of single factor productivity, particularly labour productivity. The average productivity of labour is defined in terms of output per worker over a given period of time. Notice that different measures of productivity can give quite different results. It is quite possible, for example, for total factor productivity to be falling while labour productivity is rising. It is important therefore to be clear and consistent when using these terms. Finally the concept, marginal productivity, is defined as the extra amount of output resulting from a given additional resource input. For example, the marginal productivity of labour is the extra output resulting from the employment of one extra worker, all other inputs being held constant. Although this concept is difficult to handle empirically it is used widely in conceptual discussion on production and students are advised to try to grasp the notion.

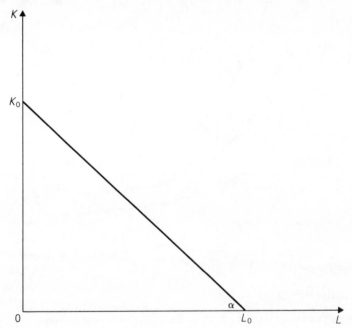

Figure 4.7 The relative price line

4.4 Economic Behaviour

Up to this point I have attempted to discuss the production function and related concepts in a purely technical/engineering sense.[4] In practice, however, actual decisions on choice of techniques are behavioural and depend upon motivations and upon economic variables (prices, costs, etc.). Productive units (firms) do not choose a technique just because it exists; they choose it because they think that it best satisfies their goals — and these goals are socio-economic in character. To make things simple we usually start off by assuming that firms are profit maximisers, although this is a very strong assumption as we shall see later on and the reason for making it is purely definitional.

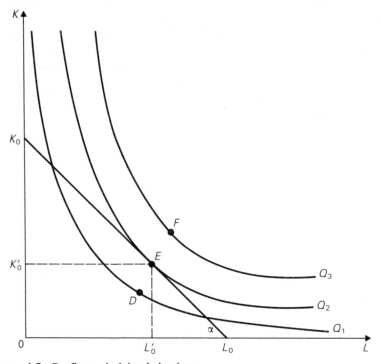

Figure 4.8   Profit maximizing behaviour

4.4.1 Factor Prices

If we designate the prices of labour and capital by W, r, then on the KL plane the relative price of labour and capital W/r may be described as a straight line with a slope equal to

$$\tan \alpha = W/r = \frac{OK_o}{OL_o} \tag{4.4}$$

The greater is α, the cheaper is K relative to L and, therefore, the more K can be purchased with a given income (Y). The *position* of the price (*or* budget *or* income) line depends upon the resources available to the firm. Assume the firm in question is faced with a given budget or income (Y_o), is producing a given product and intends to employ only two homogeneous factors, capital and labour, at prices which it cannot influence. Let Q_1, Q_2, Q_3 represent successively greater output levels on the firm's production function. Since its income is given by K_oL_o the maximum output the firm can achieve is given by E. It cannot operate beyond E (say at F) because of an income constraint. Nor is it efficient to operate below E (say at D). E, then, is the point of maximum efficiency or optimality where:

$$Q_2 = WL_o{}^1 + r K_o{}^1 \tag{4.5}$$

and where $W/r = \dfrac{\partial K}{\partial L}$ (4.6)

In other words equilibrium is established where relative factor prices are equal to the marginal rate of technical substitution of labour for capital.

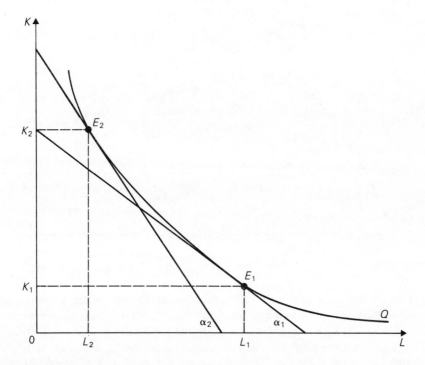

Figure 4.9 Change in relative factor prices

4.4.2 Changes in Factor Prices

If relative factor prices change, then under our assumptions an economically rational firm will shift to a new technique. In this case the relative cheapening of capital ($\alpha_1 \rightarrow \alpha_2$) leads to a switch of technique in a more capital intensive direction $(E_1 \rightarrow E_2)$.

4.4.3 The LQ and KQ Planes

Precisely analogous relationships may be demonstrated on the other planes of the production function. On the LQ plane (i.e. with K held constant) the wage rate, W_1, is

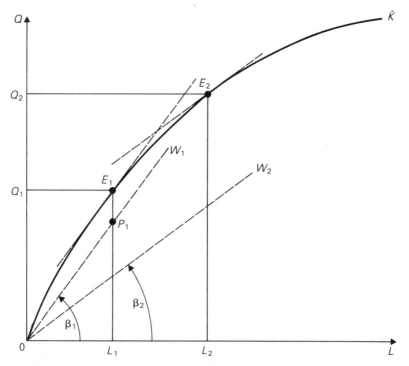

Figure 4.10   Change in relative factor prices — the LQ plane

given by the slope of the line OW_1, $\tan \beta_1$. Profit maximising output, Q_1, takes place at E_1 where it can be shown that $\partial Q/\partial L = \tan \beta_1$ represents the equilibrium condition (wage rate = marginal productivity of labour). Profits are $E_1 P_1$ and wages $P_1 L_1$. OL_1 workers are employed with capital $\bar{K}$. A reduction in the wage rate from W_1 to W_2 will lead to a new equilibrium position E_2.

4.4.4 Technological Change and Switch of Techniques

It should now be clear why there is a logical distinction between technological change (where the state of knowledge changes) and switches of techniques (where technique alters as a response to economic signals). Unfortunately it is very difficult to separate these effects in practice, since the choice of technique decision takes place at the moment of investment (additions to the capital stock) and each round of investment involves new technology. This may be seen graphically when we come to examine how technological changes have occurred historically.

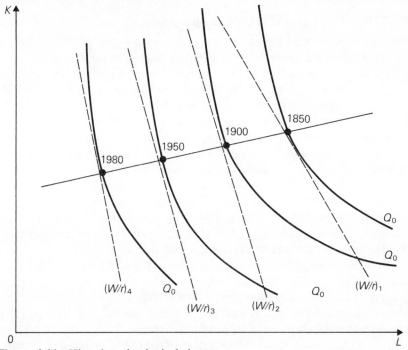

Figure 4.11 Historic technological change

Figure 4.11 represents a stylised account of what we know to have taken place progressively over the last 100 to 150 years. Technological changes appear to have been labour saving in so far as capital/output ratios in most branches of economic production have remained fairly constant while labour-output ratios have fallen dramatically. But has this been due to the *nature* of technological change itself (biased in a labour-saving direction) *or* have economic factors intruded? Salter[5] has argued against the former view, pointing out that factor prices tend to intrude at an early stage in the design process, since engineers will normally build economic factors into their

R & D work. According to Salter the evidence is consistent with the view, illustrated in figure 4.11, that there has been a constant cheapening of capital goods over the decades as a result of technological changes within the capital goods sector. Technological dynamism of the kind analysed by Rosenberg[6] has reduced the prices of machines relative to those of consumer goods and this along with other social forces has engendered factor substitution. Salter produces empirical evidence to back up his contention. Conversely, he argues that the alternative view has been fostered by a number of misapprehensions, particularly a misreading of surface phenomena. The 'fact' of labour-saving seems so self-evident that it is easy to ignore the point that technological changes also save capital as well.

4.4.5 Habakkuk and US/UK Comparisons

It is useful also to note that such social processes can operate differentially in different geographical areas and at different times. Habakkuk[7] has attempted to use an analysis similar to that of Salter to explain the very different industrialisation experiences of the US and the UK during the first half of the nineteenth century. Over this period (and also afterwards to some extent) US industrial growth was characterised by much faster rates of investment and innovation and by much greater simplicity and functionalism in industrial design. His argument, put simply, was that this occurred due to radically differing economic conditions. In the US, labour was scarce relative to land as a factor of production; this had several economic effects including raising the price of labour substantially and lowering its elasticity of supply at the margin (i.e. even fairly large wage rises were not enough to bring significant numbers of extra workers on to the labour market). Another important factor was the level of profitability of agricultural land, especially that resulting from realising capital gains as values rose. Because of these factors there was heavy pressure within the manufacturing sector to mechanise production, thus raising substantially machinery prices and creating further incentives to economise in the production and use of capital goods. This in turn led to pressures to innovate more rapidly and to economise through making designs simpler, more standardised and receptive to the interchangeability of parts. Conversely in the UK, labour was at this stage abundant relative to land and there were never the same incentives to economise. In fact Habakkuk's argument is rather more complex and sophisticated than this, but it is a good example of the applicability of the kind of conceptual discussions we have been having.

4.5 Costs and Scale Effects

I described earlier a formal model of the way a profit maximising firm might behave under various circumstances relating to technology and technological changes. Analogous relationships can be described in terms of how a firm's costs vary with changing levels of output under given technological conditions. Broadly speaking analysis takes place within the context of three 'states of nature' − the short run, the long run and the very long run. The short run defines how labour costs vary with output in a plant of a given capacity producing a given product. In the long run the size of the plant is allowed to vary while in the very long run technological conditions are allowed to change. These states are in figure 4.12

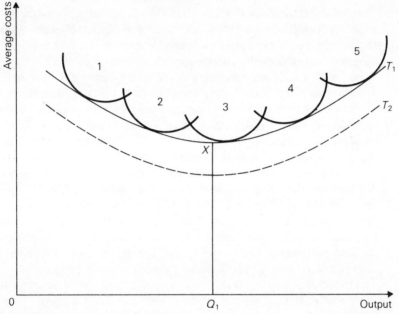

Figure 4.12 Costs and scale effects

In the short run costs are assumed to exhibit a 'U' form to reflect the presumption that average costs are lowest when the firm is operating at its optimal capacity output. At lower output levels average costs are higher because of the influence of 'fixed' or 'overhead' costs. At higher levels, diminishing returns begin to set in. The short-run cost curve is therefore analogous to the production function described in figure 4.4. However, at any point of time it is possible to have plants of different capacities. The long-run envelope curve (T_1) shows how average costs vary for five representative plants of different sizes. The way it is drawn reveals 'decreasing costs' or 'increasing returns' as the *scale* of plant increases up to output Q_1. Beyond this point returns to scale begin to fall correspondingly. Such 'economies of scale' and 'diseconomies of scale' are held to arise for a variety of reasons, some of which will be explored in detail later. Indeed the whole notion of the relative economic advantages and disadvantages of 'bigness' is a very important one in science and technology policy discussion. Finally, whereas the 'long run' is defined in terms of a given level of technology, in the 'very long run' technological change is allowed to take place. In terms of our diagram the new level, T_2, is such that average costs are now lower for all plant sizes.

A number of points should be noted about this treatment of costs and scale effects:

1   There is no presumption that in reality cost curves actually take the sorts of 'U' shapes portrayed. These are based upon hypotheses about how various combinations of inputs will behave under prescribed conditions, but the actual empirical evidence is much more ambiguous.

2   Economies of scale are sometimes classified into two types (a) technical and (b) pecuniary. The former relate to technical and organisational conditions of production, for example the lower costs associated with spreading overhead resources such as power, insurance and management time *or* the greater *flexibility* in deploying resources in a multiproduct firm where there is a greater possibility of 'hedging' against market uncertainty, thereby lowering average costs for the firm as a whole. Another well-known example is the capacity to afford R & D expenditure at the level necessary to stay abreast of relevant innovative developments and thereby to lower costs in the future. Pecuniary economies of scale concern the greater market power that large firms sometimes possess − for example, to force suppliers to cut the prices of their products under threat of withdrawing custom altogether.

3   The treatment of 'time' in the above exposition is ambiguous since the 'long run' is defined in terms of the capacity to alter the size of plants. Obviously, once having built a factory a business organisation will operate it until it no longer pays the organisation to do so − and this sort of decision depends upon factors such as the rate of obsolescence of machinery and changing market conditions. In any case by the time such a decision is taken technical conditions will have changed and so we would then be in the 'very long run'. In order to accommodate this ambiguity Sutcliffe[8] has differentiated *static* from *dynamic* economies of scale with the latter referring to the process by which firms become bigger through time while simultaneously cutting average production costs. In this sense there is a *strategic* aspect to dynamic growth on the part of firms which cannot really be incorporated into the 'comparative statics' of our definitions.[9] And yet it is precisely this growth (and decline) process which is so closely related to technological changes, as we shall see later on. The point about 'economies of growth' mentioned previously in this chapter is pertinent here.

4   It is important to point out that in some industries and industrial sectors small firms do very well in terms of economic performance, particularly in areas of very rapid technological change where R & D — intensive firms produce high value specialist equipment for a small range of equally specialist buyers. Indeed, some authorities argue that the evidence about the economic advantages of bigness is not by any means conclusive.[10]

5   Almost always, changing technical and economic conditions in one sector or firm will have effects on others and on the economic system as a whole. Such effects are described as being *external* to the sector or firm under immediate study and are often classified as 'external economies' or 'diseconomies'. For example, a technological change which reduces the market price for commodity A will induce external economic benefits in those industries which purchase A as an input in their own production processes. Similarly the introduction of microprocessor technology may have widespread 'downstream' effects on a large number of capital-goods-producing industries involving a reduction in the overall cost of capital. Such capital-saving impacts are viewed as *external* to the microprocessor industry itself. In general 'externalities' are an important aspect of all science and technology policy discussion since usually they will encompass second order effects of much greater importance than the initial impact.

4.6 Invention and Innovation

Finally it is worth summarising a range of concepts associated with the development and application of new technologies in economic production. In the main I shall use Freeman's definitions contained in his book the *Economics of Industrial Innovation*.[11]

4.6.1 Categories of R & D

(a)   **Basic Research** − Creative work undertaken on a systematic basis to increase the stock of scientific knowledge. It is not primarily directed towards any specific practical aim or application. Sometimes a category called *oriented* or *strategic* basic research is distinguished to denote work in a field of present or potential scientific, economic or social interest (e.g. biotechnology).

(b)   **Applied Research** − Original research directed towards a specific practical aim or objective which may be predetermined. Sometimes the word is used to denote the articulation of basic research findings in practical form.

(c)   **Experimental Development** – The use of scientific knowledge in order to produce new or substantially improved materials, devices, products, processes, systems or services.

It should be noted that the above do not necessarily relate to sequential stages although often they will. An example of where they do not is where a problem at the development stage requires recourse to more fundamental work for its solution. The time taken to develop a new product or process through to the end of the development phase is sometimes called the *development lead time*. In his earlier work on electronic capital goods Freeman[12] showed how lead times can vary quite widely over different product types with implications for industrial structure and government policy.

4.6.2 Innovative vs. Non-Innovative Activity

Freeman argues that R & D, as defined above, should be distinguished from other related activities which serve a routine/back-up function but which do not possess 'an appreciable element of novelty'. Such 'scientific services' may be listed as:

(a)   Scientific education (except R & D carried out as part of student training).
(b)   The provision of scientific and technological information.
(c)   General purpose data collection (e.g. resource surveys).
(d)   Testing/standardisation facilities.
(e)   Feasibility studies for engineering projects.
(f)   Specialised medical care.
(g)   Administrative/legal work connected with patents and licences (see below).

Conversely activities which *should* be included are: 'prototype' and 'pilot plant' activities since these are intrinsically part of the development process. Having made these points of definition/convention it is important to point out that the provision of scientific services is a very necessary feature of much contemporary production. However, they are in the nature of necessary 'back up' rather than innovative activity and in this sense data about them should be handled with great care since often such statistics do not follow the general guidelines laid out above.

4.6.3 Invention and Innovation

Freeman, following Schumpeter, distinguishes between '*invention*' ('idea, sketch, or a model for a new or improved device, product, process or system') and '*innovation*' ('the first commercial transaction involving the new product, process, system or device, although the word is also used to describe the whole process'). Sometimes an innovation is *patented*, a *patent* being defined as a legal right to the exclusive exploitation of a particular invention; but not always. A patent registration may provoke retaliatory competition from potential imitators, and in any case a firm may possess sufficient necessary ancillary knowledge to enable it to maintain a technical lead over potential rivals without having to go to the bother of patenting. The holder of a patent can permit another manufacturer to exploit it under *licence*, usually in return for some kind of fee and under stipulated legal conditions. And since there is now an international patent convention which is widely recognised there is also a well-established trade in licences both within and between countries. Occasionally the international trade in licence payments is used as a proxy for measuring international *technology flows* and while it has some uses at an aggregate level, the data tend to be subject to many inaccuracies. In reality, as Freeman and Schumpeter recognise, the social process (or chain) from invention to innovation, and beyond, is a long and complex one. Rosenberg, in particular, as we have seen, provides many examples where an original innovation has been subject to continuous adaptation and improvement over long periods, and where these subsequent improvements have been a far more important source of productivity growth than the original innovation. Recent work on technological 'trajectories' or 'paradigms' represents an extension of this theme, as we shall see in chapter 6.

4.6.4 Product and Process Innovations

Very often a distinction is made between the innovation of a new *product* (e.g. rayon) and that of a new *process* (e.g. the catalytic cracking of petroleum). A major reason for making this distinction is that the ,two types of innovation often relate to economic analysis in different ways (and take place for different sets of reasons and under different circumstances). For example, product innovations are often associated with an expansive economic phase where new technologies have been discovered and new demands identified. The wide range of new pharmaceutical products produced in the 1950s and 1960s are a good example of this sort of innovation. Conversely, process innovations often take place under conditions of economic stress where the resultant capacity to cut the costs of production of a given product may enable a firm to cope with stagnant conditions of market demand. Again, however, as with so many concepts in this field, the distinction is by no means hard-and-fast. New products often require process innovation for their production, while new processes can change the character of the final product as for example in the case of the introduction of the Bessemer process in the manufacture of steel. A more subtle caveat relates to the nature of final 'consumer demands' since if, as Lancaster[13] holds, it makes more sense to view consumers as demanding product *characteristics* rather than the products themselves, then our distinction takes on a new analytical meeting since product innovation can be regarded as a form of process innovation which is close to the final consumption stage. An example might be a new type of textile which could require much less cleaning than other textiles and which would therefore satisfy a range of consumer 'garment needs' at lower cost. In this sense innovation should properly be regarded as taking place potentially over all production stages with subsequent 'upstream' and 'downstream' effects which may take a variety of different forms. It may still make sense, for analytical purposes, to distinguish product and process innovations but this distinction should be regarded as very much a qualitative one.

4.7 Some Concluding Remarks

At the risk of repeating myself, I should like to re-emphasise that my purpose in this chapter has been largely definitional. There *is* a school of thought in conventional economics which uses the material covered in sections 4.3 and 4.4 as the point of departure for rather complex research into the nature and consequences of industrial innovation. We shall see in chapters 5 and 6 and to some extent in chapter 8 that this approach, sometimes called the 'production function' approach, has come under increasing criticism in recent years as a sterile and misleading set of ideas. I shall in fact argue that there are serious problems in the way economics as a 'profession' handles questions of technical change and science and technology policy. Meanwhile students are advised to treat literature based exclusively upon the production function with a great deal of care.

Bibliography

A very useful general text in this area is G. Rosegger, *The Economics of Production and Innovation: An Industrial Perspective* (Oxford, Pergamon, 1980) particularly chapters 1, 3, 4, 11, but there are also a variety of more general microeconomic textbooks which contain sections on production and cost theory. Examples are R. G. Lipsey, *Positive Economics* (London, Weidenfeld and Nicolson, 1979, 5th edn), Part IV; E. Mansfield, *Micro-Economics Theory and Applications* (London, Norton, 1979, 3rd edn); W. J. Baumol and A. S. Blinder, *Economics; Principles and Policy* (London, Harcourt-Brace Jovanovich, 1979). For criticisms of the 'Production Function' Approach, see C. Freeman and L. Sòete (eds.), *Technical Change and Full Employment* (Oxford, Basil Blackwell, 1985), chapter 2, and A. Atkinson and J. Stiglitz, 'A New View of Technological Change', *Economic Journal*, Vol. 79, pp. 573–8.

Notes

1 To make things even more confusing, you will find that the term 'plant' is sometimes used to define a piece of machinery or a collection of machines and related equipment.
2 Discussed in detail in chapter 8 where an important policy debate relates to the responsiveness of firms to changing relative factor prices in terms of choice of technique.
3 R. Solow, 'Technical Change and the Aggregate Production Function', *Review of Economcis and Statistics*, Vol. 59, 1957, pp. 312–20.
4 In fact I have cheated since the assumption of homogeneity implies the act of converting discrete types of resources to a common unit of value. The only practicable way of doing this is to use relative prices.
5 W. E. G. Salter, *Productivity and Technical Change* (Cambridge, Cambridge University Press, 1966, 2nd edn). By 'nature' I mean an inherent tendency to labour-saving within the technology itself.
6 Rosenberg, *Perspectives on Technology*, chapter 1. See chapter 2, section 2.6 above for a discussion of Rosenberg's ideas.
7 E. J. Habakkuk, *American and British Technology in the Nineteenth Century* (Cambridge, Cambridge University Press, 1967).
8 R. Sutcliffe, *Industry and Underdevelopment* (London, Addison-Wesley, 1971), chapter 5.
9 See chapter 1 for a discussion of this point.
10 See, for example, Freeman, *The Economics of Industrial Innovation*, pp. 213 *et seq.* for a discussion of this point.
11 Freeman, *The Economics of Industrial Innovation*, pp. 313–31.
12 C. Freeman, 'Research and Development in Electronics Capital Goods', *National Institute Economic Review*, Vol. 34, November 1965, pp. 40–95.
13 See, for example, K. J. Lancaster, 'New Approach to Consumer Theory', *Journal of Political Economy*, Vol. LXXIV, No. 2, 1966.

Chapter 5

ECONOMIC THEORY AND TECHNOLOGICAL CHANGE

5.1 Introduction

Returning to the discussion summarised in the opening chapters, you will recall that I defined science policy studies in terms of the allocation of national resources to science and technology, the mechanisms through which this is done and the kinds of problems which arise as a result of these social processes. You will recall also that I argued a rather limited role for economic 'theory' in policy analysis and drew attention to a range of conceptual and methodological difficulties in this context.

Having made these points, it is nonetheless the case that the economics literature has, at various times, tried to deal seriously with technological change putting forward propositions regarding how it occurs, under what sorts of socio-economic conditions it takes place, and who benefits or suffers from it. Many of these propositions have been 'tested' using fairly standard statistical techniques and have more generally become the 'stuff' of debate and controversy. As such they have an important bearing on 'policy' since they influence the view of decision-makers about how the economic system 'works' and how it can be made to 'work better', particularly in so far as science and technology are concerned. For this reason alone it is necessary to examine these 'theories' or 'traditions' and the social/intellectual climate within which they occurred.

The way that I have chosen to do so is to locate the discussion within the context of the history of economic thought — at least to begin with. I have done so partly for the sake of convenience but partly also to reiterate a theme that was central to the previous chapter, namely that science and technology only became important in an economic sense once a certain stage of economic development had been reached. Similarly how their impact was (and is) viewed was very much a function of the prevailing intellectual climate which in turn was a function of what issues people held to be important. In this sense, therefore, it is necessary to understand quite clearly that at various times political interests, metaphysical positions and ideological preconception were often at the heart of such debates. Even modern theoretical discussions are far more ideologically 'loaded' than their empirical content would appear to indicate. Such influences should be taken into account, therefore, when interpreting and evaluating theoretical contributions.

In the following section I begin by reviewing certain key features of the earlier 'classical' tradition, the period of intellectual thought spanning very roughly the beginnings of industrialisation in Europe (up until 1870). The way I have chosen to do this is to use Ricardo's Corn Model as an illustration of the way that classical economists typically thought about problems of economic production and distribution, although this model is relevant also in so far as it presaged and anticipated important economic debates that were to arise in the twentieth century. Section 5.3 reviews the 'neo-classical' tradition which followed on from the classical tradition, and developed into an intellectual framework of quite remarkable coherence and elegance. Indeed its systemic elegance is such that even today the 'economics profession' continues in a number of respects to behave as if it corresponds to reality, sometimes with unfortunate results.

Section 5.4 deals with Keynes's attempt to generalise neo-classical theory, in response to the inter-war depression. Keynes was an important figure for many reasons but particularly because his attack on the neo-classical tradition (which incidentally he himself did not regard as an attack) opened up fundamental policy issues concerning the role of government in economic management, issues which are still being hotly debated today. Although the debate does not concern science policy directly, section 5.4 ends with a summarised outline of the modern 'controversy' between 'Keynesianism' and 'monetarism'. Finally section 5.5 examines some of the ideas put forward by Schumpeter, perhaps the only major economist writing in the early part of this century who attempted to integrate the analysis of economic processes with that of technological change. And although Schumpeter became for a time marginal in relation to economic debate, more recently he has become 're-discovered' and has influenced profoundly modern thinking about the social analysis of technological change.

5.2 The Classical Tradition

We have already discussed in chapter 2 the contributions of Smith and Marx to the analysis of technological changes in an emergent industrialising economy (UK). Of course, the classical economists were not interested in technology as such. They were preoccupied by much grander issues, in particular the need to understand the underlying dynamics of the new social order and to justify the special views which they individually held about it.

Smith, for example, was primarily interested in economic growth and what brought it about, but he also had strong views on the subject which he argued through in his very influential work *The Wealth of Nations*. In particular he argued against the numerous restrictions on trade and industry which had been inherited from the mercantilist era, and in favour of the new 'economic bourgeoisie', the employers of labour whose liberated energies he felt would prove to be the main driving force behind economic production.

Writing nearly a century later, Marx took a rather different view of industrial capitalism. He did not like it nor the industrial classes who were increasingly holding political power within it. Accordingly his analysis set out to show that industrial capitalism was an unstable economic system which would inevitably break down under the pressures of its own internal contradictions, to be replaced by another and more humane social order. To both writers the understanding of technology and technological change was an essential plank or 'building block' in their overall arguments, but this represented only one part of a complex chain of reasoning and not necessarily the most important. For example, for all the classical economists (and for Marx and Ricardo in particular) the definition of the relative 'value' of goods and services was of fundamental importance since only against an invariant measure of this could the important exchange and distributional relationships be understood and developed. In fact the classical economists spent a great deal of time and energy attempting to establish a satisfactory 'labour theory' of value i.e. value reckoned in terms of labour input into production per unit of time − although Robinson maintains that they never really succeeded and 'the subject has remained a plentiful source of confusion to this day'.[1]

Another central preoccupation of classical political economy concerned income distribution amongst major social classes, namely capitalists, workers and landlords. Since each of these classes disposed of their incomes differently, income distribution became a key determinant of the pace and pattern of economic development. One eminent writer in particular, David Ricardo (1772−1823) developed a theory of distribution which he used to support his argument that the English Corn Laws should be abolished. Up until the middle of the nineteenth century English agriculture had been protected from the import of cheap grain from Europe by a series of prohibitive measures, and this, argued Ricardo, effectively redistributed the national product from those who would use it productively (the capitalists who would invest it to create more wealth) to those who would not (the landlords who would consume it unproductively). Conversely, removal of restrictions on grain imports would raise the rate of economic growth and put off, perhaps for ever, the 'stationary state' of no growth which was otherwise inevitable.

5.2.1 Ricardo's Corn Model

Ricardo's method of developing his argument was to construct a model of a simple agricultural economy where capitalist farmers rent land from land-owners and supply their own capital stock in the form of seed corn and a 'wages fund' to pay their labourers while the crop (corn) is growing. All three social classes (landowners, farmers and labourers) attempt to maximise income but there is an abundance of labour which forces wage rates down to subsistence level. Farmers re-invest all their profits, but landlords (*rentiers*) consume all their rents and have no interest in improving the productivity of their land through their own investments. Land varies in quality such that net output/hectare is higher on the better land. Finally in this simple model there is no manufacturing sector and therefore no possibility for mechanised farming.

Of course, Ricardo's model contains a range of what we would regard as heroic assumptions about ruling technical and social conditions, but it should be noted that these were probably not all that unrealistic at the time of writing (1817). Moreover, Ricardo was too able an economist to try to build his assumptions into his conclusions. Rather his aim was to 'abstract from' relatively unimportant features of the economic universe so as to concentrate his attention more systematically on the important ones. In so doing he was able to show how production and accumulation occurred, what pace and pattern economic growth took, how income was distributed amongst broad social classes and what kinds of conflicts arose thereby. His model was essentially heuristic, designed to lay bare the essentials of an important issue of national policy.

Ricardo proceeded as follows. First, he assumed that on all plots of land the ratio of worker to land area remains constant. Total output and total employment then depends upon the stock of 'corn capital' invested each year. When this employment is spread over the whole cultivated area there is some land which yields the lowest yield per hectare. This land defines the *extensive margin* of cultivation where competition amongst landlords for tenants drives rents down to zero (provided there is still some vacant land unused). Thus Ricardo concluded that marginal land exacts no rent. However, since on the intra-marginal land the rate of profit is everywhere the same (through competition), variations in the quality of cultivated land are reflected only in rent payments − the best land yielding the highest rent.

But what about the farmer's ability to alter the amount of labour employed on any given plot of land? At this point in his analysis Ricardo relaxed his assumption of a fixed land/labour ratio arguing that on all plots of land owned the farmer would vary the intensity of cultivation such that the 'marginal productivity of labour' (the *intensive margin*) is not less than the average productivity of labour on an *additional* plot of land once rent had been

deducted. Competitive forces would then ensure that the marginal productivity of labour was everywhere the same and equal to the average
productivity of labour on the poorest land.

Hence it is relatively easy to follow Ricardo's broad line of reasoning. Each
year farmers invest to meet economic needs over the coming period. These
needs are growing constantly because of population pressure (Ricardo accepted Malthus's argument that populations expand at a geometric rate) and
therefore recourse is necessary to progressively poorer quality land. Wages
remain constant, rents rise and profits fall. As profits fall accumulation slows
down and eventually the economy ends up in a condition of immiserization —
the *stationary state*, which Ricardo (but not John Stuart Mill) anticipated with
dread. Diagramatically the story may be seen with reference to figure 5.1
where output/hectare is described as falling progressively as the margin of
cultivated land is extended. At any point, say E_1, profits are given by PE_1BW
and rent by RPE_1. Eventually, however, at point E_2 all land has been used up
and the national product is divided between the subsistence income of the
labouring class, OWE_2A_2, and the rental income of the landlords, RWE_2.
There are no profits left.

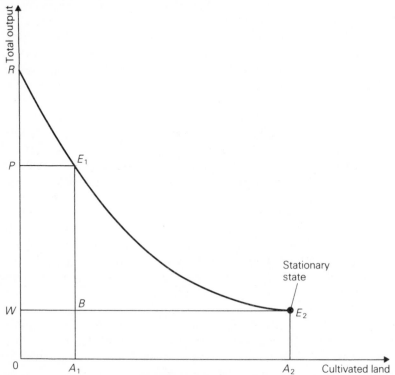

Figure 5.1   Regress to the stationary state

Ricardo's is a typically classical line of argument. Since the logic of his analysis was clear, the existing pattern of income distribution ought to be changed. One way of doing this was to allow foreign grain to enter free of duty, thereby lowering the price of wage goods, lowering rents and increasing the rate of profit. And that was what Ricardo argued for. But his argument was only as strong as the validity of his logic and the realism of his assumptions. In the latter case a basic problem was the elision of the manufacturing sector since by so doing Ricardo was not only being manifestly unrealistic, he was also cutting out possibilities for productivity improvements through the substitution of fixed capital for labour. For this reason, having established what he felt were the broad principles underlying economic development, Ricardo then introduced more lines of production, and at once got tangled up with problems of relative value which he never managed to sort out satisfactorily. On the substitution of machines for labour he did finally accept that the tendency towards stagnation 'is happily checked at repeated intervals by the improvements in machinery, connected with the production of necessaries, as well as by discoveries in the science of agriculture and therefore to lower the price of the prime necessary of the labourer'.[2] However, he appears to have regarded technological changes only as a series of temporary checks to what was essentially a gloomy prognosis.

A major criticism of Ricardo's *logic* was propounded by Thomas Malthus (1766–1834) who argued that it ignored the demands of consumers. Here he was in effect taking issue with a basic tenet of classical thinking which was that competitive forces would ensure that anything produced would always eventually be sold – that supply would create its own demand. This view, called Say's Law after the French economist J. B. Say (1767–1832) was sharply contested by Malthus on the grounds that general overproduction could take place and in fact had taken place in the period following the Napoleonic Wars. His proposals to deal with this included public works expenditures of the kind later to be advocated by Kéynes *and* encouragement of 'luxury consumption' on the part of the rich, thus providing a legitimate social role for the landed classes whom Ricardo had been so keen to attack. Ricardo's reply to this was that Malthus could not have it both ways. To redistribute the national product back to the rentier classes would simply serve to reduce the re-investible surplus thereby bringing nearer in time the stationary state. In effect Ricardo won the debate. It was not until Keynes's development of the notion of a deficiency in aggregate *investment* demand that the matter became resolved a century later.

Finally, it is interesting to note the echo of these debates in more recent times associated with the 'Malthusian pessimism' about the capacity of the Earth to maintain growing living standards in the years ahead. In the early 1970s it became fashionable in certain circles to focus attention on the Earth itself as an ecological system with a constrained potential for meeting the economic demands placed on it. A well-known example of this 'genre' was the 'Limits to Growth' book of Meadows *et al*. (1972)[3] which argued on the basis of certain (restrictive) assumptions about resources, income distribution, population growth and technological change that international policies to curb economic expansion were vitally necessary if the Earth were to remain viable as an ecological system. The Meadows view contrasted radically with the more optimistic (and earlier) position of Herman Kahn and his colleagues at the Hudson Institute, who had put forward 'futuristic scenarios' of great economic abundance. The resultant debates were interesting mainly because they revealed how complex 'global modelling' is, rather than because they produced any specific consensus as a result. At the time of writing this book it is probably fair to say that the onset of world recession has produced a narrower and more focused set of international issues for discussion. In some ways this is a pity since the broader approach raises questions of great significance which ought really to be at the forefront of policy debate. Some of these will be outlined in later chapters.

5.3 Neo-Classical Economics

According to Robinson[4] the classical tradition of economic thought suffered chiefly from two defects:

(a)   Classical theories could offer no satisfactory explanation (or set of explanations) of price determination *or* of the distribution of incomes.
(b)   They opened the door to unwelcome political doctrines, especially in the hands of Marx.

However, as the nineteenth century drew to a close a number of writers were beginning to develop a new set of explanations about economic affairs, explanations which concerned themselves almost exclusively with 'resource exchange' − the buying and selling of goods, services and factors of production in *markets*. The essential contrasts with the older tradition are interesting and indeed reflect debates that are still taking place to this day. For example, those on the political 'left' still tend to take inspiration from the more supply-oriented classical tradition, with its distinction between 'use value' and 'exchange value', its preoccupation with social class and economic (and hence political) power, *and* its relative subordination of 'demand' influences. Conversely, those on the 'right' tend to emphasise consumer demand and the 'free market', believing (or assuming) that productive forces will react automatically (or at least without significant delays) to changing consumer preferences.

The essence of the neo-classical view was as follows. *First*, production of goods and services takes place as much due to the pressure of consumer demands as due to the desire to earn income on the part of producers. In turn demand for goods exists because goods possess *utility*, defined as the capacity to satisfy 'wants'. Exchange takes place in *markets* where the *price* of any commodity reflects the strength of influences on both the supply and the demand side.

Markets are never inherently unstable because every market has a tendency to seek *equilibrium* (a state defined as that where the demand for and supply of the commodity in question is exactly equal). Thus any change in demand or supply conditions, for example a cost-reducing technological change, will lead to price changes depending upon the actual market structure obtaining. These will lead to further economising behaviour on the part of consumers, leading in this case to a new and lower equilibrium price. The well-known demand and supply diagram, illustrated in figure 5.2 for the case of cabbages, is the classic simple description of this process. Suppliers (farmers) are assumed to wish to produce more cabbages the higher the market price (hence the increasing supply function $S_1 S_1$) whereas consumers will buy more, the lower the market price (demand function $D_1 D_1$).

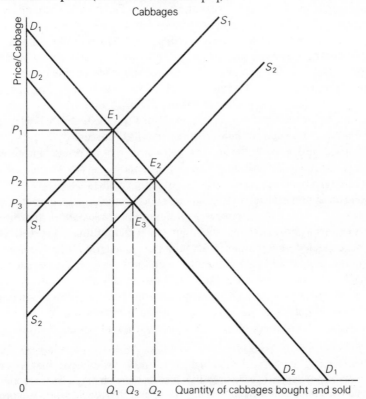

Figure 5.2   Price determination in the market for cabbages

Only at E_1 will demand and supply be exactly in balance. If supply conditions improve (to $S_2 S_2$), then a new equilibrium will be established at E_2. If subsequently demand conditions change (in this case fall to $D_2 D_2$ because of, say, a change in consumer preferences in favour of brussels sprouts), then the equilibrium position will be E_3, − and so on.

Similar forces will operate in the case of factors of production and in this way the neo-classicals developed a theory of income distribution which, they argued, was more precise than that of the classicals for whom distribution was analysed in terms of broad social class. Thus the income of a plumber in Bradford could be viewed as a function of prevailing market forces in that town and analysed separately from other types of labour market in other geographical locations. More generally the neo-classicals believed that they had developed a realistic account of how the price mechanism provided an impersonal means for resource allocation amongst competing ends.

What then were the essential differences compared to the old tradition? To begin with neo-classical analysis was more *finely tuned*. Arguments could be phrased in terms of the economic behaviour of decision-making units rather than in terms of broad social class and hence could provide a *more detailed set of statements* about how the economic system worked at any point in time. It also made economic propositions *easier to test* since unlike 'labour values' prices can be observed and measured (though not necessarily equilibrium prices, which can sometimes cause problems). One problem with propositions emanating from Marxian economics, a modern inheritor of the older tradition, is that if the predicted result (like a secular falling rate of profit) does not occur, it can always be argued by the true believer that market prices have not yet adjusted to their 'real' or 'natural' values. Indeed the classical economists did not see the necessity for a theory of prices and took it for granted that the normal functioning of the economic system would establish a convergence between market prices and labour values.

Barber argues that changing social conditions were an important factor behind the change in intellectual climate. The first half of the nineteenth century was a period of great social upheaval and political unrest. It was only to be expected that emphasis should be placed on imperfections in the economic system and the reputation of economics as the 'dismal science' was indeed well merited. By the latter half of the century, however, industrial development was solidly under way, economic growth was beginning to be felt more widely and the Victorian faith in progress was well-established. Neo-classical writers absorbed this optimism and although

> their conclusions pointed to the existence of certain 'imperfections' in the
> economic system that called for policy remedies, nevertheless, they restored a
> temper of optimism to economic discourse that − with only a few exceptions −
> had been suppressed since Malthus. Progress, they could hold, appeared to
> resolve social tensions rather than to aggravate them.[5]

But there were important *ideological* factors operating as well. The classical emphasis upon social class (and hence class conflict) needed to be defused since it opened the door to dangerous political doctrines. By focusing on the detailed 'mechanics' of the price system and by concentrating attention on the sheer complexity of the new industrial order, the neo-classicals (wittingly or unwittingly) went some way towards doing this. But they did more. In the capable hands of authorities such as Marshall (1842–1924) neo-classical economics became a powerful system of thought which served to legitimate the new social order simply because of its sheer elegance. Hence, it could be shown that *provided perfectly competitive conditions obtained* (a very important proviso) no one part of the system could hold any other part to ransom. Provided governments did not interfere beyond the minimum necessary to ensure its efficient operation, 'market forces' would allocate resources in an entirely impersonal way and economic output, and hence 'welfare', would be maximised. Moreover, economic propositions could now be portrayed in mathematical form thereby lending 'scientific' legitimacy to the system they helped to establish. By what was almost an intellectual sleight of hand, neo-classical analysis went a long way towards defusing social criticism for many decades to come.

Finally, and most importantly from our point of view, neo-classical economics concerned itself mainly with (and lent itself most easily to) matters of resource allocation in the short run – i.e. at any point in time. Conversely it had very little to say about the 'long period', for example about how economic growth and capital accumulation took place. In so far as they were concerned about economic growth, neo-classical economists assumed that it was a function of the rates of savings and of investment in the economy as a whole. These were equilibrated by the 'rate of interest' or the 'market price of loanable funds'. The process by which new technology became absorbed into the productive process was ignored, or treated as an exogenous factor in the analysis of economic systems. This is an important reason why, as was pointed out in chapter 1, neo-classical economic analysis has only limited applicability to questions of science and technology policy.

The neo-classical tradition has often been criticised for its lack of realism and for its apparent association with right-wing political doctrines. However, with the resurgence of (some) nineteenth-century ideas regarding the role of government in the modern nation state it is perhaps useful to say a last word in its defence – which is that it tends often to be both misused and misunderstood. Essentially it was, and is even in its modern form, a philosophical system designed to aid in the explanation of economic processes. But its efficacy in so doing is only as good as the realism of its underlying assumptions and many of the supposed 'defects' of the neo-classical approach are due not so much to the approach itself, but to the way it has come to be used. Regrettably the economics 'profession' is as much to blame here as anybody else. Galbraith has argued powerfully[6] (and I agree with him) that by adopting an over-simplified, and largely mistaken, view of the scientific method, and by concentrating attention only on those propositions whose variables and parameters can be expressed and manipulated mathematically, modern economics has not only cut itself off from real policy relevance, it has become almost akin to a type of religious dogma used by politicians to lend intellectual legitimacy to broad policy perspectives in a manner similar to the functioning of the Oracle at Delphi in Ancient Greece. And that has occurred for reasons associated with the 'socialisation' of knowledge and the 'professionalisation' of a discipline. Certainly students should not be unduly impressed by its apparent technical facade.

5.4 The Keynesian Critique

I have suggested above that by Keynes's time the neo-classical system had become more than just a disaggregated way of looking at an economic system in which utility and consumer demand were given a central analytical role. It had become a powerful system of thought which in many ways legitimated existing power structures, the prevailing income distribution and, most important, a particular view of the proper role of government in national affairs.

It achieved this through the doctrine of *laissez-faire*. For in principle the concentration of attention on *utility* would argue in favour of egalitarianism, and hence social interventionism, since the notion could be tied up with Benthamite ideals of the 'greatest happiness for the greatest number of people'. If income itself was subject to 'diminishing marginal utility', then clearly economic inequality could not be justified. On the other hand *laissez-faire*, which argued complete economic freedom for all, was clearly contradictory to goals of economic equality since the latter could only be brought about through the intervention of the state. Evidently a way had to be found to reconcile the two doctrines and this was achieved by emphasising the importance of capital accumulation. Since only the rich save, a redistribution of national income, it was held, would only serve to reduce drastically the rate of growth and hence *utility for everyone in the future*. In any case redistribution would not change poor people's income by very much since there were so many poor people and so few rich ones. What emerged, therefore, was an economic doctrine which frowned upon *any* sort of interference with 'market forces' (except where the government had to get involved, as with the provision of defence and law and order, for example), and which argued that if everybody behaved as they ought to behave, then all would be, if not for the best, at least as good as could reasonably be expected.

Unfortunately social conditions in the period between the wars did not reflect this optimism. From late in 1920 the UK began to suffer from a series of recessions which by the early 1930s had degenerated into an economic slump of very great severity. Economic output declined and levels of unemployment rose dramatically, in some parts of the country to well over 50% of the available working population. Hobsbawm writes graphically of communities such as that of Merthyr where 70% of the labour force 'had nothing to do except stand at street corners and curse the system which put them there'.[7] Overall, from an average of around 6% of the insured working population before the First World War, unemployment during the 18 years from 1921–3 rose to an average of over 14%. And these data relate only to workers covered under the national insurance scheme.

Of course, the neo-classicals had never been so naive as to imagine that economic evolution could be painless. But their emphasis was that any shock to the system would be strictly a temporary phenomenon mediated by appropriate price adjustments. If demand fell for the products of industry X and rose for those of industry Y then resources, including labour, would shift correspondingly and although there might be bottlenecks these would represent merely 'stickiness' in the system which would return naturally to a new equilibrium. Similarly with the booms and slumps of the 'business' or 'trade' cycle. What was so devastating to the neo-classical view was the simple fact that those departures from equilibrium, far from being temporary aberrations, showed every sign of being very permanent indeed. Nor did they respond to the normal neo-classical panaceas – cut backs in public expenditure, wage cuts and all the panoply of 'sound' and 'limited' government which were widely advocated (and practised) at the time. Clearly something was very wrong.

Keynes's (1883–1946) attack on the neo-classical position, published in his book the *General Theory of Employment, Interest and Money*[8] in 1936, was not, however, a direct attack on many of the assumptions behind neo-classical economics. Rather he argued that the neo-classical system could only work in the *special case* where resources are fully utilised and there is no unemployment. However, *laissez-faire* could not in itself ensure full employment since one of its fundamental precepts – the injunction to save – actually helped to *produce* unemployment. Thus he went on to postulate a general theory which advocated state intervention to ensure that the economy's productive resources were always fully utilised, much in the same way as Einstein's theory of relativity subsumed Newtonian physics as a special case.[9]

5.4.1 The General Theory

Keynes proceeded as follows. National savings (abstinence from consumption) will only increase employment if they are productively used – that is if they are *invested* in new capital stock. This will not automatically happen since those who save are not in general the same people/institutions who invest. In particular businessmen will not invest unless there is *sufficient demand* expected for the extra goods which the new machines will produce. And it is precisely during a period of slump that these expectations will be low, so low in fact that investment activity will be likely to fall to very low levels indeed. Furthermore the falling off in investment demand will reduce incomes and employment in the capital goods industries, thereby reducing still more consumption and investment demands, and so on in a continuous recessionary spiral until eventually the economic system stabilises at a level well below that at which productive resources are being fully utilised. This being the case, Keynes argued, it is quite reasonable to expect the capitalist economic system, in its natural operations, to seek equilibrium at *any* level of employment. Only if there is some external intervention, in the form of government action, will that level be equivalent to one of full employment.

It is sometimes helpful to portray Keynes's argument with the aid of a simple diagram portraying various categories of aggregate demand, con-sumption (C), investment (I) and government expenditures (G), on the 'y' axis as a function of national output ($=$ national income) on the 'x' axis. At all points on the 45° line aggregate demand is equal to national output.

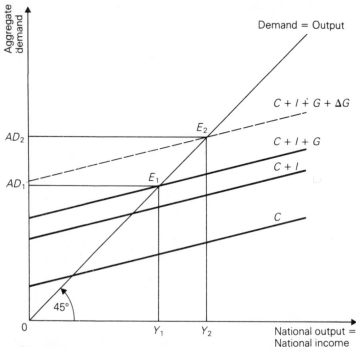

Figure 5.3 National income determination

Ignoring foreign trade, aggregate demand in any economic system is composed of three broad categories:

consumption expenditure − assumed to be an increasing function of incomes
investment expenditure
$$\left.\begin{array}{l} \text{investment expenditure} \\ \text{government expenditure} \end{array}\right\} \text{both assumed independent of incomes}$$
government expenditure

At any level of national output, Y_1, say, there will be only one level of demand, AD_1, at which supply and demand are in balance (point E_1). If production proceeds beyond Y_1 goods will remain unsold, stocks will rise, prices will fall and production will fall back towards point Y_1. If, however, production falls below Y_1 there will be excess demand, stocks will fall, prices rise and production will rise again. Only at Y_1 will there be equilibrium.

But suppose that Y_1 is a level of national output *below* that corresponding to full deployment of the nation's resources (Y_2). Under such circumstances there will be a demand deficiency or a 'deflationary gap' equivalent to $AD_2 - AD_1$, forcing the economy to operate well below its full potential, both in terms of output *and* employment. Keynes's position was that it was essentially the role of government to ameliorate social waste of this type by stepping in to ensure the necessary increase in aggregate demand (ΔG). One way of doing this was through direct expenditures on public works (e.g. a road-building programme). Other mechanisms were by means of the 'fiscal' system (e.g. reducing taxes which might encourage consumers to spend more)[10] or through public purchasing schemes.

What was so radical about Keynes's view was that it provided legitimation for the state to intervene in the workings of the economy, thereby conflicting directly with the dictates of *laissez-faire*. Moreover, the corollary argument − that governments should spend in excess of their incomes − was a blatant contradiction of an important tenet of Victorian morality. Keynes was arguing that private virtues were often public vices and, by the same token, that those who saved were not *ipso facto* productive, hence attacking the prime case for unequal income distribution and opening the door to social conflict once again. In this way the harmonious, 'value free' world of the neo-classical system broke down, a world in which 'policy' had been unnecessary because there was no need for government action.

However, it is important not to exaggerate this radicalism. Despite the rage which he aroused, Keynes was a firm believer in the capitalist system which he saw himself as trying to save. He was well aware of its defects, of course, but felt it to be preferable to the only other form of economic organisation apparently available as an alternative − the command economy as exemplified by Soviet central planning. Such an economy was bound to be inefficient, in his view, because it is impossible to plan a complex industrial system in this way. Moreover, subjecting the bulk of economic decisions to a state apparatus would inevitably reduce the freedom of the individual to the convenience of bureaucratic elites, a prospect he did not look forward to with pleasure. However, Keynes believed that with a re-establishment of full employment the neo-classical system would come into its own again, reason would prevail and social progress would continue. Nowadays we are not so sure.

5.4.2 Monetary and Fiscal Policy

It is worth noting that the neo-classical tradition by no means took Keynes's strictures lying down, and they fought a long and hard battle before Keynesian ideas became finally accepted after the Second World War. One important issue they raised was associated with investment behaviour of businessmen which the neo-classicals had always felt to be responsive to primarily *monetary* influences. In the neo-classical view the level of investment was a decreasing function of the rate of interest prevailing. If aggregate consumption demand fell for any reason then this would increase savings thereby increasing the supply of loanable funds available from monetary institutions, particularly the banking system. The rate of interest would fall and businessmen would invest more as a result, the net effects upon the whole system being a re-allocation of resources from the consumption goods to the investment goods sector with no deficiency in aggregate demand.

Keynes spent some considerable effort in rebutting this argument which we need not go into here. However, it does raise an important set of issues which have reappeared nowadays as a significant controversy in economic management associated with the resurrection of more traditional neo-classical ideas, underlying public policy. The economic doctrine behind this policy shift is sometimes called 'monetarism' because those adhering to it believe that in reality the economy does regulate itself fairly well, always provided that the supply of money in the system is appropriate to the level of real activity with which the economy can cope. Under this view (which has an ancient pedigree) monetary causes are the major source of national income fluctuations and in our present times the excessive supply of money emanating from the banking system has been the prime cause of inflation. It remains, therefore, for the money supply to be reduced through strong central action. This will raise the cost of credit (the rate of interest) both to producers and to consumers, thereby reducing the level of aggregate expenditure in the economy as a whole with a corresponding reduction in the rate of inflation (defined in terms of the rate of increase in the average price level for a given 'basket' of goods and services).

To the charge that this action apparently raises unemployment to very high levels, with enormous social costs, monetarists reply that such repercussions are the responsibility of the trades union movement which acts so as to raise wages in areas where bargaining power is strong thereby pricing other workers out of jobs. The effect is both to redistribute the national 'wage bill' from those without work to those with work *and* to redistribute national income from profits to wages thereby forcing employers to cut back on investment. Only when workers see the necessity of matching wages with the 'social opportunity cost' of labour and put corresponding pressure on their representative bodies will investment pick up, thereby bringing about further economic growth and a fall in unemployment levels. governments themselves can and should do very little, apart from providing an equitable framework of law within which economic life may be conducted.

Those of a 'Keynesian' persuasion take a different view in so far as they believe that changes in the money supply make little difference to real economic activity except in the very long term when all sorts of other changes will have taken place anyway. Hence in times of inflation the crude deflationary impact of a harsh monetary policy will not only cause waste in terms of unutilised resources, it will also absorb potential savings in the form of unemployment benefits. Moreover, since investment is not a function of the rate of interest, but responds rather to demand expectations on the part of businessmen, it will stagnate and hence economic recovery will take place at best sluggishly. Even where it does take place there are those who argue that in a monetary slump R & D will have fallen dramatically so that investment when it does take place will often be inefficient compared to 'best practice' standards in other competing countries. The Keynesian response, then, to national income fluctuations is to rely much more heavily on the fiscal system (tax policy) and public expenditures, to attempt to control inflation through direct legal action on prices and incomes and generally to be more tolerant of an increased public share in national economic activity. It tends also to believe that monetary factors react to, rather than lead to real economic behaviour.

I have, of course, over-simplified and polarised the two positions and students should consult some of the recommended texts if they wish to go further into these matters. However, it is worth making a few observations at this stage. *First*, it is undoubtedly the case that the resurrection of some of the older neo-classical ideas has occurred as a result of a perceived failure of Keynesian policies in the 1970s. In particular 'stagflation', the simultaneous occurrence of economic stagnation *and* rising prices, cannot be handled by the simple Keynesian analysis outlined above. It should not happen according to the theory, and hence where it does there is great uncertainty as to what to do about it. A *second* factor is that the revival of older ideas is probably something of a reaction against the growing involvement of the state in national affairs. Before the Second World War, the British government's share of the national product was of the order of 16%. By the late 1960s/early 1970s, and after two decades of rapid economic growth, the political ethos had changed to one in which governments were expected to get involved in the provision of a whole range of (better) goods and services, and to take responsibility for ensuring the equitable functioning of a 'caring welfare state'. Hand in hand with this new *dirigiste* role grew a much larger civil service staffed by people whose 'professional skills' had scarcely been heard of 30 years before. Social services, for example, were no longer characterised by poorly staffed, under-financed council offices coping as best they could with the more intractable problems of the poor (and helped out by voluntary groups). They had become fully-fledged bureaucracies whose many-layered managerial hierarchies were staffed by university graduates well versed in the intricacies of Freudian psychology.

These activities were supported by greater levels of taxation the burden of which was not really noticed in a period of rapid economic growth but which became more apparent as recession began to bite during the 1970s. The problem was that the creation of bureaucracy tends to be self-sustaining. Indeed we find writers such as Bacon and Eltis writing in 1976[11] that successive British governments had actually helped to create public service jobs in the period since 1965 to absorb those who could no longer be employed in a contracting private sector. Certainly it became very difficult to explain to people that their hard-won (and specialised) skills were no longer socially necessary after all. Nevertheless it can scarcely be accidental that the revival of pre-Keynesian notions has taken place at precisely the same time as it has become politically feasible to curtail the activities of the public sector.

A *third*, and related, point to make is that in reality differences between Keynesian and monetarist positions have a very strong ideological component. Thus monetarists have recently had a great deal of trouble showing that there is indeed empirical evidence to support the proposition that changes in the money supply influence real economic activity, and in fact one major piece of recent empirical research concludes that very probably there is no such simple relationship.[12] Nevertheless it is doubtful whether empirical evidence of this kind will sway the opinions of a convinced monetarist. Similar strictures apply to Keynesians. *Finally*, and very importantly from our point of view, the debate we have been discussing tends to be peripheral to science and technology policy issues simply because monetary and fiscal policies are concerned with the short-run stability (or lack of it) of the economic system whereas issues of science policy concern, as we have seen, longer-term prospects and problems of economic development. Indeed Keynes specifically excluded the 'long run' from his analysis in the sense that changes in aggregate investment demand were not permitted to affect the economy's output *by virtue of the increased capital stock available*. Although he did have points to make about the long-run prospects of industrial capitalism, Keynes's primary concern, at the time of writing the *General Theory*, was to set the story right as he saw it regarding the possibilities for the economic system to stabilise at a level where all available resources, including both capital and labour, were fully utilised.

5.5 The Schumpeterian Tradition

You will recall that I have emphasised repeatedly throughout the text an important deficiency in neo-classical economic analysis relating to its treatment of capital accumulation and economic growth. This is so because most of its propositions tend to be postulated in the short run with technical conditions taken as given. Even where technical conditions are allowed to change (through the analytical device of comparative statics), this tells you virtually nothing about the rate, direction or causation of economic growth.

It was Joseph Schumpeter's great contribution that he tried to deal with this problem and in doing so he has provided the inspiration and starting point from which a variety of more modern approaches have developed. He was, of course, very much a neo-classical economist but he was also one who understood very well the older classical tradition and he made a break with neo-classical thinking in two important respects. *First*, he developed a theory of economic progress; *secondly*, in this theory technological changes played a key role.

Schumpeter's starting point was the role of business profits in the evolution of the capitalist system, which he saw as providing an important motivating function. It must be remembered that in the neo-classical tradition, profits, beyond those necessary as a competitive return to invested capital funds, were viewed mainly as a sign of market imperfections, the result of some form of monopolistic practice which allowed the seller to hold the buying public to ransom. While not disagreeing with this, nevertheless Schumpeter argued that profits, or rather the expectation of profits, had another role − that of a *lure to the entrepreneur to innovate*, to make new combinations of inputs thus lowering production costs *or* to develop entirely new products. Profits, therefore, had a positive, energising role − that of a return to *entrepreneurship* without which capitalist growth and development would not take place at all. Moreover these profits would be temporary since imitation from competitors would erode them. In this sense there was nothing in Schumpeter's theory which contradicted the assumptions of the static neo-classical model. In essence what he was doing was adding a theory of growth (*and* a theory of profit) to it, thereby showing how growth took place in the system as a whole, but he did not disagree with the neo-classical metaphor.[13]

5.5.1 Some Points of Elaboration

An important concept in Schumpeterian thinking is that of the *entrepreneur*. It is clear that Schumpeter regarded him as an heroic figure comparable to the famous philosophers, knights and statesmen of earlier periods. He has the courage, imagination and foresight to glimpse possibilities for innovation, to mobilise the necessary resources and to see development through to a successful conclusion. Strictly speaking he is not a person but a quality, *entrepreneurship*, which is manifested by different sorts of people at different times and is defined as a distinct business category both from the person who runs things, the manager, and from the person who provides finance and undertakes financial risk, the capitalist.

> As it is the carrying out of new combinations that constitutes the entrepreneur, it is not necessary that he should be permanently connected with an individual firm; . . . on the other hand our concept . . . does not include all heads of firms or managers or industrialists who merely operate an established business, but [rather] only those who actually profess that [entrepreneurial] function. . . . [Also] shareholders, *per se*, . . . are never entrepreneurs, but merely capitalists, who in consideration of their submitting to certain risks participate in profits.[14]

It follows that we can all be 'entrepreneurs' at certain points in our lives and that 'entrepreneurship' can be applied equally to 'non-productive' activities (for example, new ways of organising church bazaars). Schumpeter of course largely applied the notion to economic production but in the way he describes it, it seems remarkably close to those qualities which produce the creative act, like the idea of 'lateral thinking' developed by de Bono.

Innovations were regarded by Schumpeter as new 'combinations' of productive resources. These would take *five* major forms;

1   The introduction of a new good *or* of a new quality of a good.
2   The introduction of a new production process (not necessarily one based upon scientific discovery).
3   The opening up of a new market.
4   The development of a new source of input supply.
5   Changes in industrial organisation.

But, broadly speaking, anything which increases the efficiency with which resources are used was regarded by Schumpeter as an innovation.*Monopoly positions* arising out of the superior market positions generated by innovations, were regarded by Schumpeter as transitory. They would 'perish in the vortex of the competition which streams after them' as the innovations were copied by other firms. Of course productive enterprises will always try to preserve their monopolies, for example by taking out patents or by holding on to key industrial secrets. But their success in so doing will always be limited because of the sheer force of competitive pressures − although observation of an economic system at any point in time, an economic photograph as it were, would tend to reveal the existence of particular monopolies.

5.5.2 Schumpeter I and Schumpeter II

The foregoing summarised account of Schumpeter's views on innovation and growth represent in fact his earlier thoughts on the subject as portrayed in his book *The Theory of Economic Development*,[15] published for the first time in German in the autumn of 1911. However, it is useful to draw attention to one or two of the evident weaknesses in this theory (sometimes called Schumpeter I), since these are precisely the points at which we can begin to develop a more complete grasp of the role of science and technology in the industrialis-ation process.

Thus while his theory was undoubtedly an advance on the *simpliste* neo-classical story, Schumpeter still lived in an artifical, nineteenth-century, world of 'perfect competition' populated by many small firms each having little market power. In reality, of course, Schumpeter was a victim of his doctrinal training since even at the turn of the century there were many industrial sectors where economic concentration, in the form of 'trusts' and 'cartels' was considerable. And it was evident also that market power could be maintained over long periods, despite the forces of competition.

A second problem is related to Schumpeter's 'entrepreneur', since although it is a very useful concept (for reasons to be discussed in later chapters) there is a certain artificiality in isolating 'entrepreneurship' in the way that Schumpeter does. As he himself admits, entrepreneurs are also other people (such as managers and capitalists) and are subject therefore to rather more complex behavioural motives. In particular, there is no reason to suppose that the successful innovating firm will stop at one innovation, but will surely attempt to *continue* to innovate so as to prevent competitive pressures and to develop market strength. Hence we find writers such as Cooper (1971)[16] maintaining that there are powerful reasons for supposing that firms will try to institutionalise the capacity for innovation in a far more permanent sense than Schumpeter I appears to allow for, for example by establishing their own R & D laboratories.

As Phillips (1971)[17] and Freeman et al. (1982)[18] have pointed out, Schumpeter came to realise these points and in a later book *Capitalism, Socialism and Democracy* (1943)[19] took the position (Schumpeter II) that corporate R & D represents a major source of industrial innovation. Indeed, since R & D is such an expensive activity only large firms are generally able to afford it. This is so for a number of reasons but it is useful to mention three particularly important ones at this stage. First of all there is the *appro-priability argument* that only large firms have the necessary productive capacity, marketing arrangements and finance to exploit a new technology quickly. This may be an especially important factor where possibilities for patent protection are weak and, therefore, where risks of imitation are likely to be high. Under such a market regime, the large firm with an established brand name may be in a very strong competitive position.

A second factor relates to *economies of scale in R & D* such that the larger the resource inputs to R & D, the greater proportionately are the innovative outputs. One reason why this might be the case is that the larger R & D department may be better able to keep abreast with a range of 'disciplines' relevant to the field and hence to mobilise resources more efficiently. *Finally* in a series of empirical studies on innovation in the electronics capital goods sector, Freeman[20] came to the conclusion that there is often a *threshold level of R & D* below which expenditure on R & D will not yield any fruit at all. Such levels will vary from industry to industry but in some (for example, telecommunications and computers) they will be quite large, thus giving a distinct advantage to the big firm.

Hence, although Schumpeter did not have access to the empirical evidence that we now have, there is no doubt that in his later writings he had come round firmly to the view that the 'entrepreneur [would] ultimately [be] . . . superceded by a "bureaucratised" type of innovation' (Freeman *et al.*). Indeed Freeman et al. (1982) point out that he viewed this tendency to be so powerful that it 'would ultimately lead to the disappearance of capitalism itself'.[21] In recent years this apparent association between size of firm and R & D effort has become the subject of considerable controversy, and we shall discuss it in more detail in a later chapter. However, it is worth pointing out probably that the logical basis for this claim (that R & D effort is proportionately greater for the larger firm) is conceptually not the same as the arguments put forward by Murray (discussed in the previous chapter) that large firms are more efficient in a *productive* sense because of their greater capacity to take advantage of the division of labour. One important writer who uses both arguments to support his views on the greater viability of large firms (Galbraith) will be discussed in more detail in chapter 6.

5.6 Some Concluding Remarks

The purpose of this chapter has been to introduce students to some of the main elements of economic theory as it has evolved over the last 200 years. The main reasons for doing so have been *first*, to bring home the extent to which economic ideas have relevance to policy-making, *secondly*, to illustrate how these ideas have evolved through time, *thirdly* to emphasise the very important role of 'received wisdom' as the basis for economic and social policy, and *fourthly* to highlight the point that it is only relatively recently that this literature has tried to come to grips with the influence of social expenditures on science and technology. Inevitably my treatment has been truncated, and in places over-simplified (but not, I feel, so much as to be misleading). Those who would like to take things further are invited to consult the texts cited below.

Bibliography

There are a number of good histories of economic thought to which students might refer. I have used W. J. Barber, *A History of Economic Thought* (Harmondsworth, Penguin, 1967) which provides a straightforward account of the writings of the major figures involved, supplemented by J. Robinson, *Economic Philosophy* (Harmondsworth, Penguin, 1983) which provides a stimulating exposition of the evolution of the underlying ideas. However, reference might also be made to G. Routh, *The Origin of Economic Ideas* (London, Macmillan, 1977), R. L. Heilbroner, *The Worldly Philosophers* (New York, Simon and Schuster, 1972) and J. Robinson and J. Eatwell, *An Introduction to Modern Economics* (London, McGraw Hill, 1973), especially pp. 1–144.

On Keynes, a good account is provided by M. Stewart, *Keynes and After* (Harmondsworth, Penguin, 1972). See also the paper by Freeman in Spiegel-Rosing and Price (eds.), *Science, Technology and Society*, and many of the references cited in the bibliographies at the end of chapters 2 and 6. On modern macroeconomic problems and policy, besides the appropriate sections of textbooks such as R. G. Lipsey, *Positive Economics*, a useful introduction is provided by J. Trevithick, *Inflation* (Harmondsworth, Penguin, 1979). An irreverent treatment of money and monetary policy is contained in J. K. Galbraith, *Money* (Harmondsworth, Penguin, 1979).

Notes

1 Robinson, *Economic Philosophy*, chapter 2.
2 Quoted in Barber, *History of Economic Thought*, pp. 88,89.
3 D. H. Meadows and D. L. Meadows et al., *The Limits to Growth* (New York, Universe Books, 1972).
4 Robinson, *Economic Philosophy*, chapter 3.
5 Barber, *History of Economic Thought*, p. 164
6 See, for example, J. K. Galbraith, 'The Language of Economics' in *Economics, Peace and Laughter* (Harmondsworth, Penguin, 1979).
7 Hobsbawm, *Industry and Empire*, p. 208.
8 J. M. Keynes, *The General Theory of Employment, Interest and Money* (London, Macmillan, 1961).
9 For a useful account of this analogy see B. R. Easlea, *Liberation and the Aims of Science* (London, Chatto and Windus, 1973).
10 Actually, in terms of figure 5.3 reducing taxes so as to increase C should be denoted as ΔC, and not ΔG.
11 See R. Bacon and W. Eltis, *Britain's Economic Problem; Too Few Producers* (London, Macmillan, 1983, 2nd edn). See chapter 1.
12 See D. F. Hendry and N. R. Ericsson, 'Assertion without Empirical Basis: An Econometric Appraisal of Friedman and Schwartz', in Bank of England Panel of Academic Consultants, Panel Paper No. 22, *Monetary Trends in the UK*, October 1983.

13 Nor indeed was he ever particularly enthusiastic about public policy intervention to bring about innovation and growth. I am grateful to Christopher Freeman for bringing this point to my attention.

14 J. Schumpeter, *The Theory of Economic Development* (New York, Oxford University Press, 1961), see p. 75.

15 For full reference, see note 14 above.

16 C. M. Cooper, 'Science, Technology and Development', *Economic and Social Review*, Vol. 2, No. 2, January 1971, pp. 184 *et seq*.

17 A. Phillips, *Technology and Market Structure* (Lexington, Lexington Books, 1971).

18 C. Freeman, J. Clark and L. Soete, *Unemployment and Technical Innovation* (London, Francis Pinter, 1982), p. 38.

19 J. Schumpeter, *Capitalism, Socialism and Democracy* (New York, Harper and Row, 1947, 2nd edn).

20 C. Freeman, 'Research and Development in Electronic Capital Goods', *National Institute Economic Review*, No. 34, November 1965, pp. 40–97.

21 Freeman, Clark and Soete, *Unemployment and Technical Innovation*, p. 41.

Chapter 6

MODERN DEVELOPMENTS

6.1 Introduction

One problem involved in trying to bring our conceptual historiography up to date is that the closer one gets to the present time the more difficult it becomes to separate oneself from on-going controversies, and debates which are far from being resolved. The way I have chosen to handle recent developments is to split them into two streams of thought, (1) attempts to include science and technology policy questions within economic 'orthodoxy' i.e. within the neo-classical tradition, (2) attempts to theorise in a more 'radical' fashion. There is a good deal of artificiality in this manner of exposition, and not everyone will agree with the way it has been done. Nevertheless it does have the advantage of system. The concentration in this chapter will be on styles of analysis. Discussion on current issues of science and technology policy will be reserved for chapter 9.

In effect what we have been witnessing in the last 20–30 years or so are a series of attempts by economists and others to come to grips with the social impact of science and technology, without really having adequate tools to carry the task out. Because, for example, there is a lack of clear understanding about how technological change actually takes place and because of difficulties involved in assimilating it into the prevailing traditions of economic thought, the late 1960s and 1970s have become a period of re-examination in which different scholars have returned to the 'drawing board' and have pursued a variety of research paths in order to establish 'how the whole thing works'. Motives too have varied. In some cases there is clearly a genuine desire to be able to say things of policy relevance. In others the interests are more detached and disinterested. All too often, unfortunately, there are keenly felt issues of doctrine lurking below the surface.

What makes it particularly difficult for the newcomer are the large number of different 'questions' to which the research is seeking answers. A central topic is clearly that of economic growth and its causes (and that is where I shall start), but behind this major question there are a range of subsidiary 'issues' which inform the main theme and interact in complex ways. Examples of these are:

— how is size of firm related to innovation?
— how is R & D expenditure related to the growth and competitive position of firms?
— is innovation stimulated mainly by the science system or does market demand predominate?
— what factors affect the rate of diffusion of innovations?
— how does the propensity to innovate affect international competitive performance at the national level?

In the main I shall make no attempt at this stage to explore these issues in any detail, but refer students to the wide range of bibliographic and other literature which now exists in abundance.

6.2 Continuation of Orthodoxy

After the end of the Second World War there was a revival of interest in economic growth. A. K. Sen[1] has pointed out that this was not only a reaction to the pre-war debates on short-run economic stability (which Keynes appeared to have won). It was as much, if not more, a symptom of the times. There was the important question of reconstruction of the war-damaged economies of Europe, assisted by US aid through the Marshall Plan. With the growing prospects for decolonization of many parts of the third world, attention became focused increasingly upon how economic growth took place and upon how the process might be accelerated through judicious action, both national and international.

But progress was rudimentary. So far as the scientific community was concerned, the war experience had brought their members into 'government' to a much greater (and more varied) extent than ever before. However, its involvement was concerned very much with the 'machinery' of warfare, the devices, systems and techniques which had rendered the conduct of hostilities quite different from anything known before — like radar, underwater systems and particularly, atomic weapons. Such a community, therefore, was not particularly well equipped to divert its (latent) talents to the often less mechanistic requirements of post-war reconstruction, and indeed the UK and the USA in particular have continued to devote a very large proportion of their respective expenditures upon science and technology to the artifacts of modern war. Nor were the economists particularly progressive. Following

Roy Harrod's well-known attempt to chart out the conditions under which an industrialised economic system could grow in a stable manner,[2] the economics literature grew replete with increasingly abstruse variations on a theme which had little or no empirical content, and therefore policy relevance.

6.2.1 The Economics of Research and Development (R & D)

The break came, as we have discussed before, with the identification of the 'residual' on the part of Solow,[3] Abramovitz[4] and others in the mid-1950s and hence the need to understand what it consisted of. Clearly R & D was seen to be very relevant. After all, if economic growth is *caused* largely by 'better ways of making things' then investment in this must surely pay off and indeed since industrial R & D expenditures had been increasing rapidly it was intuitively plausible to suggest that this must be one of the major factors involved. There followed a series of attempts to establish such an association with, however, very inconclusive results. In fact the evidence from cross-industry and economy-wide studies tended to show that although it was sometimes possible to identify a statistical association between R & D expenditures and economic performance, the strength of the relationship was often small in comparison with other factors and appeared to act in a reverse direction, namely improvements in economic performance *leading to* greater expenditures on R & D rather than the other way about. At the 'macro' level, therefore, it appeared almost that R & D represented an item of 'luxury consumption' expenditure on the part of firms.

In retrospect it is not at all difficult to find explanations for this (rather deflating) evidence. The most important of these are as follows:

(i) **Other Causal Factors**. R & D is only one potential influence. Others might well be of greater importance. Some examples are economies of scale, greater industrial concentration, better organisation of production, education improvements.

(ii) **Differential Receptivity to R & D**. Industries vary in terms of how much their economic performance can be improved through their own R & D expenditures. This could be a function of the quality of their science base or their age. Very often technological change occurs through inter-industry complementarities and in such cases cross-industry regression analyses would not pick up the influence of R & D expenditures.

(iii) **Other Statistical Problems**. It is very difficult to develop unambiguous measures of economic performance, particularly those relating to productivity where, for example, Stigler[5] has pointed to a number of problems associated with the choice of prices for capital and labour inputs and has laid particular emphasis upon the difficulties involved in measuring capital services. Very often, therefore, an apparent change in productivity is little more than a statistical illusion.

(iv) **Unmeasurable Effects of R & D**. The impact of much R & D may be felt in areas where objective measurements of costs and benefits cannot be made, as for example in medicine, health technology, warfare, environmental pollution, and so on. Hence statistical relationships would prove very hard to identify.

Nevertheless, if for these and other reasons the social productivity of R & D expenditures appeared to be relatively dubious, why did firms spend money on it? The answer to this appeared to lie in two directions. First, it came to be understood that a good part of *observed* R & D expenditures represented necessary inputs in the productive process rather than expenditures upon innovation *per se*. For example, in industries connected with electronics or electrical equipment one cannot manufacture devices without at the same time possessing facilities for routine trouble-shooting, quality control, testing, calibration and so on. More generally much of observed R & D expenditures are largely determined by the nature of the industry under consideration. The second explanation was that R & D expenditures represented a necessary element in a firm's competitive strategy either as part of product differentiation activities *or* as a device to reduce risk and uncertainty in an uncertain environment. Freeman,[6] for example, has argued that in any industry the establishment of a technical lead is a powerful instrument of competitive strength, and we shall see below that recently Nelson and Winter have developed a theory of firm behaviour in which competitive R & D plays an important role.

Certainly these explanations were consistent with the empirical evidence at the 'micro' level where a number of studies, such as those associated with Mansfield[7] and Minasian[8] for example, showed quite clear relationships between R & D expenditures and subsequent economic performance. Hence the general conclusion appeared to be consistent with the proposition that while the *social* productivity of R & D might be small (or even negative), nevertheless within any one industry or sector it might be dangerous for an enterprise to opt out of R & D spending since that would be tantamount to reducing its *private* productivity. R & D has the properties of an escalator moving downwards at an increasing rate through time. The firm may have to climb it since otherwise it goes out of business, but the effort required actually to move up becomes progressively greater.

But does this conclusion mean that possibilities for economic progress by means of technological change are inherently limited? The pessimistic view on this is 'yes'. A writer like Illich,[9] for example, would argue that the more industrialised societies become, the more science and technology through its institutions and through professionalisation becomes virtually self-justifying. In a series of books on subjects such as education and health, Illich has argued not only that humankind has abandoned whole areas of life to 'professional experts' at great cost but also that the outcome is often profoundly *damaging* to the 'consumer'. Moreover, 'professional groups' use scientific knowledge to acquire social prestige and political power, which are subsquently used to redistribute wealth to their members regardless of the usefulness of their services. Such 'radical monopolies' are achieved through various forms of certification and accreditation, and legitimated by association with 'science' even where there is little empirical foundation for the practice. This is true as much within the state sector as in the private sector.

We shall return to this point in chapter 9 but an important question arises as to whether this is true of economically oriented expenditures upon science. The adherers to the orthodox neo-classical tradition would certainly answer 'no'. It is true that it is difficult to relate R & D expenditures with economic performance but that is largely because of the reasons outlined above, e.g. complementarities amongst variables (of which R & D is only one) and hence statistical problems in establishing the associated relationships. They would also argue that innovation is a continuous process and thus not liable to be observed easily at any point of time. For more recent years a relevant argument might be that the current pessimism is the result of recessionary social conditions and tends therefore to overlook innovations which hold out promise for radical (and beneficial) social change, including shortening of the working week. Not to pursue them vigorously would be reactionary in a fundamental sense.

6.2.2 Understanding the Residual

An early point of attack was a series of attempts to 'explain' the results of Solow and others regarding the relative importance of technological change as an 'explicator' of economic growth. As Kennedy and Thirwall[10] have pointed out, the major purpose of these investigations was to reassimilate Solow's conclusions into the mainstream of orthodoxy, although researchers like Denison[11] clearly also felt that if the main components of the residual could be established accurately then this would have important implications for subsequent policy. From a doctrinal viewpoint, however, the problem was that Solow's conclusions diminished the importance of investment (and hence capital) in the growth process thus creating yet one more 'empty box' for economic theory to puzzle over.

In practice the attack on Solow took two forms: the first was a criticism of his production function specification which was of a Cobb—Douglas form and hence assumed no economies of scale through time and neutral technical change. Solow had actually dealt with the second of these in his original paper, concluding that it was in fact a reasonable assumption. On economies of scale it appears to have been concluded that at least part of the observed technological change factor (around one-third) was in fact due to a scale effect, although much of what is attributed to scale may still be technologically determined. Overall Kennedy and Thirwall conclude that there was no systematic bias arising from misspecification of the production function.

A second set of criticisms related to the specification of the inputs. Thus a number of writers, for example, argued that since capital and labour inputs had been measured at 'historic cost' no account had therefore been taken of quality improvements through time. If this had been done, observed productivity changes would have been much lower and hence the contribution of, say, R & D expenditures to 'true' technological change much larger than appeared to have been the case. Other sources criticised the treatment of cyclical fluctuations and the lack of account taken of substitution of capital for labour due to relative price movements (labour having become relatively dearer). Yet others emphasised the importance of education and 'on-the-job learning'. It is difficult, however, to avoid the conclusion that much of this research (which is still continuing) relates more to a deep desire to demonstrate that economic theory still 'works' than to the genuine wish to understand the forces of technological change.

Part of the problem is clearly semantic (or definitional) since if we define technological progress in terms *only* of 'new technology' then a high residual (called something different, like 'productivity increase') is obviously unacceptable. But to criticise the models of Solow and Abramonitz on the grounds that sequential additions to the capital stock actually 'embody' new technology, surely smacks of scholasticism. What is important is that economic performance at the aggregate level could not be 'explained' on the basis of conventional aggregates, clearly suggesting an 'agenda' for research.

Perhaps the most determined effort in this direction was mounted by Denison[12] who in a series of statistical studies on the US and Europe over the period 1909 to 1957 attempted to disaggregate the residual into its constituent parts, a truly heroic exercise in reductionism. What is interesting about Denison's research was his 'low' finding for organised R & D as a component of the residual. The US economy grew by 2.93% p.a., between 1929 and 1957 and Denison argued that as much as 2.00% was made up of a 0.43% increase in capital stock, the remaining 1.57% being due to a range of influences of which 'advances in knowledge' (0.58%) and 'economies of scale' (0.43%) were the main ones. Only 0.12% could be ascribed to organised R & D expenditures. Denison's results have been supplemented by more disaggregated studies such as that of Griliches[13] on hybrid corn, where Griliches estimated that over the period 1910–55 'the social rate of return on private and public resources committed to research on this *highly* successful innovation was at least 700%'.[14] More recently Rosenberg has pointed out that economic historians have conducted a wide range of historical studies into the role of technological changes in a number of industries, although the conclusions are indeterminate.

Students may well ask at this point, however, what is the policy significance of such studies? Is it the case that, following Denison for example, governments should allocate only a small effort to promoting R & D in comparison with promoting 'advances in knowledge'? Looked at in this light there are evident problems with the 'residual' analysis and these relate mainly to the attempt to *compartmentalise* influences. For surely factors such as R & D, education, scale effects etc. cannot be viewed in isolation from each other when they so clearly act and interact together. Indeed it is difficult to avoid the conclusion that very often results of the kinds reached by Denison beg much more fundamental questions about the nature of the methodologies used. It may not be so much a question of Rosenberg's 'Black Boxes' being unfilled, as one of the wrong sorts of boxes being examined altogether. We shall return to this point later in the text, but it is appropriate to quote the conclusions of Freeman at this stage.

> Although some enthusiasts continue to advocate the use of the aggregate production function approach, most economists now seem more sceptical about the feasibility of this method, and increasingly, about the theoretical assumptions underlying the work (Lave, 1966; Kennedy and Thirlwall, 1972). Studies based on this method may be particularly criticised for their failure to recognise the importance of complementarities in social and technical change, for their neglect of all other social science disciplines, for their lack of historical sense, and for their reductionism in relation to 'technical change'. The use of the concept of technical change in aggregate production function work departs so far from the concept in all other disciplines, and especially in the natural sciences and engineering, that it is unlikly to gain any general acceptance outside economics. Even within economics it is a source of confusion . . .[15]

6.2.3 The Role of Demand in Technological Changes

A very important strand of thinking within neo-classical orthodoxy is represented in the work of those who argue that inventions and innovations are 'called forth' by consumer demands as and when required. In a seminal paper written in 1974 Rosenberg put the matter as follows:

> Not too many years ago most economists were content to treat the process of technological change as an exogenous variable. Technological change − and the underlying body of growing scientific knowledge upon which it drew − was regarded as moving along according to certain internal processes or laws of its

own, in any case independently of economic forces. Intermittently, technological changes were introduced and adopted in economic activity, at which point the economic *consequences* of inventive activity were regarded as interesting and important — both for the contribution to long-term economic growth and to short-term cyclical instability.[16]

As Rosenberg quite rightly goes on to point out, by consigning the development of science and technology to a 'limbo' of autonomous activity producing a 'shelf' of technologies which may be drawn upon at will, it was thereby possible to resurrect the primacy of neo-classical economics in the analysis of this rather difficult area of social life.

The person usually given the credit for developing systematically the theory of demand-led technical change is Jacob Schmookler whose book *Invention and Economic Growth* was published in 1966. Schmookler's aim was to demonstrate, using data on patents and investments for a number of industrial sectors, that variations in consumer demands as reflected in rates of investment, varied systematically with *subsequent* variations in patenting activity. This was true both across industrial sectors at any point in time as well as for any one industrial sector through time. His studies revealed high correlation coefficients and hence he concluded that inventive activity could be regarded as similar to any other economic magnitude and hence as being subject to the interplay of market forces '. . . the belief that invention, or the production of technology generally, is in most instances, essentially a non-economic activity is false. . . . [The] production of inventions, and much other technological knowledge whether routinized or not . . . is in most instances as much an economic activity as is the production of bread.'[17] A similar sort of argument had previously been put forward by Hessen in 1931 but in that case it concerned the pattern of expenditures upon basic science which Hessen[18] argued was determined largely by industrial needs.

Both Schmookler's and Hessen's arguments have been subjected to considerable criticism in recent years, and the criticism has been both empirical and conceptual. Walsh et al.,[19] for example, have carried out a detailed empirical investigation into an industry (chemicals) which is more R & D intensive than those studied by Schmookler and have concluded for the four sub-sectors of plastics, dye-stuffs, pharmaceuticals and petrochemicals that the evidence broadly goes against Schmookler's view. Again Mowery and Rosenberg have published a detailed analysis of a series of *ex post* studies into the origins of innovations each of which purported to demonstrate the importance of demand factors in bringing about technological changes, and conclude that 'the primacy of market demand forces within the innovation process is simply not demonstrated'.[20] It is clear in fact that although demand factors do have a role, innovations are not equally available at equivalent cost for all industries. On the contrary the ease with which new technologies can be assimilated into economic production depends fundamentally upon the state of development of a variety of scientific and technological sub-disciplines and that varies very widely indeed. By way of caricature Rosenberg drives home the point in the following way.

> It is unlikely that any amount of money devoted to inventive activity in 1800 could have produced modern, wide-spectrum antibiotics, any more than vast sums of money at that time could have produced a satellite capable of orbiting the moon. The supply of certain classes of inventions is, at some times, completely inelastic – zero output at all levels of prices. Admittedly, extreme cases readily suggest arguments of a *reductio ad absurdum* sort. On the other hand, the purely demand-oriented approach virtually assumes the problem away. The interesting economic situations surely lie in that vast intermediate region of possibilities where supply elasticities are greater than zero but less than infinity![21]

6.2.4 International Effects – the Product Cycle

Controversy regarding the impact of technology was not, however, confined to the domestic economy only but became involved also with international trade and investment. We shall explore the issue of science and underdevelopment in the following two chapters, but at this stage it is useful to introduce the notion of the 'product cycle', first put forward as an analytical idea in relation to international trade by Michael Posner in 1961,[22] and then later refined and adapted by Hirsch, Hufbauer, Vernon and others.[23] A major reason for its introduction was to attempt to deal with two major weaknesses in inter-national trade theory as this had developed within the neo-classical tradition; first, neo-classical theory did not appear to be a very good 'predictor' of the pattern of trade between countries, and secondly, it had little to say about the dynamics of trade, about why and how trade patterns changed.

Actually 'technology' appeared to have very little *at all* to do with trade. Trade took place, according to the neo-classicals, because factor endowments varied between countries. A country which was particularly favoured by factor of production X_1, for example, would by that token possess a *comparative advantage* in the production of those commodities for which this was an important quantitative input, since X_1 was *comparatively* cheaper than other factors $X_2, X_3, X_4 \ldots$, and so on. It would then pay that country to specialise in the production of such commodities, exporting the surplus beyond domes-tic requirements and using the proceeds to import commodities manufactured using those inputs which were comparatively cheaper in other countries. In this way the promotion of international trade would ensure that world resources were optimised and output maximised. It would tend also to equalise the income of any given factor of production across countries. Much of international trade theory was, and still is, a series of articulations and elaborations of this basic theme. Since 'technology' was simply defined in terms of a combination of inputs[24] (cf. chapter 4) and was assumed to be freely available at zero cost from an international 'shelf', it played no part by definition in the pattern of trade.

However, as a scientific 'theory', the neo-classical view was unsatisfactory. Leontieff,[25] for example, had demonstrated empirically that the USA, a country manifestly well endowed with capital, appeared paradoxically to be a net exporter of labour-intensive commodities and a net importer of capital-intensive commodities. The incomes of factors of production (e.g. wages) demonstrated a stubborn unwillingness to equalise across international boundaries and it was becoming abundantly evident to all but the most committed of the faithful that 'technology' was by no means freely available at zero cost to all potential producers of a good. Moreover, the established theory provided no account of changing trade patterns through time. It was with this background that the product cycle appeared on the scene.

The argument ran as follows. Products do not suddenly appear on markets as fully-fledged mature commodities but rather demonstrate a 'life cycle' of techno-economic maturation which may be approximated as three broad phases of development. In the first phase, the *innovative* phase, the product in question is first placed upon the market as a 'new good'. This tends to happen in advanced economies since only there do you have the technological infrastructure necessary to support product innovation — access to skills, a technically advanced capital goods sector, an abundant supply of risk capital, etc. The advanced economy firm, then, has a comparative advantage in the marketing of new products which it exploits to gain monopolistic rents *à la* Schumpeter. Prices are high but there tends also to be very rapid growth of output and sales. Since the market is a high income one, there tends to be buoyant receptivity on the part of consumers.

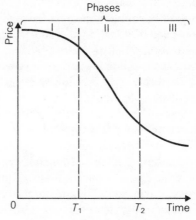
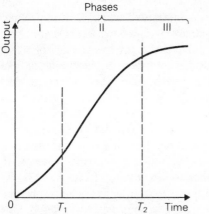

Figure 6.1 The product cycle

As time T_1 approaches in figure 6.1, the monopolistic position of the inventor begins to be eroded as patents run out and other competing firms begin to copy or introduce substitutes. The rate of profit falls along with price, and production moves out of the small, advanced, innovative firm into the larger, integrated, science-based enterprise which has the capacity to benefit from scale economies. This then is Phase II, the *intermediate* phase, when output steadies down to a 'normal' growth rate. The role of science now becomes the more standard one of the routine testing, quality control and marginal (defensive) improvements which occupy most of the time of the conventional R & D laboratory. At this stage too there will be some internationalisation of production.

Finally, in Phase III the product becomes fully *mature* in the sense that its production technology is now completely understood and standardised. Possibilities for further innovation are rare, monopolies are eroded, output falls off and price falls to a minimum 'competitive' level. It is at this stage, so the story goes, that underdeveloped countries (LDCs) have a comparative advantage in production since unskilled and semi-skilled labour have become the major inputs, and these of course are cheaper in LDCs.

But product cycle theory was not only an explanation of changing trade patterns. It was also implicitly (and sometimes explicitly) a theoretical statement about the transfer of technology, since this would be expected to take place at the 'mature' phase of the cycle. There are a number of problems with the product cycle at this level. Cooper[26] has pointed out that in practice firms 'transfer' technology and other resources at a much earlier stage in the 'life' of products often for reasons connected with defensive investment strategies where local markets are protected. In other cases firms are known to separate off labour-intensive parts of the production process and carry on what are essentially cheap-labour assembly operations overseas, re-exporting the finished parts back to headquarters. Enclave activities of this type are especially common in some far-eastern countries (Taiwan, S. Korea, Singapore) and often relate to products which are by no means exhausted from an innovation point of view. A second point is that where certain spheres of economic production are monopolistically controlled by large international firms, technology may not be transferred even where the relevant products are mature in this sense.

There is, however, a further problem with the product cycle and that is the ease with which it is turned from a 'positive' analytic device into a 'normative' description of the way things ought to be. Thus if the product cycle is a true description of the dynamics of international production patterns, the underdeveloped countries are destined to be forever technological 'followers', constantly picking up the scraps of technology which have become obsolete in the rich countries. Griffin,[27] for example, has attempted to show that in a world where the product cycle is allowed to operate unhampered by institutional restrictions there would be a continuous redistribution of income from the poor to the rich countries through the process of unequal exchange, the R & D-intensive, modern, high-priced products exported from the rich countries being exchanged for 'mature', low-priced products from the poor countries. It is, of course, precisely because the underdeveloped countries are aware of the dangers of this type of dependence that they try to ensure the transfer of technology at a much earlier stage in the 'life' of products. To the extent that they succeed, the *simpliste* product cycle model no longer works. In fact a major issue in recent years concerns the extent to which the underdeveloped countries will be able to benefit (or not) from the rapid international diffusion of technology. We shall discuss this issue in more detail in chapter 8 but already there are indications that some LDCs have begun to assimilate imported technology quite effectively.

6.2.5 The Diffusion of Technology

In recent years the literature on the diffusion of innovations has expanded enormously, and it is worth mentioning briefly one or two features of it at this stage since it relates to much of the current debate about the social impact of science and technology. A useful starting point is the *uncertainty* which attaches to all innovative activity whether it be the launching of a new product for the first time or the imitation of an innovation already introduced by a competitor. You will recall that Schumpeter I placed a great deal of emphasis on the competitive pressures which acted so as to stimulate the imitative diffusion of an innovation throughout the economic system, but he was also very much aware of the risks involved for the firm. Not to adopt a crucial innovation might mean going out of business altogether as existing product types became progressively more obsolete. On the other hand the act of adoption itself was fraught with its own uncertainties caused by factors such as the lack of access to important elements of ancillary technology, unpredictability of demand, possible changed requirements for marketing and distribution, *and* very importantly the possibility that further radical breakthroughs might yet be made. Rosenberg has pointed out that under expectations of further radical technological changes it will make sense for a firm *not* to adopt an innovation even where all other risks are low and such action makes clear economic sense.

As soon as we accept the perspective of the ongoing nature of much technological change, the optimal timing of an innovation becomes heavily influenced by expectations concerning the timing and the significance of *future* improvements. Even when a new process innovation passes the stringent test of reducing new average total costs below old average variable costs, it may not be adopted. The reason for this is that the entrepreneur's views about the pace of technological improvements may reflect expectations of a higher rate of technological obsolescence than that allowed for by conventional accounting procedures in valuing the investment. Moreover, accounting formulae may not give adequate recognition to the 'disruption costs' involved in introducing new methods, especially when such disruptions are frequent. Thus, a firm may be unwilling to introduce the new technology if it seems highly probable that further techological improvements will shortly be forthcoming.[28]

He goes on to cite a series of examples which support the view that an initial 'innovation' is often a very imperfect entity, full of 'bugs' which need to be ironed out and teething problems that require to be solved. At this stage, which has clear similarities with Phase I of the product cycle, the sensible course for potential competitors is to await developments while keeping at the same time a weather eye upon events. Only when the innovation has become relatively 'mature' will it make sense to undertake direct imitative investment. This is often true in practice even for the relatively large firms which according to writers like Schumpeter II, Galbraith and Scherer are better placed to 'hedge' against the risks of innovative failure because of sheer financial power and market control.[29]

Further support for this (rather conservative) view on the rate of diffusion of innovations is given by Freeman (1977) who draws attention to the relatively routine and defensive nature of much R & D activity in modern industry. This is in general 'not devoted to the major new product or process but to relatively minor changes and modifications'.[30] Rosenberg[31] himself has documented a whole series of historical cases where the older (and apparently superceded) technology continued to remain in existence for decades after the new technology came on to the scene. In such cases the rearguard success of the older vintage was almost always due to effective technological improvements on the part of firms which for one reason or another were not able to adopt the new technology.

Actually, within the neo-classical tradition of economic analysis the treatment of diffusion has been much more robust. The reaction of competing firms to an innovation of a rival is assumed to be a function entirely of expectations of its likely economic profitability, mediated by the uncertainty which always attaches to something new and which will have a differential impact on being taken up by other firms simply because of their different circumstances. To begin with firms are cautious but gradually as they learn from the experience of others, they leap on to the 'bandwagon' providing for the industry as a whole the classic 'S'-shaped diffusion curve, verified empirically by a range of writers such as Mansfield[32] and Davies[33] and depicted as something akin to the 'product cycle' function outlined in figure 6.1.

However, as Soete[34] has pointed out in a recent paper reviewing some of this literature, such a view of diffusion places an excessive amount of emphasis on demand factors, with adopting firms viewed as responding entirely to 'market signals' of an economic type. Rosenberg has shown quite clearly that firms often behave according to perceptions of a more technological nature (i.e. their perceptions about the likely prospects for a new technology) and there is evidence internationally that countries (e.g. Japan)[35] have been able to 'leapfrog' technologically by committing substantial resources to specific technological developments even where 'market signals' have not indicated such a strategy. We shall see in the following section that for this, and other, reasons the standard approach of neo-classical economic analysis has come increasingly under attack leading to a range of new (though probably not yet fully thought out) views about the nature of technological changes and their relation to social development.

6.3 More Radical Developments

Students will by now have gathered that the essence of the 'orthodox' view regarding the impact of science and technology on socio-economic development, is that more needs to be done *within the existing paradigm*, i.e. with the methodological and conceptual tools already available. These tend to emphasise the 'comparative static' nature of much of economic theorising, the relative importance of demand factors which 'call forth' responses on the part of the productive sector, the accompanying passivity and 'shelf-like' nature of technological developments, and the primacy of conventional economic aggregates. They tend also to gloss over important issues of political economy through which technological changes may be viewed as an intrinsic part of the bureaucratic and political operations of the modern industrial economy. There are, however, so many evident problems inherent in this position that a variety of quite radically new approaches have been put forward in recent years. The remainder of this chapter is devoted to an outline of the more important of these.

6.3.1 Science Push

Diametrically opposite to the notion of the 'technological shelf' is the view that all innovations stem mainly from advances in scientific research. Of course, in its most extreme sense, namely that basic science *causes* technical change — the notion is clearly untenable. Not only does disinterested research produce much work which could under no stretch of the imagination be translated into commercial devices. History is replete with examples of important innovations which manifestly did not emanate from basic scientific research, even if later scientific work may have played a role in bringing the ideas to commercial production. However, the notion of 'science push' is a rather more sophisticated one in which the role of professional R & D is given a primary place. Thus in a series of detailed industrial case studies Freeman[36] has shown how in this respect the twentieth century has differed from the nineteenth century precisely by virtue of a full-time professional R & D sector, attached to industry, whose function it is to search for and articulate commercial innovations by means of organised scientific research.

The starting point was the very rapid development of new process technology in the chemicals sector towards the end of the nineteenth century. Beginning with the exploitation of synthetic aniline dyes in the 1860s based on coal-tar chemistry, and then progressing through the synthesis of nitrogenous fertilisers and the catalytic cracking of petroleum, Freeman demonstrates in graphic detail how firms (mainly in Germany and the USA) very quickly came to understand that the 'organised search for knowledge' represented a systematic means of ensuring a continuous flow of innovations thereby helping to ensure market strength and corporate growth and survival. Six major developments assisted the 'shift to flow production techniques' which in turn 'facilitated the growth of professional in-house industrial R & D, and were stimulated by it'. These were:

1   The enormous growth of the market for the basic chemicals such as soda, ammonia, chlorine, sulphuric acid, ethylene and propylene. These 'building blocks' (were) used as intermediate materials for a great variety of other chemicals as well as in many other industrial applications, outside the chemical industry.

2   The switch in base materials for organic chemicals from coal derivatives to oil and natural gas. This stimulated the development of continuous processes and chemical complexes linked to refineries.

3   The increasing availability of electricity as a source of energy and the development of electrothermal and electrolytic processes. Faraday had demonstrated the electrolysis of salt in 1833 but it was not until the end of the century that cheap power became generally available and a large-scale process was developed.

4   Improvements in materials for plant construction and in components such as pumps, compressors, filters, valves and pressure vessels. These were essential to permit the use of large-scale processes, and more severe operating conditions such as high pressures and extremes of temperature.

5   The development of new instruments for monitoring and controlling flow processes, as well as for laboratory analysis and testing.

6   The application of basic scientific knowledge to the production processes, and the development of the new discipline of chemical engineering. The design of new flow processes was linked to physical chemistry whereas the old batch processes were often based on purely empirical knowledge and mechanical engineering.[37]

Nowadays the importance of design engineering and contracting have led to a very high degree of specialised division of labour as exemplified, for example, in the design and development of the modern nuclear reactor. In a very real sense, then, much of modern industrial production depends upon the search for, the verification of and the processing of scientific information, and its subsequent articulation in engineering forms. Freeman's view is that in many areas of economic production, particularly those which have experienced fast industrial growth, it is the close and pervasive link with a scientific base which really provides the thrust for technological change. The corollary is that governments wishing to promote international industrial competitiveness cannot sit back and await 'entrepreneurs' to do the job by themselves, since the complexity of the innovative act is now such that often only an organised team effort is likely to be successful.

Here he takes issue with writers such as the historian Derek de Solla Price who argued in 1965 that 'science' and 'technology' have always been two entirely separate professional activities, that contact between them while occasionally very fruitful has tended to be spasmodic, and that for long periods technology has progressed without any major inputs from science.[38] He also takes issue with a seminal piece of empirical work carried out by Jewkes and his associates in 1958.[39] In a study of around 60 important twentieth-century innovations Jewkes et al. concluded that the role of the corporate R & D laboratory had been greatly exaggerated. In Jewkes's view the 'creative independent inventor, frustrated but persistent, remains today as in the past the principal source of important industrial inventions. The large corporate R & D environment may often inhibit rather than stimulate the work of such individuals, but they frequently flourish in the more tolerant university atmosphere or in small new firms.'[40] However, both writers according to Freeman do not take sufficient account of how things have changed as this century has progressed. Price tends to draw his examples from earlier epochs, particularly during the nineteenth century, while Jewkes's own sample is biased in a similar direction, including for example the zip-fastener but excluding nuclear technology. Moreover there are important methodological problems in Jewkes's study concerning the economic importance of the innovations (and therefore their relative 'weighting') and the extent to which stress should be given to the very important 'development' phase during which the raw invention is turned into a useful commercial product. Freeman cites work by Mansfield[41] and Stead[42] which indicate that such R & D costs vary 'typically between 25% and 60% of total innovation costs'[43] so that even in cases where the original 'invention' came from one person, it has become increasingly necessary for substantial 'developmental' resources to be put in before it reaches commercial viability. This tends to take place within the R & D laboratory. Of course, all disputants agree that such trends vary across industry and in particular that the more traditional industries (like textiles) are by their very nature less research intensive. However, the position of authorities such as Freeman is that it is precisely the fast-growing industries such as chemicals, pharmaceuticals, plastics, electronics, computers, aircraft and nuclear power generation which are characterised by high in-house R & D spending and which are at the same time linked to advances in basic scientific research. In industries such as these the lone inventor is conspicuous by his or her absence.

To the extent that Freeman's view on the importance of professional R & D holds, it offers considerable support to the position of Schumpeter II, Galbraith and others that large firms are likely to be better innovators than small firms. This follows from the 'scale' arguments outlined in chapter 5. On the whole the modern evidence appears to support this view although there are areas of high technology where small firms still make substantial inroads, such as branches of electronics capital goods. A related point is that industry cannot normally substitute access to publicly funded scientific research (through universities and other research institutes) for its own in-house efforts. Although there is still much ambiguity regarding the precise nature of the links between university-based research and technological development in firms, it is generally agreed that in-house R & D provides a necessary 'filter' for external R & D inputs. It is only through the act of conducting R & D itself that the firm can keep abreast with progress in the relevant scientific disciplines, recognise the significance of particular 'advances', and have access to the appropriate 'invisible college' of university-based scientists and engineers.[44]

Hence, the notion of 'science push' in its modern form is intended not so much to convey an impression of scientific research *forcing the pace* of industrial innovation, but rather attempts to bring out the much more complex nature of industrial innovations which *relate* to basic science (as most nowadays appear to do). In many sectors firms *must* invest a given absolute sum in R & D, the precise amount determined by the nature of the industry in question, simply because if they do not they will find it increasingly difficult to compete with their rivals. Investment in science does not so much 'push innovation' as acts as a necessary condition for industrial survival.

Equally, however, the very fact of industrial R & D makes a nonsense of the idea of the 'technological shelf', which is readily available to all firms, of all sizes and wherever they may be located. A more accurate analogy is that there are many technological shelves whose stocks are constantly being changed as a result of the direct investment action of firms and of the (uncontrollable) actions of others. Sometimes the contents of the shelves are private and appropriable by the firm. Sometimes they are not. Often the existence of the shelves and their contents is simply not known about. In reality, therefore, all firms live in a world of great technological uncertainty. How to cope with this uncertainty is thus a major problem which continually faces them.

6.3.2 Technological Systems

A notion which is related to that of 'science push', although conceptually distinct from it, is that of the technological 'system', sometimes also called the technological 'paradigm' or 'family'. What the concept is intended to convey is the idea of a network of proven engineering relationships which have been articulated into a variety of designs, blueprints, systems and sub-systems of machinery, jigs and fixtures, and agendas for engineering research, all held together by a common technological thread which has shown some promise in economic production. Examples of a technological system might be machine-tool technology in the nineteenth century, transistor technology in the 1950s and 1960s, and computer aided design technology in recent years. In each case the technology cannot be regarded as an invariant 'piece of know how' which is applied to economic production in a mechanistic fashion. Rather it shows all the hallmarks of an organic system, often associated with a new industry, but not necessarily, which develops along paths determined by and unique to itself often in a very speculative 'trial and error' manner. As Rosenberg has articulated in great detail,[45] the history of technology shows quite clearly that this is the case in most areas of economic production.

One of the neatest treatments of the subject is contained in a recent paper by Giovanni Dosi[46] in which the author compares the technological system with Kuhn's scientific paradigm.[47] You will recall that according to Kuhn the 'paradigm' determines all the activities subsumed under what he defines as 'normal science' — the bread and butter, routine activity which characterises most scientific work. In somewhat similar fashion, there is at any point of time and for any industry (defined in terms of particular commodities) a dominant technological paradigm which holds sway as being seen as the most likely set of ideas/techniques/devices/materials etc. required to underpin economic production both at that time and in terms of future technical change. The technology 'trajectory', which is somewhat analogous to the idea of 'normal science', then represents the path which research/action programmes take and which itself may be sub-divided into a range of possible technological directions.

A technological trajectory, i.e. to repeat, the 'normal' problem solving activity determined by a paradigm, can be represented by the movement of multi-dimensional trade-offs among the technological variables which the paradigm defines as relevant. Progress can be defined as the improvement of these trade-offs. One could thus imagine the trajectory as a 'cylinder' in the multi-dimensional space defined by these technological and economic variables. (Thus the technological trajectory is a cluster of possible technological directions whose outer boundaries are defined by the nature of the paradigm itself).[48]

In Dosi's view the role of the market is to act as a series of 'guiding posts' or 'filters' which will constrain the technological trajectory as it is being developed into those innovative activities which look likely to be successful. But 'success' need not be immediate, of course. This is why the actual decision-making on R & D in real life often takes on the characteristics of a political battle (but within the firm) with different factions arguing the respective merits of their own particular projects, and drawing upon whatever evidential and institutional support they can muster so as to win the day. Often firms handle the inherent uncertainty involved in R & D investment by establishing a number of concurrent research projects. As each of these develops, some begin to appear more promising than others so that gradually resources are concentrated upon the 'winners' while the 'losers' are brought to a halt.[49]

In order to bring out the point that the market is not by any means the only filter for discriminating among projects and otherwise 'steering' the technological trajectory, Nelson and Winter have put forward the idea of the 'selection environment' which acts in the following manner.

> We propose the concept of a 'selection environment' as a useful theoretical organiser. Given the flow of new innovations, the selection environment (as we are employing the term) determines how relative use of different technologies changes over time. The selection environment influences the path of productivity growth generated by any given innovation, and also it feeds back the influence strongly of the kinds of R & D that firms and industry will find profitable to undertake.[50]

Certainly the market is one feature of such an environment but it is not the only one. In cases where the 'productive act' is not subject to market forces (e.g. weapons production) or where there are important government regulations (e.g. regarding automobile emissions), choice of technology will rest heavily upon a 'dialogue of experts' at all stages of development. Public agencies will certainly be involved as well.[51]

Authorities such as Dosi, and Nelson and Winter, argue persuasively that this view of technological change has many advantages over the orthodox neo-classical position. To begin with, it opens up Rosenberg's 'Black Box' in the sense that it actually provides the beginnings of a realistic explanation of the phenomenon itself, instead of relegating it to the role of an exogenous 'catch all'. Secondly, it is consistent with what we know about technological changes as these have occurred since the industrial revolution. For example, Rosenberg's interesting cases of older technological vintages coexisting with the newer ones, and indeed improving progressively, are perfectly in keeping with the notion of an older 'paradigm' struggling to maintain its *raison d'être* in the face of an apparently successful newcomer. Thirdly it permits the introduction of important questions of political economy (like, for example, the role of government agencies) which are evidently germane to science policy issues as these relate to innovation. Finally it provides some kind of reconciliation between the 'demand pull' and 'science push' theories about the genesis of technological change in modern industrial capitalism. The ideas are by no means complete. For example, there are difficult problems involved in actually defining a technological system. However, they hold out for the first time the hope of being able to explain the behaviour of production units, and indeed national policies, in so far as these make decisions on technology policy which evidently have very little to do with conventional economic aggregates.

6.3.3 An Evolutionary Theory of Firm Behaviour and Technological Change

In a series of articles in recent years Nelson and Winter[52] have attempted to weld these new approaches to technological dynamics into a theory of firm behaviour which is essentially biological in character. This theory is of interest to us because it takes issue with the neo-classical position in a number of important respects, because it has a number of important points to make about technology and technical change, because the authors are evidently concerned with the pace and pattern of economic progress and because they are clearly influenced by Schumpeterian thinking.

It is unreal, they argue, to treat firms as if they exist in a world of perfect knowledge and foresight, maximising some set of objectives in an environment of given choice sets and well-defined constraints. By so doing 'orthodox theory' has little or nothing to say about how or why economic conditions change (for example, about how firms respond to changing market conditions), and therefore about a significant area of economic activity. They go on to claim that their own approach can produce precisely the same theoretical propositions as orthodoxy, but with less restrictive and more realistic assumptions about technical conditions and organisational behaviour. For example, firms are categorised as 'profit-seeking' rather than 'profit-maximising', and 'uncertainty' is explicitly included as an essential feature of economic activity. Finally, they argue, their approach relates more directly to matters of public policy.

Nelson and Winter then proceed as follows. Economic change takes place in an 'evolutionary' fashion, where firms are constantly in competition with each other in an unstable environment. Thus firms are viewed as behaving like organisms constantly under threat and using whatever means available to perpetuate their existence. Like biological organisms their 'genes' are institutional 'routines' which define the ways they behave. Some of these 'routines' are 'search routines' which allow institutions to respond (or mutate) in the face of uncertainty and changing external conditions. The successful firms are those which remain in existence and grow. The unsuccessful firms simply go out of business. Economic life is essentially Darwinian.

Nelson and Winter's ideas have an intuitive appeal. Firms do spend resources on R & D and thereby establish a competitive lead over rivals. They take over other firms (or parts of firms) where this is in their interests. They diversify horizontally and vertically as an insurance against future risks. They clearly do not *just* maximise profits but have complicated sets of goals which themselves change in response to influences both within and outside the firms. Amongst these security and growth are clearly very important. In short, firms behave in a Schumpeterian manner where time is important and uncertainty very great. One very important determinant of their behaviour is technology and technological change. Nelson and Winter argue that tech-nological choice does not at all take place as a sort of disembodied selection 'from the shelf' but is, on the contrary, programmed into the organic behaviour of the firm. At any point of time, and with respect to any given industry, firms operate on a natural technological trajectory which is partly historically determined and which defines the 'paradigm' for current product-ive behaviour and R & D for the future. Although this trajectory is common to the industry, each firm has its own room for manoeuvre (and competitive edge) determined by its in-house expertise, technical skills, patents, reputa-tion, links to specialist suppliers, and so on. It is here that the competitive game is played out. Clearly no firm is going to undertake the enormous costs of moving on to a radically different technological trajectory, unless it is entirely convinced that the long-term economic gains are going to be large indeed in relation to the risks. Looked at in this light it is not surprising to find businessmen often responding conservatively to economic signals.

In their book *An Evolutionary Theory of Economic Change*, the authors proceed to articulate their ideas in a formal modelling schema of competitive dynamics in which all innovation is treated as process innovation. However, since much of this discussion is addressed directly to fellow economists, students need not engage with it unless they have a direct interest in modern economic analysis. In fact from a science policy standpoint the book is rather disappointing for this very reason. Nelson and Winter seem more concerned with relating their paradigm to neo-classical orthodoxy than with developing it into a set of useful policy instruments. Their chief policy conclusion − that public policy should abandon attempts to ensure 'efficient markets' in favour of a more 'pluralistic' stance of treating every issue on its merits − might well have been reached, one would think, without the benefit of their model.

The main problem appears to be that the authors provide no adequate account of what they understand a scientific theory to be, and hence of how economic modelling and analysis stand up to canons of scientific enquiry. Not only does this permit them to use concepts such as 'orthodox', 'heterodox', and 'normative' without ever really defining them; it also permits the inclusion of statements such as '. . . the failure of the heterodox tradition to influence the profession stems from its lack of appreciation of the importance and nature of theory in economics. Heterodox critics also tend not to understand the varied and extremely flexible nature of prevailing theory.'[53] It is clear that this rather vague position is designed to distance the authors from more robust critics, like Galbraith, who not only argue that 'orthodoxy' possesses very few of these qualities but indeed that the economics profession is engaged, knowingly or not, in the suppression of social criticism and the validation of existing patterns of institutional power and privilege.

6.3.4 Kondratiev Long Waves

Stagnation and recession in the 1970s and 1980s combined with associated high levels of unemployment have revived interest in problems of long-term structural change in advanced capitalist economies, and particularly in long-term cycles of economic activity. In this interest, innovation and technological change play a major explanatory role and again Schumpeter has a clear influence on the discussion. Like Nelson and Winter, the long-wave theorists are dissatisfied with orthodoxy, but their quarrel (and its resolution) takes place at the 'macro' level and with respect to long-term economic growth. For example, Freeman and his colleagues, who in recent years have played a leading role in articulating the notion of long waves,[54] argue the following propositions:

(i)   That long waves are statistically discernible.
(ii)   That they are closely associated with cycles of innovative activity.
(iii) That during each cycle the relevant technologies are related to each other in a systemic way.
(iv)   That, therefore, in so far as long-term structural problems are associated with such cycles (e.g. unemployment and stagflation), their resolution requires technology policy as a primary ingredient.

Freeman's starting point is Schumpeter's treatment of business cycles, articulated in a book of the same name published in 1939. In this book Schumpeter made use of the notion of long waves of economic activity, first identified by van Gelderen[55] in 1913 and subsequently given an extended treatment by the Marxist economist Kondratiev[56] in 1925. These superimposed themselves on the shorter 'trade' or 'juglar' cycle, normally associated with cyclical activity and lasting around five to seven years. In contrast the typical Kondratiev wave was observed to last 50 years or so during which time the economic system ran the full gamut of boom, recession, depression and back again to boom.

Schumpeter's position was not only that such waves were historically discernible, they were also clearly and primarily associated with bursts of innovative activity and the rise and decline of particular industrial sectors. The first 'Kondratiev' (or 'K') was linked to the emergence of the sequence of industries leading the industrial revolution − cotton textiles, coal and iron. The second 'K' was generated by the railway boom of the period 1850−70 while the third involved the development of automobiles, electricity and radio in the 20 or so years before the First World War. The years following each 'K' were those of long-term depression typified by the major depressions of 1870−90 and the inter-war period. To these three 'K's, Freeman adds a fourth associated with the years of fast economic growth in Europe, the USA and Japan between 1950 and 1970, led by industries such as bulk chemicals, pharmaceuticals, electronics, aerospace and nuclear power.

The way each cycle unfolds is as follows. To begin with a major technology is innovated and takes root. Often the groundwork for it has already taken place in a previous 'K', in terms of inventions and development of ancillary technologies. However, the major technology itself is a many-headed hydra involving whole clusters (swarms) of new innovations 'affecting processes, components, sub-systems, materials and management systems, skills and finance, as well as the products themselves'.[57] Moreover, there are many different product types involved. The railway boom was not simply concerned with the building of steam engines and the laying of track. It involved also the development of signalling systems, the building of rolling stock, the manufacture of appropriate forging and machine-tool facilities, the establishment of stations and marshalling yards, and the inculcation of the whole vast range of technical and managerial skills required to run a railway system.

Once the boom gets underway the explosive growth creates a climate of investment optimism which is self-fulfilling. New and related products are introduced, demand increases as does employment and the general level of wages. Eventually, however, the 'long boom' comes to an end as the new technological system becomes fully integrated within the economy. As productive potential falls off, new investment drops to zero and what is sometimes called a 'multiplier/accelerator' mechanism comes into operation bringing with it rapidly diminishing incomes and demand. During this phase price competition between productive units becomes particularly fierce as innovative activity becomes focused upon cost reducing forms (process innovation) rather than those of creating new products (product innovation). Nevertheless many firms go bankrupt and the overall rate of unemployment increases. Eventually once a 'low point' is reached a radically new technology appears upon the scene whereupon a new Kondratiev cycle begins. 'For Schumpeter the long waves in economic life were a succession of (such) technological transformations of the economic system. This necessitated deep structural change − a process which he called "creative destruction".'[58]

Freeman and his colleagues have taken these ideas of Schumpeter and have subjected them to careful empirical scrutiny using new evidence on patents and innovation for the period 1930 to the present day. They conclude that although long waves do provide a useful 'heuristic' within which to analyse industrial capitalism, they should by no means be viewed as a form of crude 'technological determinism' whereby a new major innovation will suddenly appear, like a phoenix out of the ashes of a deep depression. Although there are regularities, technological changes are extremely uneven over time and geographically (i.e. between regions and countries). There are also apparent differences between successive 'K's. Thus the recent long wave is characterised by much greater institutional rigidities than previous ones, with consequently high rates of inflation coexisting with recessionary unemployment. Moreover, there is a very real possibility that service sector employment may not be the ever-ready 'sponge' to mop up redundancy in manufacturing employment that it has been in the past.[59] These features plus the surprisingly rapid internationalisation of technology to the NICs make it at least arguable that any long-term resurgence into a new (fifth) Kondratiev (fuelled, say, by the microprocessor or biotechnology) will have very different social implications from anything that has transpired in previous periods, particularly in the areas of occupational employment and income distribution.

We shall explore these and related issues in chapter 9 but it is worth drawing attention at this stage to Freeman's major conclusion, which is that deliberate technology policies associated with greater public expenditures may be necessary if countries such as the UK are successfully to 'climb on' to the next long wave. Three main types are outlined:

(i)   Policies aimed 'directly at encouraging firms to take up radical inventions/innovations', including support for fundamental research and help to 'improve the coupling between the various parts of the science-technology- industrial system'.

(ii) Policies aimed at promoting the diffusion of technologies, particularly to 'sheltered' sectors which for one reason or another are reluctant to promote the adoption of radically new systems (e.g. through public purchase schemes).

(iii) Policies aimed at 'improving the import and the internal diffusion of foreign technology' somewhat akin to the post-war strategy promoted so successfully by the Japanese.

Certainly traditional 'demand management' policies by themselves are unlikely to act an effective means for promoting economic development in the increasingly competitive (and international) environment of the 1980s and 1990s.

6.3.5 Galbraith and the Modern Industrial State

Up to now in this section, most of the 'radical' conceptual developments I have surveyed have tended to focus directly on the essential fabric of technological changes as these take place within modern industrial capitalism. While the arguments deployed are often critical of established economic orthodoxy, they are not intended as the building blocks in any larger social critique of the kind developed by modern Marxist thinkers, for example, Baran and Sweezy.[60] In this respect John Kenneth Galbraith occupies rather a unique position in so far as he places very strong emphasis upon the influence of science and technology on modern industry and government and hence upon practically every aspect of our daily lives − an influence he clearly finds profoundly depressing. He represents therefore a throwback, as it were, to the older classical tradition of political economy where it was expected that social scientists would involve themselves more deeply in grand matters of public debate, using their analytical tools as a means towards a larger end. Hence, although I have included him in the 'radical' camp and although many of his arguments have a close affinity with them, he should really be viewed as qualitatively different from those we have been discussing up to this point.

Galbraith's concerns relate to a range of apparent irrationalities in modern industrialised societies whose capacity for systematic social waste he clearly finds quite extraordinary. Thus in one of his earlier books *The Affluent Society*, he wonders why it is that with all the economic and technological resources available to us, there is still so much 'private affluence' coexistent with so much 'public squalor'. Writing in 1958 he draws attention to the many serious social problems facing post-war US capitalism, such as poverty, inner city decay and the atrophy of many public services, noting that nevertheless the US economy could still afford to spend considerable sums of money on defence and aerospace. By 1967, in the *New Industrial State*, he had begun to set these problems within an analytical context of political economy which placed strong explanatory emphasis upon the exigencies or 'imperatives' that modern science and technology brought to bear on relations of political and economic power. Finally in *Economics and the Public Purpose* (1974), he developed his critique into what he claims to be a general theory of advanced capitalist development which is characterised by considerable social and economic inequalities of various kinds (including those relating to gender) and which cuts across traditional class lines as viewed, for example, by Marxist analysts. In this theory the social role, or 'purpose' of the modern neo-classical economist, he argues, is one of systematic obfuscation since neo-classical orthodoxy 'explains' an economic system which no longer exists. The policy pronouncements of economists, however, are not held to be irrelevant since there is a tacit understanding that their social role is ritualistic rather than substantive.

However, the key to much of his thinking is contained in the *New Industrial State* and relates to the differentiation of economic production which is associated with the history of technological changes, a point also brought out by Cooper[61] and Rosenberg.[62] Using the automobile industry as his 'case study' he shows how the extent to which scientific knowledge may be applied systematically to economic production is a function of the degree of specialisation of the production system. But specialisation also brings with it the need for co-ordination and control, greater complexity of production, heightened risks and the need for much larger sums of investment capital. Nowadays the development lead time for a new model is often five years or more. In Henry Ford's time it was a matter of months.

Thus we have a series of the *inevitable* consequences of the use of modern technology which are programmed into the very fabric of much of economic production. The obverse of the coin of the high productivity effects of science and technology, is the sheer scale and inflexibility of the modern industrial combine. Nor is this all. The large corporate organisation is itself a power centre which is self-justifying. Profit-maximisation is no longer the main motivation since the bureaucratic nature of the modern corporation has shifted power from the owners (the shareholders or capitalists) to the managerial elite (the technostructure) who run things. Shareholders are kept in a state of quiescence with a minimum level of profits sufficient to permit moderate dividends, thereby allowing the technostructure to pursue corporate goals of a more complex variety but of which 'growth' and 'survival' are clearly important elements. So far as possible the external environment has to be kept firmly under control. Sources of supply are ensured through long-term contracts and, where necessary, backward integration. Consumers are 'programmed' into the acceptance of products by means of advertising, sales promotion, market research and similar devices. In this way the traditional rule of consumer sovereignty, so beloved of neo-classical orthodoxy, is tempered to the exigencies of modern productive forces. What Galbraith has called 'producer sovereignty' takes over.

In the later book, *Economics and the Public Purpose*, Galbraith tries to put his argument within the broader context of the political economy of advanced capitalism which he sees as moving inexorably towards an Orwellian system of bureaucratic privilege and power. Modern economic production, he argues, is conducted within two broad types of sector which stand in a relationship of dynamic inequality to each other — the 'Planning System' and the 'Market System'. The Planning System is comprised of large corporations, departments of state and powerful trade unions, all of which are heavily bureaucratised. It is characterised by advanced technology, monopolistic control over market and hence the ability to control prices and wages. As with the corporations analysed in the *New Industrial State*, organisation and producer sovereignty reign supreme, and there are close organic links between its various components.

Conversely the Market System is composed of small entrepreneurial businesses dealing with personal services, agriculture and geographically dispersed functions. The labour force is often not unionised, or only weakly so, there is little access to the state bureaucracy and competitive market conditions tend to obtain along with, correspondingly, a substantial degree of consumer sovereignty. The relations between the two systems are such that the Planning System constantly gains at the expense of the Market System in terms of resources, incomes and power. Since competitive pressures are relatively absent, the Planning System can hike wages and prices during inflationary periods and can protect itself conversely during periods of recession. The Market System, on the other hand, cannot protect itself in this way and hence bears the full brunt of cyclical fluctuations. It follows, of course, that conventional counter-cyclical policy of the kind mentioned in chapter 5 will not work in the ways intended, at least not so far as the Planning System is concerned. A monetary 'squeeze' can be absorbed by large corporations which have their own sources of finance, while tax and expenditure fiscal changes can either be absorbed directly or passed on to the Market System which tends therefore to suffer disproportionately. In this way power, wealth and privilege are allocated in a manner which has little to do with 'marginal productivity', but rather is a function of increasingly rigid institutional patterns.

But Galbraith goes further than merely suggesting a new model of social development, arguing that neo-classical economics, as a professionalised activity, actively colludes in the prevailing set of power relations by postulating a body of ideas (or doctrine) which describes a world totally at variance with reality − a world in which the *whole* economic system is subject to the discipline of the market. The fact that neo-classical 'market forces' are simply not capable of functioning over large areas of economic activity is treated with a heavy, if rather embarassed, silence. Finally, his model postulates a form of class conflict which cuts across traditional Marxist categories. No longer is the antagonism one between homogeneous 'workers' and 'capitalists'. It is between 'organised' workers and 'unorganised' workers, between 'organised' industry and 'unorganised' industry. Even within the various public services (like medical care, for example), Galbraith would not see in the British National Health Service an institution devoted to the care of the masses. Rather he would regard it as a centre of privileged power, dominated by a (male) establishment with a 'high technology' approach to medical science, closely linked with large and powerful drug companies, and where the interests of the health 'consumer' play second fiddle to the certificated 'expertise' of the 'producer'. More generally, the close tie-in between scientific expertise and bureaucratic privilege in health, warfare, education, energy supply, and many other areas of modern economic and social activity, has produced a new form of bureaucratic centralism becoming ever more remote from popular understanding and control. Even at central government level, the various 'departments of state' have great difficulty in keeping abreast with each others' activities, particularly where 'high technology' is concerned. In countries such as the UK, where there is a long tradition of departmental autonomy and responsibility, this is a much greater problem than in countries such as Japan, say, where departments of state tend to be more organic and functionalist.

Not everyone finds it easy to accept Galbraith's pessimism and there is more than a hint of technological determinism in his writings. Moreover, on the whole the depth of this 'diagnosis' is not matched by the acuity of his policy prescription where he appears to place much faith on exhortation and on the good sense of the 'experts', whom he calls the Educational and Scientific Estate. Finally, although he has argued for the conscious use of state power to mitigate the pervasive tendencies to socio-economic inequality, it is not easy to see how powerful bureaucratic entities will connive at their own emasculation. Nevertheless his views need more confrontation than they appear to have received. One has to suspect that economic orthodoxy is more than a little afraid to take him on.

6.4 Some Concluding Comments

This chapter has comprised a broad survey of modern developments in the study of technological innovation. It has been written in such a way as to link these developments both with the conceptual discussion outlined in the first five chapters and with those on policy 'issues' to be covered in chapter 9. Students may well feel by this stage that the sheer range and complexity of this discussion is hardly matched by the resultant light shed on social policy. This, I am afraid, is a well-known failing of social science. Perhaps it is best to leave the last word with Keith Pavitt who, with his colleagues, has spent a great deal of the past few years in empirical study of industrial innovation, and who has come to the conclusion that as yet not enough is known empirically about the nature of technological change − its pattern, rate and direction.

Certainly from the existing evidence there is no one single pattern. On the basis of a survey of 2,000 innovations commercialised in the UK between 1945 and 1980, he and his colleagues conclude that there is wide variation in (a) size of innovating firm, (b) balance between product and process innovation and (c) intersectoral innovation patterns.

> These patterns suggest that over-general statements about the characteristics of technical change are likely to be wrong. At the same time, to say simply that 'things vary a lot' and that 'it all depends' is not satisfactory, either for theory or for policy. Such variety should at least be classified and if possible explained.[63]

Pavitt then goes on to suggest a three-fold classification of innovating firms into 'supplier-dominated', 'production-intensive' and 'science-based' which he argues provides the basis for further much needed empirical work. Only when this stage has been carried through will we be in a position to make valid theoretical statements about industrial innovation. Finally, however, I should like to point out that much of the conceptual debate surveyed both in this chapter and in the previous one has a distinctly scholastic flavour. Perhaps we should not be too sanguine about how far the existence of better evidence will take us in our search for better theory.

Bibliography

The literature in this area has become truly immense in recent years. However, particularly useful as review articles are C. Kennedy and A. Thirlwall, 'Technical Progress: A Survey', *Economic Journal*, Vol. 82, March 1972, pp. 11–72 (but written, I must add, for economists); N. Rosenberg, 'The Historiography of Technical Progress', in Rosenberg, *Inside the Black Box: Technology and Economics*, pp. 3–33; M. Fransman, 'Conceptualising Technological Change in the Third World: An Interpretive Survey', *Journal of Development Studies* (forthcoming). Other helpful source texts in addition to those cited at the end of chapter 1 are A. K. Sen (ed.), *Growth Economics* (Harmondsworth, Penguin, 1970) and N. Rosenberg (ed.), *The Economics of Technological Change* (Harmondsworth, Penguin, 1971). See also the chapter by Freeman in Spiegel-Rosing and Price (eds.), *Science, Technology and Society*.

A good critical review of product cycle and related theories is contained in W. B. Walker, *Industrial Innovation and International Trading Performance* (Greenwich, Jai Press, 1979). On Long Waves and structural change see C. Freeman, J. Clark and L. Soete, *Unemployment and Technical Innovation* (London, Frances Pinter, 1982), a shortened version of which is contained in their article 'Long Waves, Inventions and Innovations', *Futures*, August 1981, pp. 308–22. See also R. Rothwell and W. Zegveld, *Reindustrialisation and Technology* (Harlow, Longmans, 1984); C. Perez, 'Structural Change and Assimilation of New Technologies in the Economic and Social Systems', *Futures*, October 1983, pp. 357–75; and C. Freeman (ed.), *Long Waves in the World Economy* (London, Butterworth, 1983).

On Galbraith, see J. K. Galbraith, *The New Industrial State* (Harmondsworth, Penguin, 1972) and *Economics and the Public Purpose* (London, Andrew Deutsch, 1972).

Notes

1 Sen, *Growth Economics*, p. 9.
2 R. Harrod, 'An Essay in Dynamic Theory', *Economic Journal*, Vol. 49, 1939, pp. i4–33. Also in Sen, *Growth Economics*, pp. 43–64.
3 R.M. Solow, 'Technical Change and the Aggregate Production Function', *Review of Economics and Statistics*, Vol. 39, 1957, pp. 312–20. Also in Sen, *Growth Economics*, pp. 401–19.
4 M. Abramovitz, 'Resources and Output in the U.S. Since 1870', *American Economic Review, Pap. Proc.*, Vol. 46, pp. 5–23.
5 G. J. Stigler, 'Economic Problems in Measuring Changes in Productivity', in NBER, *Output, Input and Productivity Measurement* (New Jersey, Princeton University Press, 1961).
6 This point is made by C. Freeman in 'Research and Development in Electronic Capital Goods', *National Institute Economic Review*, No. 34, 1965, although it is only fair to point out that Freeman has always argued that R & D does indeed contribute to overall economic growth, through this process, and others.

7 E. Mansfield, *The Economics of Technological Change* (London, Longmans, 1968).

8 J. R. Minasian, 'The Economics of Research and Development', in National Bureau of Economic Research, *The Rate and Direction of Inventive Activity* (New Jersey, Princeton University Press, 1962).

9 I. Illich, *Tools for Conviviality* (London, Fontana, 1975) represents a good introduction to Illich's point of view.

10 Kennedy and Thirlwall, 'Technical Progress: A Survey', pp. 13–20.

11 E. Denison, 'United States Economic Growth', *Journal of Business*, Vol. 35, April 1962, pp. 109–21. Also in Rosenberg, *The Economics of Technological Change*, pp. 363–81.

12 Denison, 'United States Economic Growth'.

13 Z. Griliches, 'Hybrid Corn: An Exploration in the Economics of Technological Change', *Econometrica*, Vol. 25, October 1957, pp. 501–22.

14 Rosenberg, *Inside the Black Box*, p. 25.

15 C. Freeman, 'Economics of Research and Development', in Spiegel-Rosing and Price, *Science, Technology and Society*, p. 244.

16 N. Rosenberg, 'Science, Invention and Economic Growth', in N. Rosenberg, *Perspectives on Technology* (Cambridge, Cambridge University Press, 1976), p. 260.

17 J. Schmookler, *Invention and Economic Growth* (Cambridge, Harvard University Press, 1966), p. 208. Quoted in R. Rothwell and W. Zegveld, *Re-industrialization and Technology* (Harlow, Essex, Longmans, 1984), p. 24.

18 B. Hessen, 'The Social and Economic Roots of Newton's *Principia*', in N. Bukharin (ed.), *Science at the Crossroads* (London, Kniga, 1931), reprinted Cass, 1971.

19 V. Walsh et al., 'Invention and Innovation in the Chemicals Industry: Demand Pull or Discovery Push', *Research Policy* (forthcoming), 1984.

20 D. C. Mowery and N. Rosenberg, 'The Influence of Market Demand upon Innovation: a Critical Review of Some Recent Empirical Studies', in Rosenberg, *Inside the Black Box*, p. 235.

21 Rosenberg, *Inside the Black Box*, p. 278.

22 M. Posner, 'International Trade and Technical Change', *Oxford Economic Papers*, Vol. 13, No. 3, pp. 323–41.

23 See Walker, *Industrial Innovation and International Trading Performance*, for references.

24 This is the economist's definition which should be contrasted with the engineer's which tends to view a 'technology' more in terms of a collection of machines, assemblies, etc.

25 W. Leontieff, 'Domestic Production and Foreign Trade; the American Capital Position Re-examined', *Proceedings of the American Philosophical Society*, Vol. 97, 1953.

26 See C. M. Cooper (ed.), *Science, Technology and Development* (London, Frank Cass, 1973, chapter 1).

27 K. Griffin, 'The International Transmission of Inequality', *World Development*, Vol. 2, No. 3, March 1974, pp. 3–16.

28 Rosenberg, *Inside the Black Box*, p. 107.

29 For a discussion of this point see Freeman, *The Economics of Industrial Innovation*, pp. 213–18.

30 Freeman in Spiegel-Rosing and Price, *Science, Technology and Society*, p. 257.

31 Rosenberg, *Inside the Black Box*, pp. 141–59.

32 E. Mansfield, 'Technical Change and the Rate of Imitation', *Econometrica*, Vol. 29, No. 4, pp. 741–66.

33 S. Davies, *The Diffusion of Process Innovation* (Cambridge, Cambridge University Press, 1979).

34 L. Soete, 'International Diffusion of Technology, Industrial Development and Technological Leapfrogging' in *World Developments* (forthcoming).

35 G. C. Allen, 'Industrial Policy and Innovation in Japan', in C. Carter (ed.), *Industrial Policy and Innovation* (London, Heineman, 1981), pp. 68–87.

36 Much of the material from these is summarised in Freeman, *The Economics of Industrial Innovation*.

37 Freeman, *The Economics of Industrial Innovation*, pp. 44–5.

38 D. de Solla Price, 'Is Technology Historically Independent of Science?', *Technology and Culture*, Vol. VI, No. 4, 1965, p. 553.

39 J. Jewkes, D. Sawers and R. Stillerman, *The Sources of Invention* (London, Macmillan, 1969, rev. edn).

40 Quoted by Freeman in Spiegel-Rosing and Price, *Science, Technology and Society*, pp. 250–1.

41 E. Mansfield et al., *Research and Innovation in the Modern Corporation* (New York, Norton and London, Macmillan, 1971).

42 H. Stead, *Statistics of Technological Innovation in Industry*, Cat. No. 13–555, Statistics Canada, 1974.

43 Freeman in Spiegel-Rosing and Price, *Science, Technology and Society*, p. 251.

44 See, for example, M. Gibbons and R. Johnston, 'The Role of Science in Technological Innovation', *Research Policy*, Vol. 3, No. 4, 1974, pp. 220–42.

45 Rosenberg, *Perspectives in Technology*, Part 3.

46 G. Dosi, 'Technological Paradigms and Technological Trajectories, a Suggested Interpretation of the Determinants and Directions of Technical Change', *Research Policy*, Vol. 11, No. 3, June 1982, pp. 147–62.

47 T. S. Kuhn, *The Structure of Scientific Revolutions* (London, Chicago University Press, 1970).

48 Dosi, 'Technological Paradigms', p. 154.

49 See Freeman, *The Economics of Industrial Innovation*, chapter 7, for a more detailed discussion of this point.

50 R. Nelson and S. Winter, 'In Search of a useful Theory of Innovation', *Research Policy*, Vol. 6, No. 1, January 1977, p. 61.

51 For a useful discussion on US experience see D. Nelkin, 'Technology and Public Policy' in Spiegel-Rosing and Price, *Science, Technology and Society*, pp. 393–441.

52 See R. Nelson and S. Winter, *An Evolutionary Theory of Economic Change* (Cambridge, Mass., Harvard University Press, 1982).

53 Nelson and Winter, *An Evolutionary Theory of Economic Change*, p. 48.

54 See Freeman, Clark and Soete, *Unemployment and Technical Innovation*.

55 J. van Gelderen, 'Springvloed: Beschouwingen over industriele ontwikkeling en prijsbeweging', *De Niewe Tijd*, Vol. 18, Nos. 4, 5 and 6, April–June 1913.

56 N. Kondratiev, 'The Major Economic Cycles'. Reprinted in *Lloyds Bank Review*, No. 129, 1978.

57 Freeman, Article in the *Guardian*, 30 August 1983.

58 Freeman, the *Guardian*, 30 August 1983.

59 For an account of this argument see J. Gershuny, *After Industrial Society* (London, Macmillan, 1978).

60 P. Baran and P. Sweezy, *Monopoly Capital* (Harmondsworth, Penguin, 1973).

61 Cooper, 'Science, Technology and Development'.

62 Rosenberg, *Perspectives on Technology*, chapter 7.

63 K. Pavitt, *Patterns of Technical Change — Evidence, Theory and Policy Implications*, Papers in Science, Technology and Public Policy, SPRU, 1983, p. 6.

Chapter 7

THE NATURE OF
UNDERDEVELOPMENT

7.1 Introduction

In previous chapters the analysis has related mainly to the evolution of the industrialised economies of Western Europe and North America. Very little has been said about the so-called 'developing countries' which, according to official estimates, make up around 82% of the world's population and consume some 23% of world income.[1] There are several reasons for this. For example, during the period of industrialisation we have been considering, the LDCs as we now know them, played a peripheral and rather specialised role. They did not industrialise themselves but acted (sometimes, but not always, in the form of colonies) as sources of food and raw materials to the metropolitan economies, and as markets for the industrial goods, including capital goods, produced by the new factory system. Indeed it was clearly not in the interests of the metropolitan powers to foster rival sources of industrial production and, by and large, they ensured that this did not happen.

Partly as a result the LDCs came to be seen as a separate type of economic system, one that had not developed into the integrated industrialised economy with which we are all rather familiar, but instead remained 'underdeveloped' or 'backward' in relation to the economic progress made by the rich countries, hence requiring its own analytical treatment. Moreover, as time went by and it became increasingly obvious that in large areas of the world living conditions were falling well below those enjoyed by the 'developed countries', and that often poverty and famine were widespread, the 'problem' of underdevelopment became the subject of international concern and focus, reflecting itself not only in terms of institutional initiatives on the part of the United Nations system and national governments, but also in terms of concentrated academic discussion and debate. Thus what has grown up in recent years is a literature on the 'third world' which should be seen as distinct from other academic literatures, with its own concepts and theories, expressed through its own journals and books and within its own professional forums. Hence, much of the discussion regarding the impact (or lack of impact) of science and technology on LDCs can only really be understood in relation to this specialised, and burgeoning, field of enquiry.

This chapter concentrates upon defining what we mean by the term 'underdevelopment', how we may measure the socio-economic gap between nations and how we may characterise institutionally those parts of the world held to be backward. In the following sections I shall try to show that attempts to 'explain' the extent and nature of underdevelopment, in the last 30–40 years or so, may be classified into two broad traditions of socio-economic thought, one which stresses the need for LDCs to 'modernise' – to take on board (some of) the characteristics of those countries they are seeking to catch up with – the other which tends to stress the obstacles which LDCs typically face in so doing. There is a certain artificiality in this construct but it does serve to place the analysis of science policy very firmly where it naturally belongs – within the latter category. Thus practically all the immense literature on technology transfer, appropriate technology, science and technology planning, institution-building for science, international technical assistance and other areas, has been predicated on the view that science and technology does not transplant easily 'from the west to the east, from the north to the south'. Rather it often acts as an alien force, in general not contributing as much as it might do to ameliorating the evils of underdevelopment and sometimes actually making matters worse. The subsequent chapter will explore these points more thoroughly.

Table 7.1   GDP/Head for Representative Countries (1979)

	$
Switzerland	13,920
USA	10,630
UK	6,320
Spain	4,380
Mexico	1,640
Kenya	380
India	190
Chad	110
Bangladesh	90

Source: The World Bank, *World Development Report, 1981*, Table 1, p. 134

7.2 Measuring Underdevelopment

The most commonly used index of underdevelopment is some measure of economic performance. This is partly a function of the widely held, and rather justifiable, belief that at bottom the problem of the third world countries is one of access to incomes on the part of the mass of their populations. It is also due to the apparent relative ease with which appropriate economic data can be collected and processed. Table 7.1 presents a typical 'league table' of GDP per head across a range of representative countries, starting from $13,290 in the case of Switzerland and falling dramatically to $110 and $90 in the cases of Chad and Bangladesh.

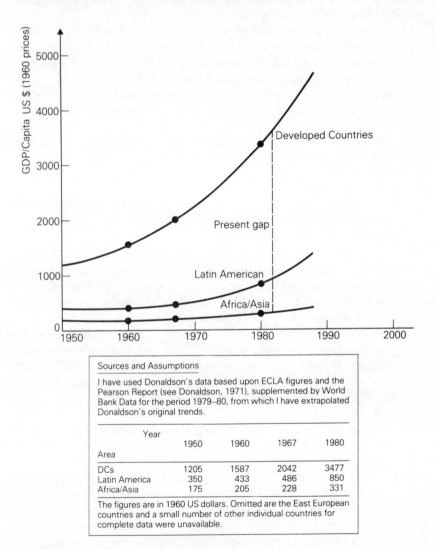

Sources and Assumptions

I have used Donaldson's data based upon ECLA figures and the Pearson Report (see Donaldson, 1971), supplemented by World Bank Data for the period 1979–80, from which I have extrapolated Donaldson's original trends.

Area	Year 1950	1960	1967	1980
DCs	1205	1587	2042	3477
Latin America	350	433	486	850
Africa/Asia	175	205	228	331

The figures are in 1960 US dollars. Omitted are the East European countries and a small number of other individual countries for complete data were unavailable.

Figure 7.1   International differences in income/head

What do these figures tell us? On the face of it, and very crudely, they show that at least in terms of overall economic production and consumption, there are huge international differences. In fact recent World Bank data (for 1981) indicate that 60% of the world's population has an income of less than $400, that half the world's population earns only 5% of world income and that the top 15% of world population earns some 75% of world income. They show us also that the economic gap between nations is increasing. Figure 7.1 portrays rates of growth of GDP per head for three development categories over the period 1950 to 1980.

How accurately do these data, then, reflect the fact of underdevelopment? To put it crudely, can we infer from table 7.1 for example, that in 1979 the average person in India was 56 times worse off than his counterpart in the USA? The answer to this is that data on national income per head give an indication of degrees of poverty, but they should be used only as very rough guides, for several reasons.

(i)   The raw data themselves are inaccurate. For example, it is usually difficult to collect even very simple economic statistics from those employed in peasant agriculture or from those employed in the 'informal' urban sector.

(ii)   How well the raw data are transformed into final aggregate figures depends heavily upon the quality of national statistical collection agencies, and this tends to be uneven.

(iii) The process of converting data from those expressed in national currencies to a common denominator (usually US dollars) builds in further bias since this is normally done at international exchange rates. The point is that exchange rates are 'market prices' which reflect the ebb and flow of internationally traded goods and services, and are not therefore a reliable mechanism for measuring the output and income of one country in terms of those of another. For this, and other rather more complex reasons which we need not go into here, it is generally accepted that international differences in incomes per head, as measured, probably tend to exaggerate 'real' differences in living standards.

(iv)   National income data tell us nothing about the distribution of incomes between social classes or between regions within a country.

Partly to compensate for these deficiencies, there has been an attempt in recent years to develop other measures of comparative living standards, sometimes called social indicators. Table 7.2 provides some examples of these for the same countries as before. It may be seen that broadly speaking they provide a similar picture − those countries with higher incomes enjoying better 'social' standards and vice versa. Again such data should be treated with caution but they are illustrative of the general conclusion that living standards do vary markedly throughout the world.

Table 7.2   Selected Social Indicators

Indicator Country	Adult Literacy (%) 1976	Life Expectancy (Years) 1979	Population/ Physician 1977	% of Labour Force Employed in Agriculture 1979
Switzerland	99	75	510	5
USA	99	74	570	2
UK	99	73	750	2
Spain	N/A	73	560	15
Mexico	82	66	1820	37
Kenya	45	55	11630	78
India	36	52	3620	71
Chad	15	41	41940	85
Bangladesh	26	49	8780	74

Source: The World Bank, *World Development Report*, 1981, Tables 1, 19, 22

However, it is clear that underdevelopment cannot really be summed up in terms of aggregate statistics of the kind we have been discussing, and most textbooks tend to stress a range of important institutional characteristics which besides providing us with a more real, if also rather qualitative, picture of underdevelopment, also bring us closer to an analytical perspective which has some policy significance. For we are interested in world poverty not as a cold fact but as a complicated and pervasive problem which has occurred as a result of given social processes and whose analysis may lead to remedial action, at least in principle. Thus many of these characteristics are both an indication and a cause of underdevelopment. Understanding more clearly what they are takes us at least some way towards policy prescription.

It might be useful at this stage if I provided a list of *typical* LDC characteristics, not by any means an exclusive one but one which will give the student at least a flavour of the problem.

(i)   In many of the poorest countries a significant proportion of the working population does not work in wage employment but instead participates in peasant farming, the fruits of which go directly towards satisfying the immediate consumption needs of the household. Very often the technological means and resources available to the peasant farmer in terms of land, tools and credit are insufficient to enable his family to subsist thereby forcing people, usually his children, to seek paid employment elsewhere, often in towns where conditions and prospects are also poor. This is one important reason why the challenge of bringing about technological changes on the land is one of the most important facing poor countries nowadays.

(ii) The drift to the cities and towns has in many LDCs created huge problems of urban squalor. Places like Jakarta, Ibadan and Calcutta seem barely able to cope with very rapidly growing populations in terms of health and sanitation, housing, transportation. Nor are there sufficient industrial or other paid jobs available for those who need them. The result is the growth of 'informal' employment of the kind demonstrated so vividly by Hart[2] — petty trading, small-scale repair and maintenance, prostitution, begging and crime. Weeks has pointed out that in countries where there is no supplementary or unemployment benefit, to be unemployed is to have no access to any income whatsoever.[3] Literally speaking, people cannot afford to be unemployed and although recourse may be had to the extended family network, much of informal employment should be seen as efforts to gain access to much-needed income.

(iii) Monetary institutions are usually underdeveloped in many LDCs, thereby hampering the extent to which potential savings may be translated into productive investment. Thus the lack of a modern commercial banking system and a differentiated capital market inhibits both the flow of investible funds from households and other institutions, *and* access to risk capital on the part of entrepreneurs. Again we have here an example of a feature of underdevelopment being both a symptom and a cause. An economy which is barely monetized, where many transactions are conducted through barter or through local specie, is hardly in a position to mobilise funds for large-scale development projects, at least not at the level required for fast economic growth. And yet the faster the population growth and the greater the poverty, the more may be the objective need for this to take place.

(iv) Sometimes poor countries may be characterised by the degree of openness of their economic systems — that is by the extent to which consumption demands are met by imports and paid for by the exports of primary products. The classic case of the 'banana republic', the monoculture export economy whose production structure is heavily dependent on one primary commodity produced for export under the ownership and control of a large foreign controlled company, is possibly a phenomenon of the past. Nevertheless its important features are still present over large parts of the world — a poorly developed industrial sector, a lack of flexibility in indigenous production structures, vulnerability to foreign trade, and reliance upon multinational companies for capital and know-how — so that even where they are no longer 'open' in the sense outlined above, nevertheless the 'symptoms' of underdevelopment are still very much extant.

(v)   Finally, a much discussed characteristic of many LDCs is that of a poorly developed administrative and political structure. This is not so much a question of the degree to which the ordinary citizen is permitted to participate in the political process (though some writers have argued in these terms). Rather it concerns the efficiency of the apparatus of government, its ability to collect taxes and administer expenditures, its access to reliable data on economic and social activity and the quality of its civil servants. It is often precisely the countries which are most poorly endowed in these respects that have the greatest need to plan development. Yet what has often happened in practice is an over-optimism on the part of governments regarding the possibilities for public action in this sphere which has resulted, in turn, in misdirected funds, cumbersome bureaucracy, corruption, and institutional developments which benefit those who work in the institutions rather than those whom the institutions are intended to serve.

Structural characteristics such as these, help us to define, albeit roughly, what we understand by underdevelopment in general. Poor countries are poor because their populations do not enjoy the incomes we enjoy in the West. Partly because of this, people do not have access to the same opportunities in terms of health, education and other services. Except for the fortunate few representing an elite oligarchy, therefore, most suffer more from disease and lack of nutrition, live shorter lives under harsher conditions and do not 'enjoy' a lifestyle remotely comparable with that experienced by those in the rich countries. Moreover, as Donaldson points out,[4] the world as a whole is a much smaller place than it was 50 or 100 years ago. A revolution in communications and transportation has increased significantly the popular awareness of international differences in income and wealth, so much so that governments in most LDCs are now under enormous pressure to provide the means whereby their own populations can enjoy a comparable lifestyle.

And the result of their efforts to do so, built upon a legacy of foreign (sometimes colonial) domination is what we now understand as 'underdevelopment' − a form of economic organisation which is neither modern nor traditional, where ancient cultures try vainly to come to terms with the modern market place, where the most glittering of modern artifacts coexist with degrading urban squalor, where institutions imported from the West take on shapes and functions infinitely (and dangerously) removed from those at first intended, where the rural sector gets neglected and impoverished, where education becomes as much a means of rationing scarce jobs as of improving people's aptitudes, and where income distribution reaches levels of inequality which would never be tolerated in the industrialised world. It is this stark reality of 'underdevelopment' which can never be captured by the cold statistics of the international league tables and which remains such a telling indictment of this world in which we live.

7.3 Theories of Development

How then has 'underdeveloment' been analysed? Throughout the years since the Second World War, the 'developing countries' have been the focus of great conceptual concern, resulting in a plethora of attempts to 'theorise' about them — to understand what causes underdevelopment, why it is so pervasive, and what can be done to ameliorate it. There have been so many attempts that it is almost impossible to give the student more than a very rough flavour of their contents and contrasts. What follows is a stylised account of two very important intellectual traditions within which most development theories may be located, which illustrate the sort of admixture of rationalism and ideology to which I have tried to draw attention in early chapters.

And here again the student must be well aware of the metaphysical positions which underlie much of this discussion, whereby theorists achieve the conclusions with which they feel most comfortable and which fit in best with their own 'belief systems' about how the world is, ought to be and can be made to be. You will find, for example, that different disciplines will view things according to their own generic categories — sociologists emphasising social class (and class conflict) and other significant institutional categories, economists emphasising resource allocation and development planning, political scientists emphasising the structure of power, representation and legitimisation of authority. On a more ideological level you will find those on the 'left' placing much more emphasis upon the 'state' and 'public action' as a solver of problems, while those on the 'right' emphasise 'market forces'. In general it is best to be highly critical about whatever you read, no matter how eminent the authority, and wherever possible to seek for empirical evidence to support (or not) propositions.

7.3.1 Modernisation

According to this tradition, which achieved prominence in the late 1950s and early 1960s, LDCs are seen to be 'backward' in a variety of important respects and will only 'advance' if they take on the characteristics of the rich industrialised countries who, accordingly, provide the paradigm for development. There have been many exponents of this tradition but arguably the most comprehensive statements have emanated from the pen of W. W. Rostow[5] who argued that 'development' takes place in sequential 'stages' which he defined independently of the historic and cultural conditions obtaining in any one country. Rostow held that although there were clear differences in such circumstances amongst countries, nevertheless they represented merely 'noise' in the system. Historically all countries pass through the same set of stages in the same sequence and if there are slight variations in terms of timing, duration and other factors, these do not detract from the main theme/process. It follows by extension that LDCs too must pass through these stages and that at any point in time a 'snapshot' of the world would reveal a hierarchy of development, from the USA and similar countries at the top right down to the poorest at the bottom. Development is an essentially linear process of modernisation and the objective of the LDCs should be to compress this process into the shortest possible time-scale.

Rostow postulated his five stages as follows:

(i)   **Traditional Society.** Traditional societies are ones where production techniques are largely primitive, where 'pre-Newtonian attitudes to the physical world prevail',[6] where innovation is sporadic but rare, where most people are employed in agricultural and related work and where power is vested in landownership. Such societies were typical histori- cally of 'the dynasties in China, the civilisation of the Middle East and the Mediterranean (and) the world of medieval Europe'.[7] There are not many around today.

(ii) **The Pre– 'Take-Off' Period.** This period is associated with some set of ideological or institutional changes which act as 'shocks' to the equilibrium of traditional society and which set in train 'ideas and sentiments which [initiate] the process by which a modern alternative to the traditional society [is] constructed out of the old culture'.[8] Often also there will be changes in technological possibilities. Rostow pinpoints the late seventeenth and early eighteenth centuries in Europe as the period when such 'preconditions' first distinguished themselves in a 'clear and marked way' and when the notion of economic progress became accepted as not only a possible but also a desirable thing.

(iii) **The Take-Off.** This Rostow defines as the period when everything comes together, when all the 'old blocks and resistances to steady growth are finally overcome' and when 'compound interest becomes built, as it were, into [society's] habits and institutional structure'.[9] During this stage there is a very rapid increase of economic activity fuelled by equally sudden spurts of savings, investments and radical technological change. A new entrepreneurial class emerges, agricul- tural productivity improves and resources, including population, begin to move into industrial activities located in towns. Rostow traces the 'take-off' period for Britain between 1780 and 1800, for Germany in the third quarter of the nineteenth century, for Russia and Canada in the period 1890–1914 and for India and China in the period since the Second World War.

(iv)   **The Drive to Maturity.** This defines the period following take-off during which industrialisation becomes consolidated. Usually this takes place in an uneven fashion with particular industries or 'leading sectors' forcing the pace e.g. machine tools, chemicals and electrical equipment in the case of the Western European economies and the USA — and with a systematic improvement in technical conditions. 'Maturity' is defined in terms of the capacity of the economic system in question 'to move beyond the original industries which powered its take-off and to absorb and to apply efficiently over a wide range of its resources . . . the most advanced fruits of [then] modern technology'.[10] This means in effect the integrated capacity and flexibility necessary to develop in any direction thought desirable, unhampered by internal constraints of a structural nature.

(v)   **The Age of Mass Consumption.** Once 'maturity' has been reached possibilities exist for expanding consumption well beyond the basic necessities of life, such as food, clothing and shelter. Now the economic system has established the capacity to produce a surplus which may be used to broaden the range of consumption goods available to the mass of the population and to ease the social strain of producing them. The advent of consumer durables, such as washing machines for example, shortens the time required for household management while the development of new labour-saving technology begins to reduce the drudgery and toil associated with unskilled and semi-skilled work in mines and factories. The working week gradually shortens allowing more people more time to pursue leisure and cultural activities, and there is a general shift in the production structure away from the provision of goods into that of services including, increasingly, a wide variety of social services provided by the state.

Such was, in outline, Rostow's general theory of economic development, a theory admitted by its author to be somewhat crude, and requiring articulation when applied in particular contexts, but one nevertheless which provided a coherent framework within which to study and evaluate the very complex phenomenon of social change. Most importantly, and this is what provided Rostow's guiding passion, it was explicitly an attack on that other great general theory of economic development associated with the name of Marx. For Marx had painted quite a different picture of the development of industrial capitalism, one in which the main 'engine' was the development of productive forces which in turn conditioned the political power structure, where history progressed in terms of class struggles, and where the newly formed industrial working class would suffer increased immiserization with stagnant and falling real wages and growing unemployment. In Marx's view there would be no neat progression from 'stage' to 'stage' but on the contrary the economic system would become increasingly unstable. The expansion of industrial capacity would tend to outreach society's capacity for consuming the resultant products, leading to an increasingly bitter struggle for markets (internationally as well as nationally), the growth of large monopolies and increasingly severe 'crises' of cyclical unemployment. Eventually revolution would take place with a socialist state acting on behalf of the proletariat taking over responsibility for economic production and distribution, which would then progress in a 'crisis-free' manner until such time as the economic problem of scarcity had been solved. As this time approached the 'state' would wither away heralding the 'final era' of communism in which all citizens would enjoy a life of abundance with the prospect of developing their own creative potentials as human beings to the full.

The debate, of course, was not about the 'ends' but about the way these may best be reached. To Rostow and people like him, the capitalist system is, in one form or another, the best means by which 'modernization' takes place. To many modern Marxist thinkers — who often differ quite considerably from the original Marx — capitalist development is ultimately flawed through its own internal contradictions and not by any means the correct path towards the eventual golden age of abundance. The Rostovian standpoint views the age of mass consumption as a desirable period, while to the Marxist it is merely a period in which a superficial gloss of consumer goods conceals a fundamentally alienated and flawed social order.

It would be wrong to pretend that so far as LDCs were concerned, theories of modernisation stemmed directly from Rostow. Nonetheless Rostow encapsulated, as it were, the essence of a very common position, which was that LDCs were *backward* in terms of their cultures, political systems, social institutions and economic resources. The way to become 'less backward' was to borrow, buy or copy those corresponding features of the rich countries felt to be instrumental in bringing about economic growth. The *act* of development became one of compressing modernisation into as short a time as possible, through singling out those aspects of rich country experience which were of most importance. In general there were advantages in being a 'latecomer',[11] first because you could avoid the mistakes, sometimes costly ones, made by the developed countries and secondly because access could be had to 'best practice' technologies produced in the interim. Moreover, new and productive technologies could be installed more readily in the LDCs because there were fewer inhibiting factors, such as vested interests. A third advantage in being a latecomer lay in possibilities for 'aid' from the rich countries.

The problem was that the modernisationists could not agree about which 'factors' to emphasise in their policy prescriptions. Some like McClelland[12] and Hagen[13] argued that what many LDCs lacked was a dynamic, thrusting middle class with the necessary entrepreneurial capacity to bring about economic growth. Others emphasised the significance of very rapid rates of population growth as fundamental constraints, and hence recommended population control measures as the first priority.[14] Some felt that in many LDCs there was plenty of latent productive capacity; what was missing was the chance to mobilise it, to provide a 'vent for surplus'.[15] Ensure the necessary market outlets, it was held, and you will soon incorporate the outlying areas into the exchange economy. And once the fruits of modernisation have been tasted there will be no holding back. Growth will represent the normal course of events.

But how do you widen markets? Promotion of primary exports was advocated by some as a means of optimising resources and maximising possibilities for earning foreign exchange.[16] But export promotion strategies are fraught with difficulties including, for example, locking the economic system into production structures which rely heavily upon a narrow range of primary products and are therefore unduly vulnerable to international trade fluctuations. In any case, in their original formulations they appeared to militate against broadening the base of economic systems through industrialisation. More direct action was felt to be necessary. Writers like Nurkse[17] and Rosenstein-Rodan[18] explored the possibilities for 'balance growth' through simultaneous investment in many industrial sectors, stimulated (partly) by central development planning and also by foreign aid. Markets would then be provided by a mechanism similar to that of Say's Law, the collective increased incomes of each sector providing the necessary aggregate demand for the resultant increased production. Others argued that balanced growth industrialisation strategies were unrealistic and that the way forward was to create possibilities for the development of Rostovian 'leading sectors', fuelled by private capital and entrepreneurship — the so-called *unbalanced growth* strategy, in which bottlenecks are deliberately created, thereby fostering the conditions in which entrepreneurial behaviour can flourish.[19]

Returning again to the resource or supply-side, there were a variety of further 'single factor' solutions or panaceas suggested by different commentators at different times, for each of which a reasonable case could be made out. Throughout these discussions and debates it is possible to distinguish a clear thread of pessimism regarding the possibilities for economic progress in LDCs. Elkan,[20] for example, writes of a 'series of interlocking vicious circles of poverty and stagnation' which act so as to perpetuate underdevelopment. The best known of these is the sequence whereby poverty leads to low rates of savings, leading in turn to low rates of investment and stagnant economic growth. In the face of rapid rates of growth of population, therefore, levels of income per head do not rise appreciably and hence poverty remains endemic. Myrdal[21] believed that development in one part of the world (the developed countries) would actually tend to impoverish the

LDCs through 'backwash effects' and there is continual reference in the literature of the period to 'low level equilibrium traps', 'backward sloping supply curves of effort', 'critical minimum efforts' all of which ideas tended to argue negatively about the future possibilities for LDCs.

7.3.2 Structural Theories

During the 1950s, and increasingly as we move into the 1960s and 1970s, many of the views and ideas of the modernisation theorists came under attack. Rostow himself, as an economic historian, received widespread criticism[22] — so much so in fact that it is doubtful if nowadays his 'stage' theory is at all widely accepted except possibly at a very general level. There are several reasons for this. The very generality of his theory as a theory of development, meant that whatever its value as an explicator of *past* trends was, and here there were many problems, as a guide to 'modernisation' it was clearly far too crude. It provided little in the way of operational clues about what *kinds* of institutional and policy changes LDCs should seek, and so as a guide to action it was very limited. Moreover, there was more than a hint of historicism about it, since there is a distinct flavour of inevitable progress towards the golden age of US capitalism (stage 5, you will remember). Seldom will you find in Rostow's writings (or in those of any other 'moderniser' for that matter) any strong emphasis on the view that there may be certain features of the rich countries which the LDCs may not wish to emulate, that there may be aspects to the march of civilisation that may be seen as undesirable. Furthermore, you will find very little in the modernisation literature which gives analytical prominence to the relations (often colonial) which existed between the present day rich countries and many of the present day LDCs and how this affected the development of each category.

Hence a major response to these and other weaknesses began to develop, the major distinguishing feature of which was that it stressed the institutional and historical 'uniqueness' of underdevelopment as a form of economic organisation, a form quite distinct in important respects from that of the present day developed countries when they were at a corresponding 'stage' in their development. Indeed explicit recognition was given to the fact that many of the current characteristics/problems experienced by LDCs are at least partially a consequence of the evolution of international political and economic relations over past periods, including those associated with colonialism. It followed that any generalised attempt to theorise about LDCs should be diagnostic in tone i.e. in the sense that the essential features of structural uniqueness were to be pin-pointed as a direct means for explanation and policy. LDCs could no longer be regarded as cardboard cut-outs of nineteenth-century Europe.

The main initial focus for this tradition were the theories of structural underdevelopment developed by a range of writers from Latin America, among whom Raoul Prebisch (one-time Director General of UNCTAD and Executive Secretary of UNECLA)[23] is usually given the credit for starting things off. Prebisch argued (in opposition to a widely held view of the time) that international trade did not in fact benefit poor countries, since the 'terms' upon which trade was conducted and the resultant 'gains from trade' systematically benefited the rich countries at the expense of their poorer trading partners.[24] Using historic data for the UK for a period of roughly 60 years prior to the Second World War, he found that the 'terms' of British trade, expressed in terms of average export prices of manufactured goods as a ratio of the average prices of primary product imports from 'peripheral' countries, improved by some two-thirds over the period. Similar evidence was produced for other 'metropolitan' economies.

The reason why international income distribution moved systematically *against* the LDCs in this way was a function of radically different structures of economic production. Technological improvements in the products typically exported by the rich countries (mainly manufactures) did not reflect themselves in falling prices through competitive pressures. Instead the growth of monopolies and trades union power acted so as to distribute benefits to capitalists in the form of higher profits and to workers in the form of higher wages. Consumers did not benefit at all. Precisely the reverse occurred in the case of the products typically exported by the poor countries − mainly food and raw materials produced under competitive conditions both domestically and internationally. Here technological progress tended not to be captured by producers, but was reflected in falling prices thereby benefiting consumers − mainly located in the rich countries.

Prebisch's ideas produced something in the nature of a Kuhnian paradigm shift. His work was criticised, often correctly, on both empirical and theoretical grounds, but it did spark off an entirely new way of viewing the nature of underdevelopment, and one that became, for a while at least, very influential indeed. One of the most succinct statements of structural underdevelopment has been presented by Dudley Seers, a British economist who spent a great deal of his career working within the agencies of the United Nations and who became very much influenced by the Latin American school of thought. He postulated a stylised 'stage theory' of economic development but one which, unlike Rostow's, appertained only to LDCs.

7.3.3 The Process of Import Substitution[25]

Seers argued as follows. One of the most characteristic features of many poor countries, especially at early periods of development, is their *dualistic* nature. A 'modern sector', often largely foreign-owned, urban/plantation based and producing for export, coexists with a 'traditional sector' in which production is dominated by subsistence agriculture and simple craft-based production, and in which the exchange economy is not very far advanced. Within the modern sector there are typically rapid developments in consumer demands, conditioned by life-styles enjoyed by people in the rich countries, while the traditional sector is in a perpetual state of 'low level' disequilibrium due to population pressures and low rates of growth of labour productivity. Sometimes it is suggested that within this broad scheme two types of dualism may be distinguished, namely the simple 'colonial enclave' case and the case where there is the beginnings of local manufacture. It was Seers's argument that there are powerful pressures forcing LDCs from the first state into the second, and beyond. This historical process he defined as that of import-substitution − an inevitable sequence of social change *conditioned* by dependent relations between rich and poor countries and *leading to* many of the features of structural underdevelopment which may be identified today.

Seers's analysis consisted of four stages. The first, that of the *open economy*, depicted a regime, usually but not necessarily colonial, completely open to foreign influences and one where much of organised economic production in the modern sector was owned and controlled by foreign capital, and oriented towards international trade. In such an economic system, growth is dependent positively upon export demand and negatively upon the income elasticity of demand for imports. The former depends upon rates of growth of incomes in the rich countries while the latter reflects the propensity to consume manufactured goods imported from these same countries. The greater this propensity to consume on the part of elites in the modern sector, the lower the rate of savings and investment for the economic system as a whole, although Seers did admit that growth often continued in practice even with high imports of foreign consumer goods, because of simultaneous imports of foreign capital. In such a regime the banking system, and hence the management of foreign exchange, was usually in the hands of foreign nationals. Also since, almost by definition, foreign interests wielded great political power, economic growth was not dependent upon internal political factors.

Seers then argued that historically such an economic system was inherently unstable and often moved quickly on to a second stage, that of the *open economy under stress*, for several reasons but mainly because there was an inherent asymmetry in foreign trade which began increasingly to put pressure on the balance of payments. While the demand for imports remained buoyant as more, and richer, potential consumers joined the ranks of those in the modern sector, the capacity to pay for imports in terms of primary product exports began to flag. This was due partly to Engel's Law − increases in the demand for food on the part of rich country consumers do not keep pace with increases in incomes − partly on lower rates of population growth in the rich countries and partly on the influence of technological changes such as the development of synthetic substitutes (e.g. synthetic rubber for natural ruboer). Factors of this kind which created shortages of foreign exchange and led increasingly to hardship for a growing urban population through rising prices and falling real wages, tended to be reflected in political opposition to foreign domination. In colonial-based dependencies a spirit of anti-colonialism led to conscious policies towards national economic development both before and after independence. In all cases the net effect was to 'close up' economic systems, as scarce foreign exchange became progressively rationed and resources became re-allocated in a drive to broaden the base of economic production.

Developments of this kind heralded Seers's third stage, that of *easy import-substitution*. Governments imposed a series of restrictions on imported consumer goods through tariffs, quotas, multiple exchange rates and direct price controls. Often these were differentially imposed on relatively 'luxurious' items on the (usually optimistic) grounds that this would lead to the equalisation of real income distribution. Policies of this kind combined with continued pressures of consumer demands created conditions ideally suited to the establishment of local manufacture of consumer goods, such as foodstuffs, beverages, garments, household equipment, cigarettes etc., since protection provided the cocoon within which the new embryonic industries could flourish. The efficiency with which economic transformation could take place depended very much upon prior factors such as the nature of the original export activity, the type of social infrastructure in existence, the level of manpower skills and other inputs available, and the size and coherence of markets. Furtado[26] compares the relatively favourable conditions in Argentina with those in Bolivia and Chile where the structural constraints on economic transformation, even during this 'easy' stage were much more severe. In general, however, it was always open to governments to speed the process along through the use of development planning as a conscious instrument of national policy, although the actual *act* of planning was rarely found to be the relatively problem-free process initially expected. A final feature of this stage was the change in the structure of imports towards capital and intermediate goods as the local manufacturing base broadened.

Whatever the initial causes, however, this stage was both easy to establish *and* relatively limited as a vehicle for industrialisation. Sooner or later these limitations became increasingly pronounced as the economic system reached the last and most *difficult stage of import-substitution*, that corresponding to the establishment of an autonomous capacity to produce capital goods. The reasons why underdeveloped economies are forced into this stage are rather complicated. They also anticipate to some extent the discussion in the next chapter. However, very roughly the argument runs as follows. As development proceeds the underlying structural deficiencies in the economic system become increasingly pronounced. This takes many forms including, for example, the low elasticity of supply of agricultural products, growing inadequacy in areas of social infrastructure such as transport and communication, failure of the fiscal system (in terms of collecting resources required for financing growing public expenditures) and shortages of skilled manpower. Bottlenecks of this kind create inflationary pressures which combined with consumer demands continue to act so as to suck in imports. Governments then react to the resultant losses in foreign exchange by placing even more stringent controls over imports and by seeking to *deepen* the base of local manufacture through the establishment of industries producing intermediate and capital goods. But the establishment of a dynamic producer goods sector depends upon the assimilation of modern technology in a far more fundamental sense than ever before and it is at this point that the very complex techno-economic relations with the industrialised countries begin to surface, creating conditions of *dependency* for LDCs which are not only very hard to break out of, but which condition in a fundamental way future development prospects.

Such then, in outline, is a typically stylised account of the 'development of underdevelopment', an account which although heavily based upon recent Latin American experience, presents quite a different picture from that of the modernisationists. In particular it argues for a theoretical position which explicitly emphasises the historical uniqueness of contemporary LDCs as a specific form of economic organisation and one which is distinct from that of the nineteenth-century European economies and that of the USA in a number of important respects. To *begin with* the motive force of industrial change comes from the side of consumer demands rather than from the pressure to reduce costs and the prospects of enormous profits. Demand-led change is both foreign-induced (the so-called demonstration effect) and foreign (demands of expatriates) and only occurs because structural conditions begin to prevent their being satisfied by direct imports. Conversely the lack of pre-existent consumer demands in nineteenth-century Europe gave the process of capital accumulation quite a different character.

A *second* point, emphasised particularly by Furtado,[27] is that for the LDCs by and large, control of the re-investible surplus remained broadly in the hands of foreigners and tended often to be re-invested in metropolitan economic systems. The capitalist class was not, therefore, the effective 'translation mechanism' which it had been in Europe but rather became a mercantile adjunct of metropolitan growth. A *third* factor differentiating LDCs was the absence of colonies which had often provided an important role for the industrialised countries as suppliers of cheap food and raw materials, and as markets for industrial products.[28] *Fourthly*, whereas rapid population growth during the industrial revolution meant a plentiful supply of cheap labour which assisted the accumulation process, for the LDCs the even more rapid rates of population growth (because of improvements in health) combined with more capital-intensive production techniques tended merely to exacerbate the problems we now associate with underemployment and urbanisation. Even to the extent that foreign investment drew labour into paid employment in urban areas, the net effect was to increase the demand for imports.

Finally, and most importantly from our point of view, the characteristics of technological change have tended to be quite different. Thus, as we have seen during the industrial revolution, technological changes were generated and responded to pressures within the economic system itself in an *endogeneous* and organic manner. This has never occurred to any marked extent for the LDCs except in very recent years and with respect to a small number of countries. Here the sources of technological changes have been geographically and culturally *exogenous* mainly because there was never a supply constraint – goods were supplied from overseas and when they were produced locally the necessary know-how was then imported. In any case, as Cooper has pointed out,[29] in an economic system where the bulk of economic production was of a subsistence/artisanal form, there was little scope for the introduction of new technology. In effect the evolution of the organisation of production, at least in the early stages, did not often reach the level where social (derived) demands for new technology required the development of an indigenous technological capacity.

7.3.4 Dependency Theory

These views of the 'structuralist school' became articulated and refined during the 1970s into what has been called 'dependency theory' a style of analysis whch is remarkably heterogeneous and, on the whole, pessimistic. It would take too much space to try to summarise the full range of dependency theory[30] in an introductory textbook of this kind but one or two general points may be made. *First* most theories of dependence stress that prospects for peripheral development in the world are hampered by the various ways that poor countries are dependent upon the rich countries, although the degree of such constraints varies widely indeed. *Secondly*, which particular *form* dependence takes varies widely from author to author, as do the consequent solutions. A well-known and extreme position is that of Gunder Frank[31] and Amin[32] both of whom assert the impossibility of peripheral development, which is due in turn to the exploitative nature of capitalist relations between rich countries and poor countries, and to the development of inequalities within poor countries themselves. Frank argues himself for a socialist revolution as a necessary pre-condition for peripheral development, while Amin is less dramatic viewing nationalism and self-reliance as a means of bringing about the transition to socialism. At the other extreme we have writers such as Cardoso[33] who assert that it is perfectly possible for some peripheral capitalist development to take place, albeit not sufficiently to resolve the severe problems of poverty experienced by the mass of the population. In between, there are a range of analyses characterised principally by different emphases on the precise mechanics of the development of underdevelopment.

A *third* point is that much of dependency theory is very much influenced by Marxist thought in its modern guise. It is important to point out, however, that traditional Marxism did not believe that backward parts of the world would remain underdeveloped. On the contrary Marx and Engels believed that 'capitalism [was] an historically progressive system, which [would] be transmitted from the advanced countries − through colonialism, free trade etc. − and which [would] spread through the backward nations by a continual process of destruction and replacement of pre-capitalist structures'.[34] Recently writers very much within this older tradition, like Warren,[35] have stressed the possibilities for peripheral capitalist development − for example through export-led growth based upon agriculture. And indeed others have argued that attempts to follow the line of some of the more extreme dependency theorists have helped to produce regimes of a particularly vicious brand, like that of Kampuchea under Pol Pot.[36]

In a sense, therefore, there is some superficial correspondence between early Marxist thought and that of Rostow, although there are still of course important differences in treatment and in ideological perspective.

7.4 Some Concluding Remarks

By now the student could be forgiven for feeling bewildered by the sheer range and complexity of development theory as expressed, even in summary form, during this chapter. Nevertheless, it is important to try to engage with these ideas since they provide an essential backcloth for the more specific science and technology policy themes to be discussed in the following chapter. At this stage it is convenient to summarise our discussion by comparing and contrasting both traditions of development theory.

First, the similarities. Both the 'modernisationists' and the 'structuralists' tend to operate at a high level of generality. Indeed at times the treatment is heavily scholastic with a great deal of energy being spent upon comparatively minor differences of emphasis or interpretation. For the policy maker this is frustrating simply because there is no direct 'way in' to the practical problems of development and, though we have not discussed this point, the *actual practice* of development planning and policy-making often touches the grand 'theoretical' issues only marginally. A related point is that much 'theoretical' discussion is heavily loaded with ideological overtones in a variety of subtle and not-so-subtle ways. A particular aspect of this on the 'structuralist' side is a tendency, as Sender and Smith have pointed out in relation to criticisms of the recent Berg Report,[37] to regard public action as a universal panacea without taking account of the many and labyrinthine complexities and constraints faced in practice by all public agencies in the exercise of their policy functions. A similar observation could reasonably be made about the tendency of some modernisationists to recommend free trade policies and to extol the virtues of market forces.

Returning to the point about policy and planning, for the moment, you will find that most public bodies concerned with these matters, both national and international, operate within a well circumscribed field of 'tried and true' policy instruments which have become enshrined in established bureaucratic practice, which are politically acceptable and which function independently of much current debate. Examples of this are the World Bank's predilection for social cost/benefit analysis as a necessary condition for project funding and the International Monetary Fund's usual insistence on devaluation of a currency as a necessary condition for stabilisation finance. At a national level the well-known example is the preparation of a (five-year) 'development plan' as a guide to public action. This is not to say that people do not have sensible things to say about the details of public administration in and for poor countries. They do, but what is said can not often be closely linked to 'grand theory'. Students coming from a background in the natural sciences may find this puzzling, but it is, I am afraid, very much the case.

There are, however, important differences between the two traditions some of which have been mentioned already, but which will nevertheless bear repeating. First, an important characteristic of the structuralist school is its insistence on the differences between LDCs as they have developed and as they are now, *and* the present day industrialised countries when they were at a corresponding stage in their development. This gives structuralist thinkers on the whole a more critical perspective on LDC prospects. A second, and related, point is the association between the ideas of the structuralists and those of the 'left' more generally, although we have seen that this association is not as clear cut as is sometimes assumed. Often ideological stances become counter-productive. A particular instance of this is the difficulty that some dependency theorists have had in explaining, within their own paradigms, the evident fact of considerable 'development' in a number of peripheral economies — the so-called 'newly industrialising countries' (or NICs) — in evident contradiction of some of their own predictions.[38] Equally, however, similar structures may be applied with justification to the more right-wing position of the modernisationists, since it is fairly clear that attempts to create LDCs in the image of the social order now present in the rich countries, are manifestly not working.

A third difference relates to the more holistic view of underdevelopment as viewed from the standpoint of the structuralists who, however clumsily, do make a greater effort to view the problems of poor countries in a less narrowly economic and a more inter-disciplinary way. Conversely the ethnocentricity of some modernisationists does in many senses inhibit them from suggesting alternative strategies for 'development' which need have little to do with what we are currently experiencing in the 'first world'. My own position on these matters is that, on the whole, attempts to improve living conditions in the LDCs are often frustrated by the limited imaginations and bureaucratic inertia of the governments and agencies who have been entrusted with this task. No doubt there is usually a genuine desire to act, although sometimes the strength of desire is questionable. The following chapter explores some of these points in relation to questions of science and technology policy.

Bibliography

A number of texts already cited at the end of earlier chapters are also relevant here, for example both references to Furtado (the later chapters in each). Two useful introductory texts are P. Donaldson, *Worlds Apart: The Economic Gulf Between Nations* (Harmondsworth, Penguin, 1978) and W. Elkan, *An Introduction to the Development of Economics* (Harmondsworth, Penguin, 1978) each of which provides further bibliographic information. See also H. Bernstein (ed.), *Underdevelopment and Development* (Harmondsworth, Penguin, 1976), I. Livingstone (ed.), *Development Economics and Policy* (London, Allen and Unwin, 1981) and from a socialist perspect J. Hill and H. Scannell, *Due South* (London, Pluto, 1983).

On questions of employment, a good range of papers is contained in R. Jolly, E. de Kadt, H. Singer and F. Wilson (eds.), *Third World Employment* (Harmondsworth, Penguin, 1973). On trade and development, see G. K. Helleiner, *International Trade and Economic Development* (Harmondsworth, Penguin, 1972). On industrialisation generally see R. B. Sutcliffe, *Industry and Underdevelopment* (London, Addison-Wesley, 1971) and on dependency theory, a useful text is D. Seers (ed.), *Dependency Theory: A Critical Re-assessment* (London, Frances Pinter, 1981) which contains a number of useful papers. Finally an older text which contains a number of early papers is A. Agarwala and S. Singh (eds.), *The Economics of Underdevelopment* (London, Oxford University Press, 1971).

Notes

1 See World Bank, *World Bank Development Report* (Washington, DC, Oxford University Press, 1981). This is an annual series which provides a useful set of summary statistics relevant to world development. For purposes of this calculation I have excluded the Eastern European economies and that of the USSR.

2 K. Hart, 'Informal Income Opportunities and Urban Employment in Ghana', in Jolly et al. *Third World Employment*, pp. 66–74.

3 J. Weeks, 'Does Employment Matter?', in Jolly et al., *Third World Employment*, pp. 61–5.

4 P. Donaldson, *Worlds Apart* (Harmondsworth, Penguin, 1978), pp. 15,16.

5 A useful account of Rostow's ideas is contained in W. W. Rostow, *The Stages of Economic Growth* (Cambridge, Cambridge University Press, 1966). Criticisms of Rostow's general approach are contained in P. Baran and E. Hobsbawm, 'The Stages of Economic Growth', *Kyklos*, Vol. XIV, 1961, pp. 234–42 and S. Kuznets, 'Notes on the Take-Off', in W. W. Rostow (ed.), *The Economics of Take-Off into Self-Sustained Growth* (London, Macmillan, 1963), pp. 22–43. This volume contains a number of other interesting papers.

6 Rostow, *Stages of Economic Growth*, p. 4.

7 Rostow, *Stages of Economic Growth*, p. 5.

8 Rostow, *Stages of Economic Growth*, p. 6.

9 Rostow, *Stages of Economic Growth*, p. 7.

10 Rostow, *Stages of Economic Growth*, p. 10.

11 The phrase 'latecomer' was initially applied to the European countries whose industrial transformation occurred during the middle to late nineteenth century. See A. Gerschenkron, *Economic Backwardness in Historical Perspective* (London, Praeger, 1965).

12 D. C. McClelland, *The Achieving Society* (New York, Van Norstrand, 1961).

13 E. E. Hagen, *On the Theory of Social Change: How Economic Growth Begins* (London, Tavistock, 1964).

14 G. Ohlin, *Population Control and Economic Development* (Paris, OECD Development Centre, 1967). Discussions on population growth as an obstacle (or not) to development are contained in W. Elkan, *Introduction to the Development of Economics*, chapter 8 and H. Myint, *The Economics of the Developing Countries* (London, Hutchinson, 1971), chapters 2, 6.

15 Discussed in G. K. Helleiner, *International Trade and Economic Development* (Harmondsworth, Penguin, 1972), pp. 17–19.

16 See, for example, Myint, *Economics of the Developing Countries*, chapter 9.

17 R. Nurkse, *Problems of Capital Formation in Underdeveloped Countries* (Oxford, Oxford University Press, 1953).

18 See, for example, P. Rosenstein-Rodan, 'Notes on the Theory of the Big Push', in H. S. Ellis and H. C. Wallich (eds.), *Economic Development for Latin America* (London, Macmillan, 1961).

19 A. Hirschman, *The Strategy of Economic Development* (New Haven, Yale University Press, 1964).

20 W. Elkan, *Introduction to the Development of Economics*, p. 28.

21 G. Myrdal, *Economic Theory and Underdeveloped Regions* (London, Methuen, 1964), pp. 27–9.

22 See references in note 5, above.

23 United Nations Economic Commission for Latin America.

24 A useful discussion of this whole topic is contained in Helleiner, *International Trade*, pp. 20 *et seq*.

25 This should be distinguished from development 'policies' or 'strategies' of an import-substituting character. Seers's account is that of a social process. See D. Seers, 'The Stages of Economic Growth of a Primary Producer in the Middle of the 20th Century', in R. I. Rhodes (ed.), *Imperialism and Underdevelopment* (New York, Monthly Review Press, 1970), pp. 163–80.

26 C. Furtado, *The Economic Development of Latin America* (Cambridge, Cambridge University Press, 1970), see particularly chapters 10–12.

27 Furtado, *Development and Underdevelopment*, chapter 4.

28 Martin Bell has pointed out to me that in many LDCs the rural areas fulfil this function, often to their detriment.

29 C. M. Cooper (ed.), *Science, Technology and Development* (London, Frank Cass, 1973).

30 See, however, Seers, *Dependency Theory*, particularly articles by Palma, Seers and Soete. Also M. Godfrey (ed.), 'Is Dependency Dead?', *IDS Bulletin*, University of Sussex, Vol. 12, No. 1, December 1980.

31 See, for example, A. G. Frank, *Capitalism and Underdevelopment in Latin America* (New York, Monthly Review Press, 1967).

32 See, for example, S. Amin, *Neocolonialism in West Africa* (Harmondsworth, Penguin, 1973). There has recently been an interesting debate on Amin's ideas. See, for example, S. Smith, 'The Ideas of Samir Amin; Theory or Tautology', *Journal of Development Studies*, Vol. 17, 1980. S. Amin, 'Expansion or Crisis of Capitalism?', *Third World Quarterly*, Vol. 5, No. 2, April 1983 and S. Smith and J. Sender, 'A Reply to Samir Amin', *Third World Quarterly*, Vol. 5, No. 3, July 1983, pp. 650–6.

33 See, for example, F. H. Cardoso, 'Dependency and Development in Latin America', *New Left Review*, No. 34, pp. 83–95.

34 G. Palma, *Dependency and Development: A Critical Overview*, in Seers, *Dependency Theory*, p. 21.

35 B. Warren, *Imperialism, Pioneer of Capitalism* (London, Verso, 1980).

36 Smith and Sender, 'A Reply to Samir Amin', p. 651.

37 J. Sender and S. Smith, 'What's Right with the Berg Report and What's Left of its Critics?', *IDS Discussion Paper*, University of Sussex, June 1984. The 'Berg Report' is: World Bank, *Accelerated Development in Sub-Saharan Africa: An Agenda for Action* (Washington, 1981). On the more general issue of public policy and what often goes wrong between planning and implementation in a particular context, see E. Clay and B. Schaffer (eds.), *Room for Manoeuvre: An Explanation of Public Policy for Agriculture and Rural Development* (London, Heinemann, 1984).

38 An attempt to answer this sort of criticism is contained in M. Bienefeld, 'Dependency and the Newly Industrialising Countries (NICs): Towards a Reappraisal', in Seers, *Dependency Theory*, pp. 79–96.

Chapter 8

SCIENCE, TECHNOLOGY AND DEVELOPMENT

8.1 Introduction

The problem of science policy in relation to developing countries is a difficult one. As we have seen a primary characteristic of many LDCs is a lack of flexibility in economic structures. For a variety of reasons these countries are 'locked into' patterns of production which not only do not provide adequate levels of consumption for their citizens but also do not contain within themselves the means for escape. There are two aspects here. One is that the economic system finds it hard to react to changing demand conditions through a smooth re-allocation of resources. There is, therefore, a strong propensity for bottlenecks to arise and tendencies towards stagnation to develop along the lines suggested by Myrdal[1] for example. Secondly, the economic system does not possess the means to advance technically and hence the rate of growth suffers. Both aspects are interrelated since an adequate technological infrastructure is, as we have seen, an important ingredient in economic transformation and since the possibilities for economic progress act as a spur to technological change.

These features may readily be seen (by contrast as it were) with reference to the integrated economic systems of the industrialised economies where there generally exists a complex scientific system of the kind discussed in chapter 3, whose services may be drawn upon fairly readily by productive units. Typical components of such a system are the R & D departments of firms, specialist engineering and consultancy firms and the network of institutions in the public 'research' sector which possess a wide range of scientific and technological facilities of relevance to the business of economic production. Moreover, we have also seen that such an integrated scientific system is the product of historic evolution in which a complex network of links between 'science' and 'production' gradually developed in an organic fashion. In contrast, for LDCs the very absence of such a set of systemic links is at one and the same time both a feature of underdevelopment and (arguably) an obstacle to its removal.

Initially the role of science in poor countries was viewed very much from a modernising standpoint. Since industrial advance was associated with investment in science and technology in rich countries, it was felt that the quicker the LDCs built up their own corresponding capacities the better. This could be done by establishing science curricula in schools, opening universities and technical colleges with substantial science departments, establishing a network of institutions connected with research and scientific services and taking full advantage of foreign aid and technical assistance. Foreign direct investment was especially to be encouraged since it was not only an unrequited resource, but provided LDCs with direct access to best practice technologies as they were being currently utilised in the rich countries. Although there might be teething problems, what Charles Cooper once called the 'take root and flourish' school of thought was optimistic about the long-run advantages that science and technology would bring.

With the advent of structuralist ideas and the spread of their influence, however, discussion took a more critical turn. Over the last 15 years or so policy analysts in this area have explored in detail the various ways in which LDC investments in science and technology have not had the effects hoped for, followed often by government responses to try to improve matters. The question of science policy thus relates to how LDC governments should respond in particular instances. I have structured this chapter around the better known of these themes. Section 8.2 explores the ways in which technology is transferred from rich country enterprise to LDC enterprise and the common socio-economic consequences of such transfers. Section 8.3 deals with the difficult topic of 'appropriate' technology and choice of technique. Section 8.4 looks at how LDCs have used the import of foreign technology as a means of progressively enhancing their own 'technological capacities'. Section 8.5 explores the very topical question of radical technical changes and the likely impact of these on prospects for LDC industrialisation. Section 8.6 examines problems associated with science, technology and rural development while section 8.7 reviews aspects of the indigenous science 'system' and explores the prospects for 'planning' science in a more coherent way. Again, because there is so much ground to be covered I shall not be able to give any of these topics the detailed treatment they deserve. Students are therefore encouraged to consult the cited texts where necessary.

8.2 The Process of Technology Transfer

Technology transfer occurs as a by-product of industrialisation. Essentially the demand for foreign technology on the part of LDCs is a derived demand, derived from demands for goods which in previous periods were met by imports from the industrialised countries. As was pointed out by many analysts of the structuralist school (see previous chapter) the process through which LDCs gradually began to replace imported commodities with local manufacture required a technological base, and since LDCs did not historically possess this to any marked degree there began to develop what might be described as a 'market for foreign technology', though one with unusual characteristics.[2] It could also have led, of course, to the development of indigenous sources of technology (and indeed some countries, like India, have attempted actively to foster this), but for a variety of reasons these developments have often tended to be stultified or 'marginalised'.

One of the clearest accounts of the nature of this 'market' for foreign technology is provided by Cooper and Sercovitch[3] in a monograph published in 1971 which has become something of a classic. It provides a useful picture of how and why technology flows from rich countries to poor countries, what kinds of problems can result and what policy options may be required. The paper begins by pointing out that 'technology' is not a homogeneous concept but is rather a term connotating a wide range of heterogenous forms or 'elements' (knowledge about plant design, process know-how, plant construction, feasibility studies, production management, marketing, distribution and so on) all of which are necessary for starting production but *not* all of which are possessed by the person or organisation wishing to establish new production facilities in an LDC. Normally it will possess few and in particular it will seldom possess the skills necessary to weld these various elements of knowledge into a viable productive effort. The shortage of this, essentially management, skill in most underdeveloped countries leads to a situation where the local firm, instead of 'shopping around' for each technological element and thereby buying technology at a low 'real' price, will tend to rely completely upon a foreign company (frequently a large multinational corporation which itself often subcontracts stages in the technical and production process) to provide the complete technology package. This factor is a very important source of 'control' for the supplying company whose bargaining position in the 'sale' of technology is thereby considerably strengthened.

We have also seen that technical knowledge is both *inappropriable* (it is difficult to treat it as a 'commodity' which may be bought and sold at a 'market price') and *differentiable*. Hence there is clearly both the incentive and the means to keep it secret, giving a highly monopolistic flavour both to the 'market' for the technology itself and to that for the products involved. Technology is not so much 'transferred' as it is used as a commercial device to serve the interests of firms, both foreign and indigenous and there is no reason in general to suppose that such interests are congruent with the developmental needs of the countries under consideration. Cooper and Sercovitch go on to explore in detail the nature of these socio-economic relations, and the kind of problems that typically arise.

The essence of much of the literature on technology transfer in the early to mid-1970s was thus one of drawing attention both empirically and theoretically to the many ways in which the 'market' for foreign technology often functioned in ways which were apparently not in the interests of LDCs. Technological dependence, it was argued, not only placed restrictions on national autonomy through various kinds of restrictive practice, it also contributed to an unequal sharing of the benefits resulting from associated investments. Three further problem areas were identified. First, much foreign technology was 'inappropriate' to LDC conditions in a number of important respects; secondly the development of an autonomous and indigenous science system was stultified by the 'superior' foreign alternative; finally many of the early technology transfer studies tended to find that genuine transfer, in the sense of a permanent capacity to build upon technology imports through enlarging domestic capabilities, often did not take place – mainly because it was not in the interests of the technology supplier to lose an important source of monopolistic control. The *private* appropriation of technical know-how, through various mechanisms, continued to permit the foreign supplier this considerable advantage.

8.3 Appropriate and Inappropriate Technology

The notion of 'appropriate technology' was developed in the 1960s as a means of drawing attention to the often quite glaring mismatches between resource endowments in poor countries and the types of technologies available for economic transformation. In its original form, as propounded by Schumacher,[4] it related to the potential and actual loss of employment and output resulting from the adoption of excessively machine-intensive techniques of manufacturing production. A derived problem was the regional inequalities which then occurred. 'Modern' capital-intensive production lent itself to location in urbanised complexes because of access to cheap overhead facilities (power, water, services), markets and 'external' economic benefits. Resources were attracted to such regions and with them, income and wealth for their inhabitants. The corollary was that if policy makers could solve the 'technology' problem (get the 'technology' right) then many of these disproportionalities would at least be mitigated, if not disappear altogether.

Although the analysis was crude and clearly over-simplified, it did highlight some evident problems. In many LDCs the agricultural sector was evidently not supporting a growing population and rural-urban migration was increasing. Reliance upon imported technology (urbanised, large-scale and capital-intensive) as the basis for indigenous industrial production was widespread, and possibilities for regionally dispersed, non-agriculture employment were not nearly sufficient to reverse the trends away from the land. There was more to it of course (e.g. foreign trade and agricultural pricing policies), but Schumacher and his followers *were* identifying an objective set of problems underlying capitalist economic development in peripheral economies and trying to show that technology choice had some relevance to them. In particular they argued that if more 'intermediate' technologies were invented/innovated/made available, then this would provide 'entrepreneurial possibilities' for small businesses in rural areas and, with some further assistance and a little luck, provide the basis for economic development in backward areas.

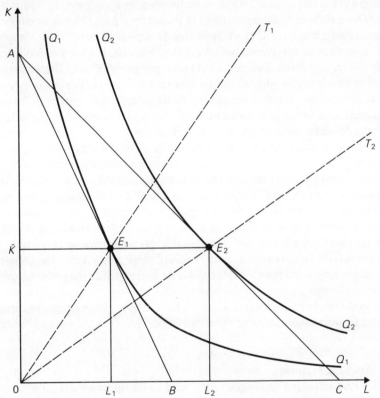

Figure 8.1 Inappropriate technology − the neo-classical analysis of relative factor price shifts

The economic treatment of this discussion according to the neo-classical tradition can be seen with reference to figure 8.1. which represents an 'aggregate production function' for any LDC, possessing the properties and characteristics described in chapter 4. The story runs as follows. In many poor countries the relative costs of labour (L) and capital (K) do not reflect their relative factor endowments, as described by price line AC. If they did, output would be maximised on isoquant Q_2, with full utilisation of all available capital and labour resources ($\bar{K}$, L_2) consistent with a labour-intensive technology T_2.

In practice, however, 'labour' is systematically 'over-priced', through a variety of social measures like minimum wage legislation, while 'capital' is correspondingly 'under-priced', through such devices as investment incentive schemes. Employers therefore face a price line corresponding to AB and, since they are operating under competitive conditions, produce at E_1, employing $\bar{K}$ of capital (the relatively scarce resource), L_1 of labour and utilising a relatively capital intensive technology in aggregate, T_1. Output is lower (Q_1) and there is unemployment in the system (L_1L_2). Since in any case the technology transferred from overseas is capital-intensive (i.e. 'appropriate' to economic conditions within the rich countries), what you have is an unholy alliance between distorted local factor prices and a set of inappropriate technologies. Basically, therefore, the problem was reduced to one of getting local factor prices 'right' through judicious government action to reduce wages and increase the price of capital. Market forces would then ensure that 'appropriate technologies' got transferred and installed in poor countries. Notice that this argument, while conceptually more rigorous than the more general arguments of Schumacher, rests firmly on a highly restrictive set of assumptions regarding technical and behavioural conditions of production. For example, inputs and outputs are assumed to be homogeneous and additive, information about technologies is assumed to be costless and accessible, there is a wide range of technologies 'on the shelf', as it were, which may be 'taken down' and installed cheaply, there are no economies of scale, and so on. To the extent that any or all of these assumptions (and others) are wrong, clearly the policy prescription on factor prices may also be quite wrong.

This point has been elaborated at length by a variety of commentators and it is useful to summarise some of the more important 'real life caveats' at this stage.

(i) **Working Capital**
     Labour intensive techniques may tend to tie up more working capital because of the greater need to finance wages, raw materials, work-in-progress and inventories of finished products.

(ii) **Homogeneity of Labour**
     Labour-intensive techniques may require greater inputs of managerial and supervisory staff so as to control and direct efficiently a larger labour force. Since such requisite 'supervisory skills' are often particularly scarce in LDCs, their price may be very high, rendering the 'real' or 'social opportunity cost' of labour at the margin much higher than would appear to be the case.

(iii)   **Economies of Scale**
Labour-intensive techniques are not susceptible to the scale economies often associated with capital-intensive techniques. This may render them absolutely less 'efficient' (see chapter 4 for definition of this) even in countries where markets are small and relatively underdeveloped, since in the long run markets do grow and there is always the possibility of entering export markets.

(iv)   **Range of Available Production Techniques**
This is often not nearly as large as assumed, since in reality 'best practice' technology has historically moved along certain (usually capital-intensive) paths. There may at one time have been efficient labour-intensive techniques in existence, but these have gradually become obsolescent. Hence factor price movements may have little impact upon labour absorption in industrial employment, merely changing the distribution of income from workers (whose wages have fallen) to capitalists (whose return on capital has increased). However this argument in particular has been criticised by a number of writers on several grounds; for example, possibilities for de-mechanising ancillary operations have been emphasised along with policies designed to shift the structure of production towards industries which tend naturally to be labour-intensive. In any case, it is held that although *actual* technologies in an operational sense may not be available which are both labour-intensive and efficient, the basic knowledge needed to 're-innovate' them does nevertheless exist. Hence, the policy imperative becomes the need to decide which mechanisms should be instituted to this end.

(v)   **Technological Dynamics**
The argument here is that even if labour-intensive techniques do exist and could be adopted, policies promoting them would lead to technological stagnation since the potential for improving on them is strictly limited. This is a particularly important point since it relates to some of the discussion in previous chapters on the organic nature of technological development, as developed for example by Rosenberg and Nelson and Winter. If it is the case that world best-practice technology moves along 'trajectories' or 'paths' which are powered by their own internal dynamic, and are to that extent removed from economic and social forces, then it is clearly not in the interests of entrepreneurs to 'opt out' of them no matter how 'appropriate' the static alternative may appear to be.

(vi)   **Confusion Between Degree of Mechanisation and Capital-Intensity**
Sometimes a mechanised production technology may appear to be more capital intensive than it really is. For example, if there are possibilities for multiple shift-working then labour absorption may be quite high, and the gains in terms of output and more rapid depreciation of machinery considerable.

For each of these reasons, and others, the *simpliste* appropriate technology argument has come under heavy criticism, at least in so far as it can be tied into the sort of economic analysis outlined in figure 8.1. However, it would be a mistake, I believe, for students to conclude that Schumacher's position can be understood, and criticised, in these terms. For Schumacher was not by any means a crude technocrat. On the contrary it is quite clear from his writings that he was appalled by the fact of 'technologised' society itself, which he saw as fundamentally dangerous to the development of the human qualities he valued most. Machine-based technologies had become not just a set of means. They had become in the rich countries at least, ends in themselves, and ends which ultimately were damaging to the human spirit. He desired, if at all possible, to prevent LDCs from following the same path. 'Employment' in Schumacher's meaning of the term was not, or should not be considered as, a means of earning income through a 40-hour working week. On the contrary it should be seen as a basic feature of human growth and development. Hence, however idealistic one considers Schumacher to be, it would be a gross over-simplification (and indeed a mistake) to accuse him of not grasping elementary economic principles. What Schumacher wanted was nothing less than a fundamental shift in human values.

8.3.1 Inappropriate Products

A second sense in which technologies imported from rich countries are sometimes classified as 'inappropriate' concerns the nature of the products the technologies are used to produce and the resultant impacts on income distribution and economic growth. The argument is fairly straightforward and runs roughly as follows. The needs of consumers in LDCs are for the basic necessities of life, food, clothing, shelter etc. However, the types of technology (and hence products) normally transferred are an expensive way of satisfying such needs since they also satisfy other needs as well. In a sense products are an indivisible, and therefore clumsy, 'mechanism' for providing consumers with what they really need.

The reason why this is so relates to the fact that every product possesses certain objective characteristics. For example, soap is not just 'soap'; it represents washing quality, smell, durability, ability to damage fabric or skin, packaging, etc. Thus each product possesses a 'consumption technology' − an ability to produce various characteristics to a certain degree and in certain proportions. To the consumer, it is the characteristics that are important because these represent the ultimate preferences and the problem arises because products are indivisible. Frances Stewart puts it very neatly as follows:

> If one acquires a particular product for one of its characteristics one unavoidably has to acquire the other characteristics too. The only way to avoid

unwanted characteristics is to find some product without them (e.g. a non-drip-dry shirt). A particular product may be described as having excessive characteristics or embodying excessive standards in relation to a particular consumer, or set of consumers, when it has characteristics which the consumer does not want, or standards in excess of those needed to fulfil the purpose for which the product is required. An example of excess standards is of a brick strong enough to support a four storey building, used for a single-storey house.[5]

Similarly any one need can be satisfied by a variety of products, but the choice becomes smaller the more narrowly one defines the need. Again, to paraphrase Stewart, basic sustenance can be provided by bread and caviare, but the body's need for calcium can be met only by a much narrower range of foodstuffs.[6]

Poor consumers in LDCs can be expected to demand those products possessing a relatively high proportion of *essential* characteristics (i.e. those related to basic needs) whereas rich consumers will tend to prefer *luxury* products. Where both product types exist, there is in theory no problem since poor consumers are able to exercise some free choice in the matter. However, the view of a number of writers has been that the transfer of technology from rich countries to poor countries has had the effect of systematically driving out 'basic goods' from the market place – a sort of 'Gresham's Law' of products. This can happen, for example, where entry of a new product takes away part of the market for competing traditional products, hence raising unit production costs for the latter and so forcing some traditional producers out of business. The net effect is to force consumers to spend more than previously to obtain an equivalent quota of the essential characteristics since they are simultaneously purchasing luxury characteristics as well; and where this practice is spread over the whole array of purchased commodities the *necessary* level of consumption rises over the whole economic system with clearly harmful implications for the mass of poor consumers.

Notice that this argument holds *independently* of advertising or consumer inefficiency. In the former case preferences are actually altered while in the latter various forms of sales promotion may produce misleading information thereby persuading consumers that the product possesses characteristics which in reality it does not. In such cases, which are arguably fairly common (e.g. certain proprietary brands of synthetic baby foods), the overall argument made above holds even more strongly. Finally the whole process becomes more solidly entrenched where a foreign firm can establish a 'brand name' or 'trade mark' which has a high selling value on local markets.

8.3.2 Policies Towards Foreign Technology

As a result of considerable empirical work carried out internationally on the transfer of technology from rich countries to poor countries, many LDCs have now established machinery to monitor and control the inflow of foreign technology in all its various guises.[7] For example, many countries have Royalty Committees to limit licence payments, and most countries will not now allow foreign direct investment to take place without close scrutiny of the terms and conditions associated with the contracting procedure, such as local sourcing of inputs, export restrictions, payments for technology and so forth.

It has proved rather more difficult for LDCs to develop concrete policies on 'appropriateness', even where the definition of appropriateness is confined to the three forms discussed above i.e. regional impact, capital-intensity, inappropriate products − , although some countries have attempted to establish relevant machinery, with what effectiveness we have yet to find out.

However, a major problem with both types of policy analysis considered, valuable though much of the work has been, is its essentially timeless or static nature which itself is derived from its roots in neo-classical economic analysis. For 'technology' is not an artifact that may be taken off the shelf and applied to the process of economic production in an automatic fashion. On the contrary (and here students are referred back to the relevant discussion in chapter 6) 'technology' can only really be understood in an evolutionary sense, constantly changing as a result of both the operation of its own dynamic in specific circumstances, and of contextual conditions. And, just as perspectives on technology are beginning to change in the theoretical literature relating to the economic development of the industrialised world, so a similar shift has taken place with respect to the role of science and technology in LDCs. It is now being realised that to tie this discussion down to an arid set of (blunt) policy instruments derived from crude empirical analysis is to trivialise the problem, and to distract attention from the infinitely complex tapestry of promise and threat which modern science and technology portends for the third world. The following sections explore some of the more recent attempts to break new ground in this sense.

8.4 Learning and Technological Capabilities

You will recall from the discussion in section 8.2 that one major problem regarding the 'import' of foreign technology was identified from the earlier literature as the difficulty many LDCs apparently have had in fully absorbing the 'transferred technology', partly due to the way in which the 'technology market' typically functions. The argument was that foreign suppliers of technology so arranged transfers (both through formal contracts and through other devices) that in effect very little actual transfer of knowledge in any permanent sense took place. The main policy recommendation which followed from this was that LDCs should develop mechanisms for 'unpackaging' foreign technology, thereby reducing the extent to which suppliers could dominate the transfer process and increasing the flow of technical know-how to individuals and institutions within LDCs. However, as Maxwell and others have pointed out, a major weakness of this approach is its timeless and mechanistic character. In their view much more needs to be known about how technological capabilities have been fostered and have taken place within developing countries, before policy recommendations can be safely implemented. In consequence recent years have witnessed an explosion of literature on the subject of 'indigenous technological capabilities', what they are, what concrete forms they take and how they evolve, or do not evolve, in particular circumstances.

The starting point for much of this very recent work is the notion of 'learning-by-doing' first formalised by Arrow in a classic paper in 1962,[8] in an attempt to help explain the high 'residual' element in economic growth identified by Solow and others. Arrow's view was that much technical change takes place within the productive unit, the firm, as a necessary counterpart to a production process where difficulties, bottlenecks etc. are being continuously tackled and solved. At the point of installation, a new investment is usually a very 'raw' collection of machinery, blueprints, rating capacities and engineering schedules, but as time goes by management and operatives gradually come to terms with the new system and 'learn' how to get the most out of it by a judicious mixture of operational change and further investment. According to Arrow, therefore, technological change was largely a function of experience, and hence of *time*. And his ideas were then elaborated and articulated in a number of theoretical models.

However, Arrow's hypothesis (and those of his followers) was seen to be inadequate in a number of respects and in particular in terms of its 'Black Box' nature, where it has the characteristics of a 'catch all' for many unexplained influences. Maxwell who has carried out a detailed literature survey in this field puts it succinctly as follows:

In summary, the main intrinsic defects of the formal learning-by-doing models in terms of offering an empirical specification of actual firm learning processes are:

(i)   The models fail to come to terms with the intrinsic heterogeneity of firm learning processes.

(ii) An unclear picture of the nature of firm learning processes due to the conflation of learning with technical change in general. Failure to incorporate the notion of learning through research as well as learning through 'doing', or to consider the interaction between these two kinds of learning; failure to specify the kinds of problems that give rise to learning, or how learning is accumulated or is wasted.

(iii) A limited picture of the objectives or fruits of learning-by-doing. Only cost reduction is considered.

(iv) No specification of the process whereby learning efforts get translated into technical change.

(v) There is no notion that firms may have a strategy for learning or an organisation to make sure it occurs; nor is it contemplated that firms may deliberately invest in learning via research or training programmes. The internal variables (i.e. firm variables) that affect learning are not characterised at all.

(vi) No specification is presented of the exogeneous variables or constraints that may provoke a firm's learning efforts.

(vii) The models refer only to post start-up learning, and do not incorporate the learning involved in the choice of techniques or in the start-up period of plants, or the carry-over of design experience from older to newer plants.

And hence he concludes:

> These intrinsic defects mean that the formal learning-by-doing models are a quite insufficient empirical guide for policy-makers concerned to promote socially valuable kinds of learning activities in firms in developing countries (or in developed countries for that matter). A much more detailed, close-up and empirically-based account of the nature and determinants of firm learning processes at all stages of the plant life-cycle seems to be needed.[9]

And indeed there have been a number of such studies carried out over the last ten or so years, relating to different industrial sectors in a number of LDCs many of which have concluded that a considerable number of minor or incremental technical changes regularly occur as a result of 'adaptive' learning *and* of conscious investment on the part of LDC firms. More specifically Bell (1985)[10] on the basis of a survey of over 30 case studies on   the development of indigeneous technological capabilities in the third world concluded that:

(i)   Technological changes in *existing* plants are often more significant than those arising as a result of the installation of *new* plants.

(ii)   That technological improvements do not just happen, but on the contrary they arise from conscious commitments of scarce resources.

(iii)   That only in a few cases, however, has post-installation technical change been sufficient to close the gap with world best practice activities.

(iv)   That sometimes state intervention has been instrumental (e.g. public purchasing policies) but never in any systematic way.

(v)   That improvements tend to take place over substantial time periods, often decades in length.

(vi)   That although the development of technological capabilities is located within the firm, in the more successful examples there have been important complementarities with supplier and customer organisations.

On a more conceptual level, writers such as Lall and Bell have attempted to discriminate between different types of learning. Lall,[11] for example, produces a six-fold classification: these are: (i) learning-by-doing; (ii) learning-by-adapting, where imported technology remains unchanged but its utilisation becomes more efficient either through the experience of workers or through minor changes made in a plant; (iii) learning-by-design, where imported technology is replicated and at this stage the setting up of capital goods industry is involved; (iv) learning by improved design, where imported technology is adapted to local materials, conditions and skills. At this stage a separate R & D department is needed; (v) learning-by-setting up complete production systems, where the ability which has already been acquired, is used to set up complete factories and plants to specific needs; (vi) learning-by-designing new processes, where R & D departments extend into basic research and development.

And Bell[12] has gone further by arguing that such learning does not happen automatically but on the contrary requires the commitment of resources on the part of the firm. Hence his own taxonomy is more active including factors such as learning-by-training where the organisation and implementation of technology training programmes takes place; learning-by-hiring, where specialised tasks require hiring of individuals; and learning-by-searching, where disembodied knowledge and information are searched out and acquired by the firm.

It is clearly too early to give a very clear picture of how this new tradition will inform the making and implementation of science and technology policy in LDCs. What is evident, however, is that henceforth it will no longer be acceptable for policy analysts to prescribe blanket remedies like 'protection' or 'unpackaging' as a means to promoting this or that objective. Also account will have to be taken of the organic and systemic attributes of technological changes, including importantly, that of uncertainty.

8.5 Radical Technical Change

This new focus on dynamic technological changes has become concentrated recently on investigations into the actual and likely impact of the 'radically' new technologies associated with the use of the microprocessor in many branches of economic production and distribution. Particularly important here are the effects upon industrialisation prospects for LDCs some of whom have done rather well in this respect in recent years. Such 'newly industrialising countries' (or NICs) have sustained quite rapid rates of industrial growth which has rested on an equally remarkable expansion of manufactured exports. For example, Deirmentzoglou[13] points out that Taiwan, South Korea and Hong Kong grew rapidly between 1965 and 1975 particularly in the areas of clothing, textiles, shoes and leather, and Kaplinsky[14] has shown that progress has taken place in more technologically-based areas like electronics and electrical machinery where, for example, the LDC share of total developed country imports rose from 2.6% in 1967 to 11.9% in 1974.

One mechanism through which such developments have taken place is that of 'off-shore assembly' of specific parts of the production process which are amenable to the employment of unskilled labour.[15] In such cases it has been possible for manufacturing enterprises, usually multinational companies, to 'export' those tasks to poor countries where wages are considerably lower, thereby cutting production costs and providing employment for local labour (often female). Completed sub-assemblies/components etc. are subsequently shipped back to the parent plant for the more technology-intensive final stages of production, quality control and distribution. LDCs have often encouraged such activities through the creation of 'export-processing zones' within which foreign firms have received special fiscal, and other, incentives.

The problem, however, is that modern technological changes associated with developments in microelectronics may be about to reduce dramatically the labour-cost advantages which have sustained the recent progress of the NICs, thereby reversing a trend which some authorities had felt might become a powerful mechanism for the redistribution of income from the rich countries to the poor countries, as we move towards the end of the twentieth century.

Broadly speaking the argument runs as follows. During the period 1950–1970 the electronics sector acted as a significant 'engine of growth' for the industrialised world. Although it was not alone in this respect (for example, the plastics industry clearly also had a major influence), the sequence of events starting with the discovery of the transistor in the 1940s was revolutionary in terms of the sheer range of products and applications which resulted in communications, computers and a wide variety of durable consumer goods including television. By the 1970s, however, this impact had become significantly smaller partly because of market saturation, partly through product cycle effects (see chapter 6) and partly as a result of the onset of world recession. Similar trends were experienced by other industries, and it was at this stage that competition from the NICs began to be felt.

One general response on the part of all manufacturing industry in the rich countries was to seek methods of cost reduction including, importantly, process innovations. These in turn tended on the whole to be labour-saving, capital-using and applicable on large production scales. This meant that the efficiency of investment fell which combined with other factors (like, for example, the OPEC price hike in 1973) had a further dampening effect upon economic growth. However, a major exception to these trends are those firms which produce capital goods incorporating microelectronics technology since it is precisely this technology which forms the basis of a wide variety of 'downstream' cost-reducing innovations. In this way microelectronics represents a focus of technological convergence in Rosenberg's sense, since those firms producing capital goods based upon it have a potential market of practically the whole of manufacturing industry. Examples of uses are:

(a) Product design and process specification (computer-aided design).
(b) The controlled movement of materials and components between work stations (automated transfer systems).
(c) The positioning of components to allow machining.
(d) Temperature, pressure and other controls (scientific instruments).
(e) The cutting, mixing and moulding of metals (numerically controlled machine tools).
(f) The planning of systemic production (office technologies, etc.).

And indeed the rate of technical change here has been dramatic. Freeman, for example, contrasts a complete computer in 1978 contained on a single silicon slice 1 cm^2 in area, costing £10 and comprising 20,000 components, with the 1970 equivalent which would have occupied several rooms and cost more than £100,000.[16] The sheer power of this new technology rests upon its revolutionary contribution to 'time economy' thereby enabling capital goods and production systems based upon it to produce at considerably lower unit cost of *both* capital and labour. This in turn comes about through two key characteristics. *First* a capacity to handle prodigious quantities of information at low unit cost; *secondly* devices using it are highly flexible in so far as they can be programmed to perform a wide range of tasks under very different conditions. These attributes then mean that such devices can often replace human beings in the workplace and produce products to a high degree of accuracy and definition. In addition they can be used as the 'building blocks' of whole production systems approaching, in the limit, the completely automated factory — although this is still some way off.

Hoffman and Rush show in a recent book[17] how technological advances in this field may be classified into two broad types:

a **incremental applications** — where microelectronics based control units have been incorporated into machinery without changing the fundamental design of the equipment.
b **systemic applications** — where the technology is applied in a generic fashion to whole production processes and combinations of processes.

(a)-type advances are clearly far more limited but easier to implement than (b)-type advances and have so far dominated innovation patterns. Nevertheless the authors argue that it is only a matter of time before (b)-type advances become increasingly common. Already they are to be found in the fields of industrial robotics and numerically controlled machine tools where, for example, the machines may be linked together using a hierarchy of computers to perform automatically a wide range of specific functions. Similar developments have taken place with regard to computer-aided design (CAD) systems, thus permitting much swifter responses to market shifts on the part of many areas of manufacturing production.[18]

And the purely economic benefits are likely to be substantial in terms of both labour productivity and capital productivity (more efficient machines and improved capital utilisation). Also further gains may be realised through reductions in training costs of labour (because of the increasingly modular nature of the technology), reductions in inventory costs (because of more efficient production programming), and shorter development lead times — and hence lower development costs. Clearly the reality will depend ultimately on both the inherent dynamism of the new technology and upon the ease with which customer industries can absorb it, but certainly there are evident implications for LDC industrialisation prospects. And here there are two broad views about the expected pattern of diffusion of microelectronics related innovations (MRIs) internationally.

The 'pessimistic' view (from the standpoint of LDCs) is that diffusion will occur much more rapidly within the rich countries thereby overcoming the labour cost advantages of LDCs and shifting the distribution of international income towards the 'centre'. This will arise partly because only in the rich countries has there been sufficient prior investment in the overhead resources involving science and technology necessary for the rapid adoption of MRIs, partly because of smaller 'barriers to entry' of new firms and partly because of the more plentiful supply of risk capital. The 'optimistic' view is that the prospective international pattern of diffusion is much more uncertain. Although on the surface rich countries would appear to have advantages, there are other features of MRIs which favour poorer countries. Hobday,[19] for example, has argued that in an industry like telecommunications, the modular nature of the new technology makes it easier to establish firms in poor countries both because of the relatively 'de-skilled' nature of labour requirements and because there is often little in the way of existing technological practice which needs to be done away with. In addition, the relevant scarce resource is not necessarily the ability to make microprocessors but rather the 'software' required for specific applications. Hence there is no reason why with the right set of technology policies, some LDCs at least could not benefit from MRIs. However, because things appear to be moving so fast in this field, and given the lack of appropriate evidence, there is little in the way of a basis for such policies at the present time.

8.6 Rural Technology Transfer

There is a tendency very often to equate the analysis of technological change exclusively with the process of industrialisation. One reason why this is so is a natural association in people's minds between 'machinery' and 'technology', − 'natural' because most of the technological advances we are aware of are to some degree embodied in equipment of various kinds. But of course, if we refer back to the discussion in chapter 4 you will remember that 'technology' was defined in terms of the conversion of inputs into outputs − if you like, the 'art' of making things − and hence equally applicable to all branches of economic production, including agriculture.

Two other possible reasons behind this relative bias are *first*, the very great stress placed upon industrialisation as the 'cutting edge' of economic development, on the part of a wide range of commentators during the 1960s and early 1970s; and *secondly*, a division of intellectual labour within development studies itself whereby all things 'agricultural' were the province of an (older) academic tradition consisting of anthropologists, rural sociologists, agricultural scientists, soil and water engineers and other associated disciplines. Hence by the time industrial engineers and economists began, relatively late in the day, to take an interest in how modern science and technology might benefit LDCs it was understandable that they should gravitate naturally towards the new industries that were being established and to their respective technological foundations.

However, probably the most important factor leading to the relative neglect of the agricultural sector is that the 'technology' of agricultural transformation is qualitatively different from its industrial counterpart in a number of important respects. Biggs and Clay, for example, have pointed out that agricultural technology is both *biologically unstable* and *locationally specific*[20] in the sense that the efficiency of economic production is indeterminate through time and through space. It is generally to be expected, therefore, that the yield per hectare on a given plot of land will vary widely from one year to another, and from other plots in different geographical areas. And these variations will not in general be under human control since they will depend upon factors such as soil chemistry, the height and composition of ground water, climate, pests, seed type, agronomic practices, crop type and a host of other 'variables' which interact in a complex and uncertain fashion. This inherent uncertainty and lack of replicability has produced an institutional approach to technological changes in LDC agriculture which is quite different from what we are familiar with in the industrial sector, as we shall see later on. For all of these reasons then, science policy analysis in respect of the development of poor rural areas has not really developed very far.

And yet rural development is vitally important for a number of very obvious reasons. In many LDCs the majority of people make their livelihood on the land, often under conditions of great hardship. To the extent that science and technology can assist in improving the productivity of rural resources, and provided the resultant gains can be appropriated by the poor themselves, it must surely be seen as a primary goal of policy makers to ensure that this happens. Moreover, any improvement in rural conditions may help to lessen the drift to the urban areas, thereby creating possibilities for more even regional development and for ameliorating the horrendous living conditions which exist in most urbanised complexes in poor countries.

A third vitally important factor concerns irreversible environmental damage which is now occurring over many parts of the third world. In many parts of sub-Saharan Africa, for example the Sahel or the Ethiopian Highlands, de-forestation has produced considerable soil erosion and desertification of land which up until recently has been capable of supporting much larger populations. Conway[21] has argued forcibly that by concentrating attention on apparently successful innovations, such as those associated with the Green Revolution, agricultural research policy has tended to neglect the longer-term problem of ensuring the ecological stability of our natural environment. In effect planners have placed short-term productivity criteria above those of 'stability', 'sustainability' and 'equity', thereby building up serious problems for future generations, and unless action is taken soon these problems may become virtually insoluble.

Finally, there is the fundamental point that *unless* the rural sector is enabled to develop, its very backwardness will place constraints on industrialisation itself. Thus not only is the rural sector a market for industrial goods, it is also a major source of food and raw materials. Rising food prices (because of shortages) tend to force up money wages and thereby reduce the competitiveness of industrial products. Rising raw material prices hamper the progress of local processing industries. In both cases there tend to result balance of payments pressures as cheaper imports are sucked in while exports stagnate.

8.6.1 Rural Agriculture

Hence for many reasons there is evident need to concentrate on rural development in LDCs and the question from our standpoint is what role can science and technology play in this endeavour? What I have done is to focus the discussion on the subsistence farming sector as the 'key' to science policy in this regard, since not only does it represent the 'productive base' of very many poor countries but at least some of the issues raised have relevance for other sectors as well. Students who wish to explore policy issues in other areas are invited to consult the references at the end of the chapter.

In poor countries dominated by subsistence farming it has long been recognised that technological change requires public sector intervention in some form or other. As far as R & D is concerned the appropriate vehicle is the publicly financed applied research institute set up to perform relevant research regarding particular forms of agricultural product. The expectation has always been that such bodies will produce 'knowledge' which will ultimately benefit the poor farmer.

Here, a major problem has been one of ensuring that scientific advances made in research institutes are communicated to farmers in ways that ensure that derived technological changes can be readily adopted. The traditional means of bringing this about has been the agricultural extension system as portrayed in figure 8.2. Agricultural ministries take on the responsibility of developing technology 'packages' based partly on research material produced by research institutes which are put together in a form which can be understood by subsistence farmers. The actual task of communicating these packages and the provision of relevant material input is given over to extension 'agents', normally secondary school or university graduates who are provided with a little extra training in agricultural development problems and who are normally given responsibility for a certain geographical area.

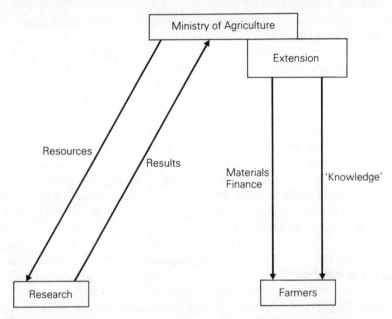

Figure 8.2   Technology transfer in agriculture – the hierarchical model

The general view is that this hierarchical model is fraught with difficulties. To begin with it is enormously expensive in its use of resources. Extension agents have to be trained in a range of appropriate skills and *enough* of them have to be so trained to allow for a reasonable amount of client coverage. However, the sheer magnitude of the problem also defies description since it would not be unreasonable to suppose that in many parts of the third world one extension worker covering 50 villages might be an optimistic scenario. When account is taken of the relative lack of experience of extension personnel, time constraints, language difficulties and distrust of them as 'outsiders' on the part of farmers, it would not be surprising if contemporary evidence concluded that agricultural extension workers have so far had little substantial impact on productive practices in rural agriculture. And indeed it does appear that in many parts of the world extension agencies are able to do little more than scratch the surface of the problem.[22]

This brings me to a third factor, that of the sheer complexity of agricultural technology. Since, as argued above, this is essentially *systemic* and *locationally specific* the character of technical change is not something that the isolated extension workers can handle. Yields per hectare will only rise to a new best-practice plateau where *all* the necessary 'elements' in the technology 'package' are handled correctly. Simply to introduce changes in one or two components will not do the job — indeed it may actually reduce output and incomes with devastating effects on poor families, which brings me to a fourth factor, that of risk and uncertainty. The perceived risks to the farmer in changing established practices are very great simply because he is normally operating at or near subsistence level. This produces an inherent *asymmetry*. If a recommended change turns out to be successful, perceptions of risks with respect to any subsequent change are not likely to change significantly. If, however, it turns out to be unsuccessful, the farmer may take the view (not unreasonably) that henceforth representatives of agricultural extension systems are not to be trusted.

A fifth problem with this approach is that it tends to take little account of traditional 'informal' R & D which, according to Bell,[23] represents an important and continual source of technological change in subsistence agriculture. Institutionally it does not facilitate the integration of 'traditional knowledge' into the 'technology packages' of the extension agents. Nor in general are these agents in a position to carry out this sort of integration exercise themselves. Finally note should be taken of the ways in which local political interests shape the orientation of agricultural development assistance in ways which benefit particular ethnic groups and particular classes of farmer (often the larger capitalist farmer).[24]

Hence, the vertical, specialised and hierarchical system of agricultural extension may be seen as costly, clumsy and inefficient. Nevertheless, there are two major reasons why it continues to be the dominant mode of rural technological change in many poor countries, and these relate to vested interests and perception of employment. Thus in most LDCs there is now a substantial public bureaucracy associated with the provision of extension services and ancillary activities. To close such a bureaucracy down or to alter radically its nature would in most cases be seen as threatening jobs and resisted accordingly.

A second reason concerns the professionalisation of agricultural science and the ways in which agricultural scientists view, and value, their own work. Here 'good science', in the sense of the empirical pursuit of knowledge, can only really be practised under conditions of controlled experimentation i.e. on experimental stations where results can be reached which are independent of interfering factors. Conversely, one cannot achieve replicable and publishable results by 'experimenting' directly with subsistence agriculture. Given the reward system associated with science as a 'profession', therefore, it would be very surprising indeed if agricultural scientists strayed much beyond the confines of their laboratories and trial plots. Far simpler, is it not, to pass the job of transferring 'knowledge' to another branch of the public services? And indeed this is now very often standard practice, the justification being that the proper role for the agricultural scientist is that of the establishment of 'basic principles' the detailed application of which is somebody else's concern.

8.6.2 Farming Systems

In recent years the 'top down' model of diffusion of agricultural technology has been confronted by an alternative model of technology transfer in which relations between science and production are viewed in a decentralised holistic way. Here the focus is directly on the geographical location as the locus of developmental attention with scientific inputs considered as only one resource along with many others necessary to raise yields per hectare, including for example the 'informal' knowledge possessed by the farmers themselves, as well as material inputs (seed, fertilisers etc.) and credit provided by central agencies.

There have been a number of recent examples of this approach sometimes called the 'farming systems' approach, to agricultural development.[25] I shall use one with which I am familiar as an examplar but many of its features will be found in other examples of this genre. In this particular case a watershed of 2,000–3,000 ha. was made the focus of concern.[26] Scientists from a local research institute were charged with a directly productive function − that of increasing yields per hectare over the whole cultivable area, with particular attention being given to the smaller farmer. Hence they were forced into a position of having to pool their various specialist types of knowledge within a given productive context and were not able to leave technology transfer to a public bureaucracy.

More specifically the elements of this approach are:

(i)   The existing 'technology' was surveyed for the area and the key deficiencies isolated and defined, particularly those affecting the smaller farmer.

(ii)   On the basis of this diagnosis and other inputs, an optimum 'package' was decided upon i.e. crop types, agronomic practices, soil/water improvements, fertilizer inputs etc.

(iii)   The scientists then worked with the farmers (in an interdisciplinary way) in a phased programme of implementation, feeding *scientific* problems back to the research station where necessary, and seeking assistance from government agencies where the obstacles were of a more practical nature (e.g. finance, seed availability).

(iv)   Farmers were encouraged to use their own investment resources but were guaranteed against financial loss in the first few years.

(v)   There was constant monitoring of technical and social transformation so as to change strategies where necessary.

(vi)   There was the expectation that imitation outside the project area would begin to occur through a process of technological diffusion (though one operating through a causal mechanism of differential *incomes* rather than differential *prices*).

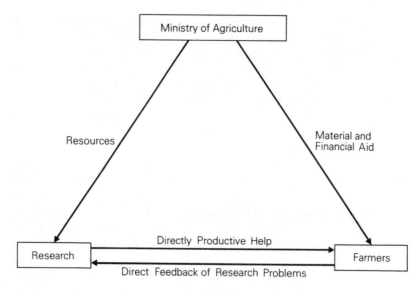

Figure 8.3   Technology transfer in agriculture − the decentralised model

Essentially, therefore, this project represented a different model of agricultural extension, one in which the transfer of technology was attempted in a decentralized, holistic and horizontal manner with potentially much less involvement of the bureaucratic hierarchy and with the concentration of resources into a geographical area within which similar techno-economic problems would be faced. Farmers were provided with very little in the way of a *direct* subsidy. On the other hand they *were* guaranteed against losses and the expectation of the model was that improved practices would be taken in neighbouring areas through a process of emulation and diffusion, the technology being modified to meet changing conditions as required. Figure 8.3 provides a rough sketch which can be compared with figure 8.2.

One way of viewing farming systems projects of this type is with reference to the notion of the technological 'paradigm' or 'trajectory' outlined in chapter 6. Here the paradigm is defined in terms of a geographical area and is 'articulated' in a practical context with a continuing set of problems (both productive and scientific) being thrown up as a result of experience. Some of these were dealt with at a common-sense level by project staff. Others required external help of a bureaucratic kind (e.g. supply of materials fr^{om} overseas *or* the state government). Still others needed further research in the research stations. Under such a regime the project organisers can never 'get things right' simply because the set of 'right' conditions can never be independently defined. Also, since conditions are constantly changing, all that project staff can be expected to do is to deal with problems as they arise in a 'satisficing' manner, the ultimate test being the extent to which project 'goals' are being met.

Here we have something akin to a 'biological' model of social development in which scientific and technological activities lend a continuous dynamic to the productive process which itself throws up scientific problems requiring feedback to the research system in a continuing series of linkages. One would imagine that these relations would continue to exist so long as this 'geographically' determined technological paradigm remained socially productive i.e. until research constraints of the area have been as fully resolved as they are likely to be, given the level of development of the basic scientific disciplines and the institutional character of agricultural production in that area.

Notice that such an approach requires the scientific community to view its professional role in a radically different way from that which it has come to expect as normal. Instead of professional goals being defined in terms of differentiated, replicable and controlled experiments, the results being published in reputable refereed journals, scientists are being asked to take on attributes of the entrepreneur and the manager. They are also being asked to relate to each other across disciplinary boundaries, including importantly those of the social sciences. No longer is it considered sufficient for the scientist to produce a 'shelf' of knowledge as his or her sole contribution while the *application* of this knowledge becomes the responsibility of some other person or group. On the contrary, the transfer of agricultural technology is seen to be akin to its industrial counterpart where successful innovations usually involve close interchange between the 'producer' and the 'consumer' of technology. Undoubtedly such a new professional role will be resisted strongly. There is, however, a growing amount of evidence that existing arrangements are in need of reform, and the farming systems approach gives at least a promise of more fruitful results in this sphere.

8.7 Indigeneous Science and Science and Technology Planning in LDCs

It is probably useful at this stage to summarise the main drift of the discussion. Questions of science policy as they relate to developing countries concern how best such countries should commit scarce resources to acquiring the benefits of and minimising the costs of modern science and technology in their quest for economic and social development. Historically access has been secured through two broad channels.

(i)   The transfer of production technologies from enterprises registered and located mainly in the industrialised countries.
(ii)   The attempt on the part of governments to invest in a scientific infrastructure consisting of a range of institutions felt to be necessary for the eventual integration of science into the social fabric.

In sections 8.2–8.5 we concentrated very much on the first of these, on the various ways in which the social transfer of foreign technology often produces results which are not in the best interests of LDCs; however, the second channel, touched on in section 8.4 and section 8.6, is clearly also germane and I should like to end this chapter with a brief discussion on the functioning of indigenous scientific systems in LDCs (and what often goes wrong with them) and with one or two points about possibilities for 'science planning'.

The major problem appears to be that research institutions established to provide a 'scientific base' which will contribute towards developmental goals, do not in fact perform this function well. Instead they become very often centres of 'academic' employment, ivory towers isolated from much of what is going on around them and increasingly oriented towards the norms and goals of the international scientific community, which they try to emulate as best they can under what are often unfavourable conditions. One reason why this happens is a lack of a social demand for their services on the part of the productive sector, where it is clearly far simpler to import a foreign technology which is known to work commercially.

A second reason concerns the way in which scientific institutions are staffed and structured – which follows very much the 'Western' model of disciplinary based organisations where scientists are provided with the facilities to follow the path of their own intellectual concerns. Once such a structural pattern has become established it is extraordinarily difficult for a research director to gear a research programme to the needs of external 'client' groups. And even where it is feasible to do so in one period (i.e. where the profile of scientific and technical skills is congruent with socio-economic requirements), it is certain that as times change mismatches will increasingly arise. Such has been the overwhelming experience in many LDCs. Furthermore academic alienation of this type tends to deepen since in the face of lack of demand for their services research institutions tend gradually to sink back into the role that they know best – that of the disinterested pursuit of knowledge – often encouraged by the organisations which provide them with their resources, the 'science councils' which themselves are staffed by senior scientists brought up in the old disciplinary tradition.

There are two broad views about this 'alienation of the scientific community in LDCs'. Writers like Moravcsik[27] and Roche,[28] for example, argue that although there are problems in the short term, these represent the price that must be paid for long-term institution-building. What is necessary is the creation of a 'scientific fabric' where habits of sound scholarship and rigorous experimentation are instilled in a critical minimum number of people and institutions. And this may take a long time. Eventually the expectation is that healthy relations between 'science' and 'production' will evolve somewhat along the lines typical of those in the industrialised world.

The opposite view, which is the one that I hold myself, is that such prospects for institution-building are altogether too sanguine. To begin with, the need for economic progress is very pressing and there is arguably a strong case for concentrating the resources to which LDCs can get access (including those relating to science and technology) directly on this major goal. Since a very large proportion of scientifically trained personnel is concentrated within the publicly-financed research and university system, this in itself implies the need for a radically different role for such institutions. Viewed in this way the (modernising) comparison with scientific systems in rich countries is misconceived since in those parts of the world the preoccupation of publicly-financed scientific research is with 'big science' (space, energy) or with armaments production (weapons research of various kinds). Conversely the purely 'economic' impact of science is left largely to the workings of the economic system itself as a series of 'spin-offs' which can be handled by already existing institutional arrangements. In any case the 'modernising' approach tends to avoid the important science policy questions in LDCs. The creation and institutionalisation of science as a resource is a very costly business indeed. The bodies in which scientists work are expensive to build and to maintain, as is the equipment and materials which they need to pursue their professional concerns. Unless conscious policies are developed and executed to carry out these aspects of social investment, the amount of social waste may be very large indeed.

8.7.1 Science Planning

But if science is to be consciously planned, how is this to be done? Can existing institutional mechanisms be used or will new ones have to be created? And how efficiently can the whole process be made to work? One obvious possibility, is to tie the making of science policy to the institutional process of national development planning. The argument is very simply that if expenditure upon science and technology has a rationale which is fundamentally economic and developmental, then this must be reflected in appropriate institutional arrangements. The process of development planning at its most general consists in setting targets for the various elements of national output and in mobilising investment resources to enable these targets to be met. There are usually additional mechanisms for reconciling inter-sectoral inconsistencies and for continuous plan revision during the planning period so as to allow for unforeseen circumstances. The comprehensiveness of plans depends further upon a variety of factors including the ideological political climate, the degree of general institutional development, the ability of the civil service and the quality of available social data.[29]

A moment's reflection, however, will indicate that while an organisational exercise of this kind might prove very useful as a rough overall guide (and certainly a number of LDCs now possess administrative machinery of a comparable kind), considerable problems still remain. There is in general, for example, no one-to-one correspondence between research 'inputs' and productivity 'outputs', especially at the level of detailed sub-sectors. Nor in any case, can scientific and technological inputs be regarded as relatively short-term inputs even if adequate statistics existed to quantify them. Furthermore we have seen that at least with respect to some aspects of science and technology, institutional structures have already been created and have established a bureaucratic momentum of their own. To force them into a radically different mould would be a difficult and possibly wasteful task, and might well run into the type of problems experienced by the Rothschild reforms in the UK — more bureaucratic expense but little in the way of substantive functional change.

However, to the extent that structural change is required for the science community in LDCs — and at the very least there is a case to answer — it is clear that governments will need to instigate reforms. Whatever these are (and they will vary widely across countries) they will probably need to be informed by the following:

(a)   Mechanisms to ensure that the professionalisation of science follows a pattern which is consistent with indigenous objectives, and is not simply a carbon copy of the Western model. Here the points of interdisciplinarity and developmental orientation, made above, apply.

(b)   A similar injunction applies to the institutionalisation of science and technology in terms of the structure, functioning and finance of establishments and parts of establishments.

(c)   Mechanisms to ensure that government agencies for planning science are linked to all potential sources of science and technology. There is no point, for example, in taking decisions about the development of indigenous technologies independently of those taken on the import of comparable foreign technologies.

(d)   Mechanisms to ensure flexibility and adaptability on the part of agencies charged with funding scientific and technological activities. In this way allowance may be made both for the unpredictability of much scientific work and also so as to counteract the tendency towards bureaucratic rigidity.

(e)   Mechanisms to ensure that overall development planning is closely integrated at all levels with scientific developments.

(f)   Mechanisms to ensure that sources of indigenous technology are fully utilised in an integral fashion with other resources.

(g)   Mechanisms to ensure that sectoral ministries are fully aware of the technological requirements necessary for the execution of departmental functions.

To stress these points, however, is really to say very little since the making of effective science and technology policy is something that can only be carried through effectively by those who have a deep knowledge of the relevant social, political and economic context. I suspect that a primary ingredient is a healthy scepticism about the benefits of Western science and technology combined with a willingness to take on board those aspects which appear to hold out most promise for long-run success. Whatever and however this is done, it is certain that the institutional context will be of fundamental importance. And there ought to be no automatic presupposition that the institutional forms appropriate to, say, the USA in 1985 should have relevance to the development prospects of countries at quite different 'stages' who may wish to choose radically different paths for the future.

Bibliography

It is difficult to find texts which give adequate coverage to all the major issues. However, students may care to consult F. Stewart, *Technology and Development* (London, Macmillan, 1977), F. Stewart and J. James (eds.), *The Economics of New Technology in Developing Countries* (London, Frances Pinter, 1982). C. Cooper (ed.), *Science, Technology and Development* (London, Frank Cass, 1973) and M. Fransman, 'Technology in the Third World: an Interpretive Survey', *Journal of Development Studies* (forthcoming). On appropriate technology, see E. F. Schumacher, *Small is Beautiful* (London, Bland and Briggs, 1973), N. Jequier (ed.), *Appropriate Technology: Problems and Promises* (Paris, Development Centre, OECD, 1976), C. Cooper, 'Choice of Techniques and Technological Change as Problems in Political Economy', *International Social Science Journal*, Vol. XXV, No. 3, 1973. On the development of LDC capacities for technological change, see M. Fransman and K. King (eds.), *Technological Capability in the Third World* (London, Macmillan, 1984). On radical technological change a useful review volume for the case of microelectronics is H. K. Hoffman (ed.), *Micro-electronics, International Competition and Development Strategies: The Unavoidable Issues*, Special Issue of *World Development*, January 1985. See also R. Kaplinsky, *Computer-Aided Design: Electronics, Comparative Advantage and Development* (London, Frances Pinter, 1982).

On problems of technical change and rural development K. Griffin, *The Political Economy of Agrarian Change* (London, Macmillan, 1974) is a good survey of the Green Revolution. For a discussion on the relations between science and agricultural production, see S. Biggs and E. Clay, 'Sources of Innovation in Agricultural Technology', *World Development*, Vol. 9, No. 4, 1981, and N. G. Clark, 'The Economic Behaviour of Research Institutions in Developing Countries: Some Methodological Points', *Social Studies of Science*, Vol. 10, No. 1, 1980. An important general source with an extensive bibliography is S. Biggs and E. Clay, 'Generation and Diffusion of Agricultural Technology', *Technology and Employment Programme*, ILO, Geneva, August 1983. A useful annotated bibliography on problems of rural energy is contained in A. Barnett, M. Bell and K. Hoffman, *Rural Energy and the Third World* (Oxford, Pergamon, 1982).

Notes

1 G. Myrdal, *Economic Theory and Underdeveloped Regions* (London, Methuen, 1964).
2 Martin Bell has pointed out to me that even now over 90%, he estimates, of trade in technology is carried out *between* the industrialised countries. Hence the transfer of technology between rich and poor countries is a small fraction of the total, although of course very important for the development prospects of poor countries.
3 C. M. Cooper and F. Sercovitch, *The Channels and Mechanisms for the Transfer of Technology from Developed to Developing Countries* (Geneva, UNCTAD, TD/B/AC.11/5, 27 April 1971). For discussions on this 'early view' of technology transfer, see also F. Stewart, 'Technology and Employment in LDCs', *World*

Development, Vol. 2, No. 3, March 1974, pp. 17–46 and N. G. Clark, 'The Multinational Company, The Transfer of Technology and Dependence', *Development and Change*, Vol. 6, No. 1, June 1975.

4 E. F. Schumacher, 'Industrialisation through Intermediate Technology', in R. Robinson (ed.), *Developing the third world; The Experience of the Sixties* (London, Cambridge University Press, 1971), pp. 85–93.

5 Stewart, 'Technology and Employment in LDCs', pp. 21, 22.

6 Stewart, 'Technology and Employment in LDCs', p. 22. This particular volume of *World Development* contains a number of useful articles on this general theme. For a more formal treatment see G. K. Helleiner, 'The Role of Multinational Corporations in the Less Developed Countries' Trade in Technology', *World Development*, Vol. 3, No. 4, April 1975, pp. 161–89.

7 For a description of some of this work see C. V. Vaitsos, *Intercountry Income Distribution and Transnational Enterprises* (Oxford, Clarenden, 1974). See also UNCTAD, *Major Issues Arising from the Transfer of Technology to Developing Countries* (Geneva, TD/B/AC.11/10, 18 December 1972).

8 K. Arrow, 'The Economic Implications of Learning-by-Doing', *Review of Economic Studies*, Vol. 29, June 1962, pp. 155–73.

9 P. M. Maxwell, *Technology Policy and Firm Learning Effects in Less-Developed Countries*, D.Phil Thesis, University of Sussex (SPRU), 1981, pp. 34, 35.

10 R. M. N. Bell, *Technical Change in Infant Industries: A Review of Empirical Evidence*, World Bank Staff Working Paper (forthcoming 1985).

11 S. Lall, 'Developing Countries as Exporters of Industrial Technology', *Research Policy*, Vol. 9, No. 1, January 1980, pp. 24–53.

12 R. M. N. Bell, ' "Learning" and the Accumulation of Industrial Technological Capacity in Developing Countries', in Fransman and King, *Technological Capability in the Third World*, pp. 187–210.

13 A. Deirmentzoglou, *Technological and Structural Change in the Greek Textiles Industry*, D.Phil Thesis, University of Sussex (SPRU), 1983.

14 R. Kaplinsky, 'Radical Change and Manufactured Export Growth Strategies', IDS, University of Sussex, 1980 (mimeo).

15 For a useful discussion of the mechanics of this, see for example, G. K. Helleiner, 'Manufactured Exports from less Developed Countries and Multinational Firms', *Economic Journal*, Vol. 83, No. 329, March 1973, pp. 21–47.

16 C. Freeman, 'The Kondratiev Long Waves, Technical Change and Unemployment', in OECD, *Structural Determinants of Employment and Unemployment* (Paris, OECD), Vol. 2, p. 193.

17 H. K. Hoffman and H. Rush, *Microelectronics and Clothing: The Impact of Technical Change on a Global Industry*, Geneva, ILO, 1985.

18 Kaplinsky, 'Radical Change and Manufactured Export Growth Strategies'.

19 M. Hobday, 'The Impact of Microelectronic Change on Developing Countries: The Case of Brazilian Telecommunications', *Development and Change*, Vol. 17, No. 1, January 1975.

20 Biggs and Clay, 'Sources of Innovation in Agricultural Technology', Martin Bell has pointed out to me that there are important senses in which *industrial* technology is also locationally specific. However, I would argue still that there is a qualitative difference between the two forms.

21 G. R. Conway, *Rural Resource Conflicts in the UK and the Third World: Issues for Research Policy*, Papers in Science, Technology and Public Policy. No. 6, Imperial College/SPRU/TCC, 1984.

22 For example, see D. Leonard, *Reaching the Peasant Farmers* (Chicago, University of Chicago Press, 1977).

23 R. M. N. Bell, 'The Exploitation of Indigenous Knowledge, or the Indigenous Exploitation of Knowledge: Whose Use of What for What?', *IDS Bulletin*, Vol. 10, No. 2, University of Sussex, 1979. Edward Clay has pointed out to me the importance of viewing indigenous knowledge as essentially dynamic, constantly evolving in response to changing contextual conditions.

24 Leonard, *Reaching the Peasant Farmers*.

25 There is a growing literature on farming systems. Useful sources are D. Byerlee and M. Collinson et al., *Planning Technologies Appropriate to Farmers: Concepts and Procedures*, CIMMYT, Mexico, 1980. D. W. Norman, 'The Farming Systems Approach: Relevancy for the Small Farmer', *MSU Rural Development Paper*, No. 5, East Lancing, Department of Agricultural Economics, Michigan State University, 1980. On the rather different notion of 'on-farm research' see S. Biggs 'Generating Agricultural Technology: Triticale for the Himalayan Hills', *Food Policy*, Vol. 7, February 1982, pp. 69–82.

26 N. G. Clark and E. J. Clay, 'The Operations Research Project at Indore (1974–80) – An Institutional Innovation in Rural Technology Transfer', mimeo (SPRU/IDS), University of Sussex, January 1984.

27 M. Moravscik, 'The Effectiveness of Research in Developing Countries', *Social Studies of Science*, Vol. 12, No. 1, February 1982, pp. 144–6. See also in same volume, pp. 147–50, N. G. Clark, 'Reply to Moravscik'.

28 M. Roche, 'Social Aspects of Science in a Developing Country', *Impact*, UNESCO, Vol. XVI, No. 1, 1966.

29 A useful treatment of many of these points is contained in K. Griffin and J. Enos, *Planning Development* (London, Addison-Wesley, 1971). On 'science planning' more generally, see F. Sagasti, *Science and Technology for Development* (Ottawa, IDRC/STPI/109e, 1978).

Chapter 9

CONTEMPORARY ISSUES OF SCIENCE AND TECHNOLOGY POLICY

9.1 Introduction

In the previous chapter I summarised a series of policy issues in so far as these reflect the impact of science and technology on third world countries. I wish now to turn to questions of science and technology policy in the industrialised countries, to explore how economic analysis does (or does not) inform such issues and to examine the extent to which analyses of this kind can actually help policy makers make sensible decisions both in mobilising resources *to* science and in coping with the social effects of such mobilisation. Since there are very many issues of great relevance which could be treated in this way, I have been forced through reasons of space to choose those which I feel are most representative for the purposes in hand. The issue of 'employment' or 'lack of employment' arising out of modern technological developments is clearly an important one both because of its very great social relevance and because it illustrates how very complex indeed are the underlying socio-economic relations. That of the sheer 'bigness' and 'irreversibility' of large-scale projects is also very important, but it raises the extra dimension of the association between the artifacts of modern science and technology and vested interests of a variety of different kinds, interests which in many respects give the development of modern capitalism the character of a juggernaut, increasingly uncontrollable by traditional political processes.

On the side of 'science', I have chosen to examine both the practice of monitoring and commissioning applied research through the customer/contractor principle as put forward by the Rothschild Report in 1971 in an attempt to orientate applied science more directly to its 'constituency' of social relevance, *and* the question of how best to evaluate the activities of basic science. Increasingly the last issue is taking the attention of policy makers if only because of the very large sums of money frequently spent, as for example in nuclear physics and radio-astronomy. Equally relevant, however, are questions about whether the overall pattern of scientific research is optimal and, if not, in which way should it change. Inevitably again I shall not be able to give anything like an adequate treatment to any of these topics, but I hope to be able to say enough to give students a flavour of the analytical problems involved. In the final section I shall return to a theme which was introduced in the first chapter, namely that the nature of science policy analysis is such that neither economics nor any other discipline can provide an adequate conceptual background for its elucidation. In this respect we are very much in a pre-paradigmatic phase − casting around for conceptual structures which will provide an adequate organising metaphor for systematic policy analysis.

9.2 Policy Issues

9.2.1 Employment

The problem of unemployment arising from the introduction of major technological changes is one which has its roots early in the development of industrial capitalism when, as we saw in chapter 2, the nature of economic production became radically more susceptible/vulnerable in this respect. One of the best known examples of this was the destruction of whole communities whose livelihood had been gained through hand-loom weaving[1] but there have been, and continue to be throughout the world, repeated cases of people's livelihoods becoming threatened in this way. Here we have a considerable moral dilemma. Do we value employment for its own sake − as an essential and vital aspect of the lives of all people and one through which the development of the human personality ultimately takes place? Certainly this view has been held in one form or another by most of the major religions and by many important social philosophies, including that of Marx, but as Routh[2] points out it is not the neo-classical view. The philosophical foundations of modern economics hold that 'work' is painful and, therefore, that people have to be bribed to do it. Conversely 'goods' are positive phenomena, naturally desired in increasing quantities by all rational beings, so that the greater the wages paid to compensate for the 'pain' of work, the greater the quanta of goods available for enjoyment. The laws of supply and demand immediately become operable, such that differentiated labour markets determine the distribution of income amongst occupations. Under this view technological unemployment is merely the price that one pays for social progress, regrettable but necessary − and sometimes made worse by the 'irrationality' of the affected workers and conservative trade unions.

In recent years the issue has become focused on the 'new technology' associated with the introduction of the microprocessor. Cooper and Clark point out that this

> is not some single technique but a set of new approaches to the organisation and control of production, which have become conceivable because of dramatic reductions in the costs of microelectronics systems, and commensurately dramatic advances in their power and flexibility[3]

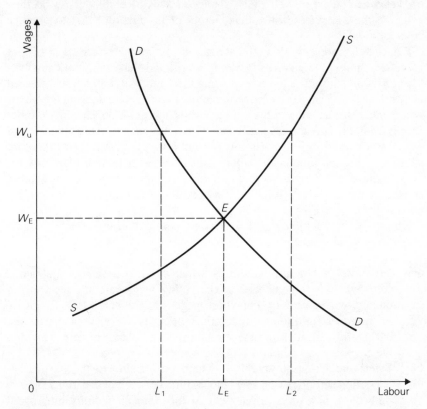

Figure 9.1   Aggregate labour market

Students are referred to the section on radical technical changes in the previous chapter for a fuller discussion on the ways in which microprocessor technology impinges on the economic system as a whole. The 'pessimistic' view is that the introduction of microprocessor technology will create conditions of permanent unemployment for a substantial proportion of the employable population, while those of a more phlegmatic persuasion believe that in practice this will not be so. Where one stands on this issue depends upon one's analysis of how the new technology will permeate through the economic system and what 'compensating mechanisms' exist to ensure that change takes place quickly. The notion of compensation[4] is important since it describes, or attempts to describe, the capacity of the economic system in question to diffuse the benefits of the technological change in such a way that new employment opportunities arise to replace jobs that have been lost.

We shall return to this point below, but first let us describe how economic analysis conventionally defines the problem in terms of a simplified labour market where workers sell their labour services to employers, who then combine these services with other factors of production so as to produce commodities.

Figure 9.1 represents an aggregate labour market where the supply curve SS reflects individual choices between 'work' and 'leisure'. Work involves 'disutility' and therefore in order to bring forth more of it higher wages need to be offered. The curve *DD* reflects employers' collective demand for labour which increases as wage rates fall and whose position depends upon other factors, notably income levels, technical conditions and the availability of capital stock. Equilibrium exists only at point *E* where on average workers are supplying just the amount of labour consistent with their preferences for income and leisure, and where employers are employing just that amount consistent with their profit-maximising ambitions (an important underlying assumption).

On this basis 'unemployment' is viewed as a market imperfection which may take several forms:

a   **Involuntary Unemployment** − which arises where more labour is supplied than is demanded at the ruling wage rate W_u resulting in unemployment of L_1L_2, but where wages are prevented from falling by institutional rigidities or restrictive practices, very often due to the bargaining activities of trade unions or to a deficiency of demand within the economy as a whole.

b   **Frictional Unemployment** − which occurs due to the normal re-allocation activities whereby labour shifts between occupations. At any time there is always an element of this even in a 'fully employed' economy.

c   **Structural Unemployment** − which happens as a result of very rapid structural shifts in economic production, usually associated with the decline of older industries, concentrated in particular regions and hence leading to overall regional decline. Within the UK, Merseyside, Central Scotland, South Wales and Northern Ireland are examples of regions where structural unemployment has become particularly severe.

d   **Seasonal Unemployment** − arising where the demand for labour only occurs at particular times of the year, e.g. at harvest periods in poor countries.

e **Disguised Unemployment** – which is the term used to connote the relatively unproductive use of labour, mainly in poor countries where work is shared so as to ensure incomes for a greater proportion of the working population. What the term means is that labour may be withdrawn from existing activities without a proportionate loss of output, so that the existing pattern of labour use is to that extent sub-optimal.

9.2.2 Compensation Effects

How then does improved technology affect this stylised labour market? In general there are a number of social processes which tend to *compensate* for the labour displacing effects of an innovation. These may be classified under three broad headings:

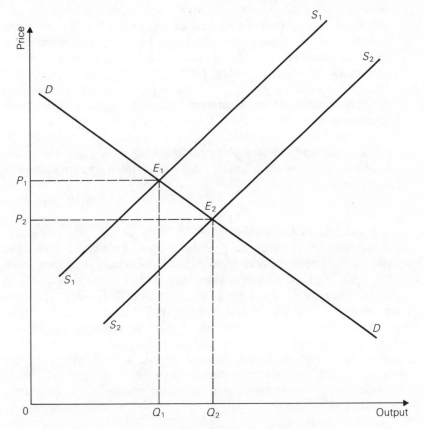

Figure 9.2 The effect of a process innovation on price and output

1   **Endogenous Adjustments** Figure 9.2 represents the result of a process innovation in any industry, which reduces unit production costs (and therefore labour requirements) and hence unit price. S_2S_2 represents the new supply function (shifted from S_1S_1) resulting in a movement from E_1 to E_2, for price and quantity bought and sold in equilibrium. Under such conditions there is clearly the possibility for some re-employment due to the expansion of output, the actual amount being determined by the slope of the demand function and the nature of the technological change which has taken place (i.e. how labour-saving it is).

2   **Exogenous Adjustments** These arise by virtue of the income effects of technological change. A fall in the price of commodities implies a rise in real incomes for the consumers who purchase them and the likelihood of increased demands for other goods, including the capital goods required for bringing about innovations. To the extent this happens, demand for other goods will increase leading to increases in employment in the relevant sectors and to further 'multiplier' increases in the economy as a whole. A second form of exogenous adjustment are the increased demands for complementary goods, of the kind discussed in chapter 6 under the general rubric of 'long cycles' of economic activity.

3   **Government Counter-Cyclical Policy** You will recall from the discussion in chapter 5 that it is possible for governments to deal with generalised unemployment through various forms of compensatory adjustment using monetary and fiscal policies. Clearly where very radical technical changes have occurred leading to a considerable degree of generalised unemployment, it is always open to governments to do precisely this and to attempt to deal with inflationary pressures in other ways.

Two points should be evident from the argument so far – *first*, the relationship between technical change and employment is a very complex one involving an intricate mechanism of social change; *secondly*, there is no need in general for technical changes, even very radical ones, *necessarily* to increase unemployment. Hence where unemployment *has* tended apparently to increase it may well be that labour-saving technical change has been an important contributing factor. On the other hand there may equally have been other influences at work which in causal terms are rather more important. Commonly cited examples are international recessionary conditions, changes in the way in which unemployment statistics are calculated, increased female participation in the labour force, and exogenous changes in labour market conditions.

An important example of the last of these has been identified by Gershuny and his colleagues at SPRU over the last few years.[5] Using time-budget data on household activity, Gershuny has concluded that an important effect of technical changes in certain industrial sectors (particularly consumer durables) has been to encourage householders to substitute their own labour time for the services that they used to buy commercially. To the extent that such 'do-it-yourself' activities spread throughout the economic system, the traditional role of the service sector for 'mopping up' labour, made redundant from manufacturing, may change radically in future years, leading in turn to the need for innovations in *social* policy to cope with what may well become a serious problem of income distribution as we move towards the end of the present century.

For very many reasons, then, the policy prescriptions in this area require a diagnosis which is infinitely more detailed than a simple concentration upon the apparent labour-saving nature of technological change would warrant. But let me return to the point made at the very beginning of this section regarding how one views employment as a personal and social activity, so as to highlight the important role that ideology plays in policy analysis. Those who believe that it is bad in a fundamental sense to alter radically people's working conditions, and occasionally the communities which depend upon threatened industries, will always find it difficult to accept technological change, notwithstanding whatever compensating mechanisms exist to 're-employ' those thus made redundant. But this should not be dismissed as mere 'Luddism', since what is in question is a fundamental debate about how 'commodities' and 'employment' should be valued relatively at this stage in the development of industrial capitalism. It may well be that the imperatives of international competition will compromise the autonomy of any one country to slow down the pace of technological change should it wish to do so. But this does not mean that there is not an important objective problem involved. To abdicate from engagement with such issues, does not in general make for good analytical practice.

9.2.3 The Planning and Control of Complex Technology

A recurrent theme throughout this textbook has been the association between the developments of modern technology and the systemic complexity of its artifacts, enshrined as they often are in huge projects involving very large sums of capital investment and lengthy development lead times, and removed from public comprehension by many layers of bureaucracy associated with an 'expertise' of impenetrable obscurity. In recent years spectacular examples, such as Concorde, the Windscale Inquiry and the recent controversy regarding the installation of a nuclear reactor at Sizewell, have focused public attention on a problem which has in fact been around for some time and shows every sign of becoming more severe.

In general there are three broad types of explanation for this growing 'rigidity' or 'fixity' in modern complex systems. The first of these is the growing *involvement of government* itself partly because the inherently expensive and risky nature of modern R & D combined with the belief that international competitiveness depends upon it, forces the state into action, and partly very often because of strategic military considerations. Once governments get involved, so the arguments run, the management of research becomes a matter for a civil service machine which finds it difficult to tolerate uncertainty not least because the normal business of running a modern nation state is a complex enough task by itself. An almost inevitable result is an attachment to given 'technological paradigms' (or 'solutions') which become guiding principles for the bureaucracy and which are only capable of being shifted with considerable effort. Indeed it has been argued by some that whole traditions of conduct become embedded into the hierarchies of the civil service such that younger staff feel inevitably constrained to adhere closely to the established canon.[6] Deviation is seen as lack of 'soundness' which may well compromise a promising career.

A second factor is the Galbraithian argument outlined at the end of chapter 6. Much of modern industrial technology is now so inherently systemic and large scale that only large organisations are able to mobilise the necessary resources, and 'hedge' against the risks of market or technical failure. Even where smaller firms are apparently able to enter into particular 'high technology' sectors it is usually the case either that they are associated in some fashion with larger combines *or* that they get taken over once their corporate lives have reached a given stage of development. In this way even the private sector has become dominated by large enterprises, corporate in their organisational structures, and immensely powerful in terms of their control over finance and their influence with government itself. Such corporations try wherever possible to control the technological and economic environment in such a way as to maintain activity along tried and true paths, although their ability to do so is not as complete as that of the government.

Finally, there are the neo-Marxist arguments of writers such as Baran and Sweezy which argue that there are inherent tendencies to under-consumption in modern capitalist economies, which can only be resolved by direct activity on the part of the state. In their book *Monopoly Capitalism*, Baran and Sweezy[7] see the 'permanent arms economy' as a means of 'realising' production surpluses which not only does not threaten established class positions (as would, for example, social investments on behalf of disadvantaged groups) but also appeases powerful military castes. Moreover an arms race with an enemy, conducted under conditions of great secrecy, has the added advantage that it is an insatiable user of resources which very rapidly become obsolete and have then to be replaced. Once substantial armaments and related industries get established the power of vested interests keeps things going along established paths, rendering any adjustment to an alternative use of resources at best marginal, and in practice increasingly unlikely.

Undoubtedly, there are elements of all three factors present. For example, Pavitt and Warboys[8] have provided us with an interesting summary of the main features of the well-known 'military/industrial complex' which include a high economic and geographical concentration closely locked into government defence departments, an overtly political justification for the pattern of public expenditures and close links with 'academic science'. And more recently Kaldor in her book *The Baroque Arsenal* portrays a terrifying scenario of a runaway military/technological machine which absorbs an increasing proportion of national resources but produces little in the way of benefit, even of a military kind.

> The outcome of this contradictory process, in which technology is simultaneously promoted and restrained, is gross, elaborate, and very expensive hardware. The Trident programme will cost the American taxpayer over $130 billion (in 1980 prices). The latest nuclear-powered aircraft carrier, the subject of controversy between Congress and President Carter, will cost, together with its associated ships and aircraft, more than $60 billion. An Air Force F−15 fighter cost $19 million; the Navy F−14 costs $22 million. The Air Force F−16 and Navy F−18, which were originally designed as cheap, lightweight fighters, are currently estimated to cost $11 million and $18 million respectively. These costs are several times greater than the cost of World War II predecessors, even when inflation is taken into account. One well-known estimate suggests that if current trends continue, the US Air Force will be able to afford only one plane in 2020.[9]

What role, then, can economic analysis play in the articulation and resolution of this sort of issue? I have selected the recent Sizewell 'B' inquiry as an appropriate case mainly because the force of the CEGB's case for building a PWR at Sizewell is fundamentally economic, but also because there are other important criteria, like public safety, which clearly have to be taken into account. The case is also important, of course, because, if built, the PWR becomes automatically a technological paradigm for some time to come − and so helps to 'lock' the British economy into a given pattern of electricity use/production. It also illustrates how important vested interests are in this sort of controversy.

The history of nuclear power in the UK goes back to the 1950s when the decision was made to develop it as an important source of electricity. By the early 1970s the apparent failure of the AGR programme combined with a perceived need to expand generating capacity for the 1990s and beyond, had led the CEGB to press for the building of a series of PWRs in order to increase the country's generating capacity by some 40 GW by the year 2010 (an increase of some 75%). The current inquiry under the chairmanship of Sir Frank Layfield QC is designed to adjudicate between the competing arguments of the CEGB position and those people/institutions who argue that the installation of this reactor should not take place.[10]

In a recent paper MacKerron[11] has outlined the CEGB's economic case as consisting of four elements:

(i)   Achieving systems costs savings.
(ii)   Meeting capacity needs.
(iii)   Providing for fuel diversity.
(iv)   Opening up future investment options.

The first two criteria are of relevance to the single investment decision at Sizewell, although MacKerron notes that 'it is clear that if Sizewell could be justified for early construction on *either* cost-saving *or* capacity needs grounds and a Westinghouse PWR was the lowest cost option available, then the longer term issues would be of much reduced importance.'[12]

On systems cost savings the calculations are based on the project appraisal SCBA technique outlined in chapter 3 with the slight difference that the key operating statistic is the so-called net effective cost (NEC), defined as the extent to which the extra costs involved in building and running a PWR at Sizewell are greater than the resultant cost savings in terms of fossil fuels which would have been used to generate the same amount of electricity. If the NEC is negative there are therefore net social benefits.

MacKerron shows how the CEGB figure of £-57/kW per year (a saving of over £60m per year) is crucially dependent on a range of assumptions regarding:

(i)   Construction costs and times.
(ii)   Operating performance and plant lifetime.
(iii)   The future world market price of fossil fuels.

and that if only marginal changes in a 'pessimistic' direction are made to each of these assumptions, the cost savings case would quickly evaporate. Whether more 'pessimistic' assumptions should be made is another question, but what MacKerron does make clear is that the uncertainty range around *any* values chosen is very large. He argues also that the capacity need argument is less pressing than the CEGB has suggested, and that the fuel diversity case, while important in the long term, is not much affected by the timing of a single investment decision. He concludes that there may be much to be gained in delaying a decision until we have more information about the likely performance of PWRs in comparison to other nuclear technologies.

The *prima facie* evidence from changes in the relative importance of the US and Europe as technological leaders in light water reactors, plus recent operating experience, is that consumers could well be saved of the order of £2−3 b., if a thorough review of international reactor technology preceded any investment commitment.[13]

Table 9.1   Impact on Sizewell NEC of Alternative Assumptions in the Investment Appraisal

	(1) CEGB Assumption	(2) ECC Closing Speech 2 Assumption	(3) Impact on NEC of Difference Between (1) and (2)
Capital Cost	£1147 m	£1350 m	+ £26/kW p.a.
Construction Time	90 months	102 months	
Settled-down load Factor	64%	58%	+ £25/kW p.a.
Plant lifetime	35 years	25 years	
Steam coal cost (Year 2000)	260 p/GJ	200p/GJ	+ £40/kW p.a.
Exchange rate (Year 2000)	$1.40/£	$1.70/£	
	CEGB	ECC Closing Speech	
Overall NEC on Scenario C (Medium Nuclear Background)	− £57/kW p.a.	+ £34/kW p.a.	+ £91/kW p.a.

Source: G. MacKerron, 'Sizewell: Good Value for Consumers' Money?', *Energy Policy*, Vol. 12, No. 3, September 1984, p. 297.

It is worth noting that the debate about Sizewell turns not only on the economic argument, complicated as that is. In addition to questions of public safety there are two further factors which clearly play an important role. One is the very heavy emphasis given to nuclear R & D, as opposed to R & D related to other potential energy sources, in the UK's technology policy towards energy (over half of a £500m total in 1981/82). There is an important element of the self-fulfilling prophecy in this: if one starts by perceiving nuclear power as an important potential energy source and, in consequence, devotes the bulk of technological resources to nuclear options, then it is hardly a surprise if nuclear solutions subsequently appear attractive. The second is the powerful effect of vested interests which take the following forms:

a   **Intellectual.** People who have an influential voice in this kind of
     decision become deeply committed to particular 'views' and harness a
     wide range of intellectual arguments to back up their cause. Often their
     'expertise' is marketable precisely because of the prevailing pattern of
     technology policy. This is particularly true in the nuclear power debate,
     where nuclear technology has become highly symbolic to both suppor-
     ters and opponents: both see nuclear power as a powerful embodiment
     of the science-led, growth-oriented and centralised urban economy,
     which is either applauded or denounced according to taste.

b   **Institutional.** Relevant institutions become similarly committed, devel-
     oping a bureaucratic inertia which is very difficult to shift.

c   **Economic.** Given decisions will have differential economic effects,
     particularly on those industrial sectors heavily involved in producing
     the relevant plant, equipment and components. Any change in policy,
     however good the apparent rationale, is bound to be resisted strongly by
     those economic sectors likely to be threatened. Most directly of all, the
     economic interests of the coal mining industry and nuclear power
     industry are now in serious conflict. Each new nuclear power station
     now displaces some 2m tonnes of coal output per year. The implacable
     opposition of the National Union of Mineworkers to nuclear power is
     therefore understandable.

It is for reasons such as these that the ultimate decision on whether Sizewell
(and no doubt further PWRs) will be built is ultimately a political one, and one
where the skills of the political scientist are no doubt more germane than those
of the economist. There are of course, important economic questions
involved (after all the expected capital cost of Sizewell alone is of the order of
£1,200m), but such is the uncertainty regarding the true nature of the costs
and benefits, and so removed is the exercise of power from any real public
awareness of the economic arguments involved, that the final decision will be
one where political consideration are paramount.

9.2.4 The Appraisal and Evaluation of Scientific
Expenditures

We have seen that the period following the Second World War was one of
rapidly increasing expenditures by all Western governments on science and
technology. In the UK by 1964 government R & D expenditures had reached
a level of £412m[14] (about 1 % of GDP) approximately half of which was being
spent 'intramurally' i.e. within institutions controlled directly by itself − and
the rest 'extramurally', mainly in industry and further education. Moreover
these expenditures were concentrated heavily on defence-related work, while

much of the civil R & D conducted within government Research Establishments seemed to be having little impact upon industrial output, and therefore
upon overall economic efficiency. Considerable worry began to be expressed
over this apparent disjunction between high rates of national R & D expenditures and poor manufacturing performance, so that with the advent of a
Labour government in 1964 a series of measures was taken to close the gap,
especially with regard to machine tools, computers, electronics and telecommunications.

One apparent problem was institutional. Unlike the USA, whose government traditionally sub-contracts a high proportion of its R & D 'extramurally', the UK's Government Laboratories and Research Establishments
(GREs) had begun to develop an internal momentum of their own whereby it
was difficult for their 'customers' or 'sponsors', the departments which
financed them, to control adequately the nature of R & D carried out. Part of
the difficulty, of course, was that government departments are really only
'surrogate' customers on behalf of a much wider public for whom they act –
as, for example, the Overseas Development Administration (ODA) acts as a
surrogate customer for the 'aid needs' of poor countries – and so it became
relatively easy for GREs to develop research programmes which fitted in with
their own internal scientific interests, while claiming always that such
programmes were in fact geared towards 'customer needs' – a claim almost
impossible to check with the organisational machinery then available, though
scientists have alway claimed with great conviction that their work is socially
relevant.

It was partly in response to perceived problems of this kind that the
Rothschild Report,[15] published in November 1971, advocated the widespread
use of the 'customer – contractor' principle whereby all government-financed
applied R & D would be managed by an R & D controller and subject to
advice and formulation by a chief scientist within the relevant department. In
the department of Trade and Industry (DTI), for example, there are now a
series of Research Requirements Boards, manned by representatives from
industry, government, higher education and other relevant bodies, each with
a given industrial remit, whose function it is to give advice on and commission research relevant to the wider responsibilities of the DTI. Other departments tend to have a more internal type of machinery manned largely by
officials.

Rothschild did not stop with the government departmental laboratories,
however, but went on to advocate that at least part of the work of the research
council system should be subject to a similar form of control, with parts of the
budgets of the ARC, MRC and NERC transferred from the DES to 'customer' ministries. The rationale for this recommendation, which was in fact
implemented though not to the full financial extent originally envisaged, was
that since the remit of these research councils was partly concerned with

'applied' research there was no reason to exempt them from the general thrust of science policy. Actually, although in the event the SRC and the SSRC were excluded, there were more general worries about the very rapid growth of British science in the 1950s and 1960s (and the lack of public accountability for this growth) which combined with the more straitened economic circumstances that began to be felt towards the late 1960s to produce an atmosphere conducive to direct political control. Thus

> Rothschild's proposals as a whole were intended, in line with one of the leitmotifs of the new (Heath) government, to increase accountability and efficiency in government R & D, and also to improve the quality of scientific advice available in departments and to orientate government-supported research more closely towards the national interest.[16]

Such, then, was the reasoning behind this major restructuring of British science policy. It did not take place without its critics, particularly from within the scientific community itself which found for the first time that its traditional autonomy was being fundamentally threatened − and in ways, it was felt, which were both crude and impractical. Typical criticisms were:

(i)   No distinction was made between 'applied research' and 'development'. The former category is of a strategic kind and, unlike development, difficult to tie in to a customer's requirements in any simple fashion. To give any departmental institution the role of a 'customer' in the purchase of this type of R & D was therefore totally inappropriate since it was not really in a position to judge its social value. This was particularly the case with respect to the applied resarch carried out by the research councils.

(ii) There was no justification given for the equation between national need and department fiat, which underlay the recommendations made. Since no overall national co-ordination was envisaged there would be bound to be social inefficiency on this account.

(iii) Long-term continuity for strategic research would be compromised, leading to poorer quality work and possibly the loss of valuable staff overseas.

(iv) There would be an increase in bureaucratic procedures as a result of the recommendations, leading to delays and other forms of inefficiency.

(v)   Greater governmental control of research might lead to greater secrecy regarding the findings of research, thereby compromising the success of the overall national scientific effort.

Despite these criticisms the Rothschild proposals were implemented by the Heath government and have now become an accepted institutional form for UK science policy, albeit with some changes. Little formal work has been carried out to assess how well the system has worked. Gummett[17] has concluded that one major advantage has been the positive one of putting the scientific community more directly in touch with civil servants in such a way that each 'estate' can better understand the nature of the other's professional work and associated constraints, although there is little evidence so far that 'markets' for the allocation of 'applied science' resources are working any more efficiently. 'That flexibility in the use of scientific resources which was explicitly sought in the United States through the introduction of the contract mechanism is not achieved any more easily in the Britain of the customer-contractor principle than it was before.'[18] Similar conclusions have been reached by Kogan and Henkel[19] who in a detailed analysis of DHSS experience paint a rather depressing picture of civil servants and scientists attempting vainly to come to terms with the practical exigencies of Rothschild through a complex bureaucracy of interlocking committees. As far as the research councils are concerned, the ARC and MRC have managed to regain some control over alienated funds while all three councils (i.e. including the NERC) have had difficulty devising suitable machinery for handling the new relationships. Certainly there have been increased administrative costs while the vulnerability of research programmes to sudden cuts may have had some adverse effects.

9.2.5 The Evaluation of Basic Science

Turning finally to the assessment of social expenditures on basic science, very little work has been done in this area. Traditionally the disposition of resources is handled by a network of disciplinary committees appointed by the research councils and consisting of eminent scientists who judge research proposals mainly according to internal scientific criteria. There are two major drawbacks with this approach. One is that decision-making becomes a 'closed' process not open to a wider public scrutiny. The other is that it becomes difficult to compare expenditures across disciplines and hence tends to create situations where a given pattern of expenditures, established in the past for valid reasons, becomes relatively fixed for reasons associated with vested interests.

In recent years Irvine and Martin have done a great deal to dispel the first drawback through the use of a range of indicators to compare the 'performance' of different institutions within the same discipline. For example in the field of radio astronomy they compared two UK centres (Jodrell Bank and Cambridge) using the following indicators:

- number of published papers over a ten-year period;
- number of published papers per 'effective researcher';
- an index of citation;
- peer evaluation;
- economic cost per published paper.

Allowance was made for a number of influential factors such as commitments to administrative duties and student supervision. For comparative purposes two overseas institutions were also examined. The authors found that there was a considerable degree of convergence with respect to the different measures calculated and hence that there was prima facie evidence to indicate the superior performance of one institution over the other.[20]

There are of course problems over how empirical data of the Irvine/Martin kind should be used in the decision-making process since it has been pointed out, for example, that there may often be extraneous contextual factors, such as instrumentation quality, which influence the results differentially. Also there are dangers inherent in simple extrapolations from what *has* happened in the past to what *may* happen in the future. Nevertheless it is clear that Irvine and Martin have opened up a promising new area of enquiry which may well improve the policy-making process in this area.

9.2.6 An Evaluation

How far does economic analysis help in the understanding of these important issues of science policy and how far does this analysis help in developing suitable policies? On both of these points, the answer is probably 'not much'. On the question of technological unemployment, what economic theory does is to highlight the very great complexity of the relationships involved and the lack of any simple 'cause-effect' connection. Technical change, certainly radical technical change, will almost certainly threaten employment prospects in the short run but what happens at the end of the day will depend upon a whole matrix of dynamic and inter-locking social and institutional circumstances, about which economics, as it is conventionally practised, has little or nothing to add beyond pointing out that there is more to things than meets the eye.

In the case of the appraisal of complex projects it is clear that even ignoring 'external' issues, such as that of safety, no responsible political authority could place much credence upon a calculus which requires to make so many 'guesstimates' about so many technological and economic variables, both in the present and in the future. For example in the debate over the respective merits of the AGR and the PWR there is an important question regarding how to 'value' the indigenous British capabilities that have arisen through the design and development of the AGR. Approving the PWR, a 'foreign' technology, implies increasing the apparent level of technological dependence. We have already seen in chapter 8 that economic analysis can tell us little about this crucial point. Economic analysis then becomes merely one of many technical inputs into a wider debate about whether or not a decision should go ahead and if so when. It does, however, have the virtue that the act of carrying out an investment appraisal becomes an efficient means of isolating some of the key 'subsidiary' questions which may be germane to the larger decision.

When we come to questions of policy regarding the disposition of resources towards scientific research, both basic and applied, economics has virtually nothing to say beyond the prosaic — such as, for example, that the committal of resources in one direction has an opportunity cost in terms of other foregone possibilities. The lack of any accurate means for evaluating the outcome of research activities combined with the uncertainty which surrounds research by definition has led in the British case to the policy of creating the social facsimile of a market situation — where consumers 'purchase' the research they need from 'contractors' who are supposed to provide it. Unfortunately the experience of trying to reproduce such a context has merely highlighted the fact that the 'market for knowledge' simply cannot be handled in this way. This does not mean that there may not have been some positive features of the Rothschild experiment, but simply that conventional economic analysis is irrelevant to the whole procedure. The same is clearly true with respect to the evaluation of basic science.

9.3 Economic Theory and Science Policy Analysis

It is now time to recap on the main themes which have been developed in a book which has been written with the major aim of explaining to the 'non-conversant' reader the nature of science and technology policy issues and the role of economic ideas in their analysis. By way of introducing the subject, chapter 2 attempted to trace the rough historic evolution of the relations between science and production, and to show how the systemic role played by technological changes is very much a feature of the nature of the economic organisation appertaining. The industrial revolution brought with it a central role for science in production but not immediately, since the degree of differentiation of the productive system had to proceed to a fairly high level of sophistication before it became possible to apply scientific knowledge in a systematic way through the industrial R & D laboratory. Nowadays, however, the sheer power of technology in the production of goods and services is very great indeed, and has undoubtedly been partly responsible for the very rapid rates of economic growth experienced by the Western powers and Japan over the course of this century — at least as measured by conventional national income statistics.

It is important, however, not to be carried away by the apparent success in harnessing science and technology to social goals, substantial as the benefits have been. For there have been costs as well. Not everybody has benefited and there are indications that in many of the poorer areas of the world economic and ecological conditions are deteriorating, sometimes irreversibly. Moreover, even within the rich countries there is increasing concern that modern technology has become unduly associated with unnecessary and often lethal products, and that the associated structures of industry and government are becoming ever more remote from popular understanding and control. Hence a recurrent theme throughout this book is that questions of science policy are not just concerned with how the UK may keep up with the Japanese, important though it is to have an international perspective on such matters. They are also concerned in a deep sense with the very fabric of civilisation, its priorities, life-styles and artifacts − if only because 'policy-making' implies making choices also at this level, at least in principle.

Chapter 3 dealt with the economic system as a whole − the 'macro-economy' − where it is possible to 'account for' broad interrelationships amongst important economic variables, such as consumption, investment, taxation, imports and exports. The importance of these aggregates lies in their significance for the management of modern economic systems and indeed much of conventional macroeconomic analysis (which we did not discuss) consists of an articulation of how such variables interrelate, and what implications there are for the solution of macroeconomic 'problems', such as inflation, for example. However, since from our standpoint the important objective is definitional, it was sufficient to develop a social accounting framework showing how a 'map' of the economic system may be developed according to straightforward conventions. The second major objective of this chapter was to illustrate the extent to which it is possible to be quantitative about the disposition of resources to science and technology and the resultant social outputs. Beginning with a description of the scientific 'infrastructure', or 'system', which typically obtains in most industrialised economies, the discussion goes on to show how in principle, at least, it is possible to measure the relevant 'inputs' and 'outputs' and in this way to provide a similar sort of 'mapping' exercise to the more general economic one. Admittedly there are considerable problems of definition and accuracy, but exercises of this kind do help to increase our understanding of how scientific resources are spent − and this is an important first step in much of science policy analysis.

Chapter 4 was devoted mainly to elements of microeconomic analysis − particularly production theory which defines many of the relevant variables, including technology, associated with the conversion of 'inputs' into 'outputs'. Here 'technological change' was viewed in the way that economists tend to see it, namely as an improvement in the efficiency of production − and *not* as an engineer, for example, might see it, as the replacement of one set of machines by another. An important conclusion of this chapter was that many of the propositions deriving from this form of analysis do not have much in the way of an empirical content which is relevant from our standpoint. Rather they should be seen as a series of intellectual 'metaphors' in which simplified assumptions about human behaviour and technical conditions are elaborated into a series of economic relationships and definitions, which in turn help to clarify our understanding of this aspect of social relations. They should *not* conversely be seen as scientific propositions in the normal sense in which these are understood.

Returning then to the question of the role of economics in the analysis of science policy issues, you will recall that in chapter 1 I defined these as interdisciplinary issues of social policy arising out of the impact of science on the social order, and thus conceptually more related to the social sciences than to the natural sciences. I suggested also that they are very much problem-focused, so that no one discipline within the social sciences can by itself provide very much enlightenment. Inevitably this means that the science policy analyst is someone who is able to exercise a range of craft skills regarding how the mobilisation and allocation of resources to science and technology takes place, what kinds of problems result, how these may be diagnosed and what policy prescriptions may be recommended. These are difficult skills to develop especially as there is no body of theory which exists to provide an unambiguous reference point.

How then can economics, as a well-established discipline within the social sciences, help in this respect? I have argued that its importance lies mainly in its role as a 'language' of description and in that of an aid to the organisation of ideas. However, when it comes to theoretical power in a more fundamental sense, the discussion in chapters 5 and 6 argued that the tradition of neo-classical analysis has not taken us very far, and that many writers are now beginning to search for new ways of conceptualising the process of techno-logical change in modern economic systems. The problems are of two broad types – conceptual and policy-related.

9.3.1 Conceptual

Our discussion shows that economic analysis is inadequate in the following respects:

(i)   It cannot handle the 'long run', since technological changes – and decisions about technological changes, take place over, and are related to, very long periods indeed. Conversely economic propositions deal mainly with resource allocation at a point in time.

(ii)   Economics cannot handle uncertainty since most of its theorems assume perfect knowledge on the part of producers and consumers. And because uncertainty is an inherent part of scientific and technological activity almost by definition, the conceptual hiatus is clear.

(iii)   Economics cannot 'explain' the fact of technological changes in any way other than by pronouncing them inexplicable. Even the leading proponent of 'growth accounting'[21] has concluded that nearly a quarter of Japanese economic growth between 1953 and 1971 was 'caused by advances in knowledge', a statement which merely postpones explanation.

(iv) Economics cannot relate its apparatus easily to the inherently inter-disciplinary nature of socio-economic change. For example, and relating to the previous point, it is not at all clear why it is conceptually valid to 'account for' growth in such a disaggregated fashion when most of the 'causes' quite evidently act and interact themselves in an inte-grated and dynamic fashion.

(v) There is now quite a lot of evidence that decision makers in industry and government make decisions on grounds which are as much concerned with long-run technological expectations as they are with conventional economic aggregates, such as prices. One would expect theory to take account of this.

It is for reasons such as these that in very recent years some writers have begun to break away from the confines of standard economic theory in order to attempt to conceptualise technology and technological changes more realistically, borrowing where appropriate from other branches of learning. Nevertheless there is still a powerful body of thought which believes that it ought to be possible somehow to relate traditional economic concepts to technical change and whose work reflects this belief, sometimes with con-sequences which appear rather contrived. Why should this be so? We have seen that one set of reasons may lie within the 'professionalisation' of economic knowledge − that is within the way in which economics as a professional activity explores the social environment, develops models which inform us about how economic behaviour takes place, and then attempts to test these models empirically.

In an interesting and scholarly account of the development of economic thought, Guy Routh has come to the conclusion that right from its inception with the seventeenth-century writings of Petty, D'Avenant, Locke, North and others, economics took on the characteristics of exercises in deductive logic, in which assumptions about human behaviour and about technical and social conditions were elaborated into complex cognitive structures which had no necessary connection with reality. Making use of the Kuhnian view of scientific development, he argues that

> the paradigm that provides the inner framework for economic thought has not changed since the seventeenth century; that neither the advent of marginalism that distinguishes classical from neo-classical economics, nor the admission of the possibility of involuntary unemployment, that distinguishes Keynesian from neo-classical economics were revolutions in the Kuhnian sense. On the contrary, they were the means by which the survival of the existing paradigm was ensured.[22]

Implicitly, therefore, although Routh does not take his analysis much beyond this point, the various 'schools' of economic thought which we discussed in chapter 5 are not capable of being differentiated according to *scientific* criteria, but rather reflect *doctrinal* conflicts where metaphysical and ideological considerations are paramount, where battle is joined with wellnigh religious fervour and where evidence has little or no impact on the basic structure of ideas. Why this should be the case must appear quite extraordinary to the natural scientist who, however conservative he/she is with regard to any particular set of theories, has always been taught, presumably, that *eventually* established theoretical positions are vulnerable to evidence of a contradictory nature.

In this sense, therefore, 'progress' in economics does not obey the type of norms conventionally laid down by philosophers of science where evidence is seen to play an important role in conceptual development. Popper,[23] for example, has argued that in whatever branch of the natural sciences scientists are pursuing their research, their constant aim should be to make their propositions as clear and simple as possible so as to avoid confusion in communication with peers and so as to render such propositions subject to unambiguous empirical tests. Furthermore scientists should *want* to be proved wrong whatever the personal and social pressures upon them may be, and the knowledge pursued must be *relevant* knowledge i.e. it must build upon what is already known about the natural world as expressed by the scientific discipline in question. In this way, Popper argued, criteria of relevance, clarity, testability and falsifiability represent strong moral/professional imperatives, vitally necessary for the pursuit of 'good' science. They are independent of the reality of how science is actually conducted though I imagine that most scientists would subscribe to them in a general sense. Judged by these criteria, however, it is clear that most economic scholarship does not perform well.

Galbraith with transparent irony argues that the answer lies within the study of social anthropology where the best analogue is that of the tribal group. Economics shares with

> members of city gangs, religious congregations, aboriginal tribes, British regiments, craft unions, fashionable clubs, learned disciplines, holders of diplomatic passports and, one is told, followers of the more intellectually demanding criminal pursuits . . . the natural desire . . . to delineate and safeguard the boundary between those who belong and those who do not.[24]

Hence the use of the complicated 'language' of economics has got nothing whatsoever to do with science but represents merely the imperatives of professional differentiation, exacerbated probably in this case by the reluctance of its adherents to render obsolete their hard-won intellectual capital.

Indeed, Galbraith argues, this professional/tribal dynamic becomes further regressive by virtue of the need to develop an intra-group hierarchy through which aspirants to high positions are required to master certain skills — in this case the use of mathematical logic to express economic relationships.[25]

If this equation of the sociology of economics with quasi-religious practice is correct, then students would be correct in concluding that they should not engage with economic analysis. In my view, however, this would be too precipitous a conclusion, since the real need which economics attempts (unsuccessfully) to fulfil is the need for an 'organising framework' within which to pattern our thoughts. For cognitive structures exist in the social sciences in order to provide some semblance of order in an otherwise incomprehensible melange of technical and social relations, and the signal failure of economic analysis is in reality the failure of a metaphor, and not the failure of a scientific theory. Very simply, the history of economic thought so clearly demonstrates the unscientific nature of much of economic analysis that only the deluded or the mischievous could seriously argue that we can evaluate it according to the same canons of scholarship as are relevant, say, to Newtonian physics.

But the failure of one metaphor will only be acceptable when another arises to take its place, and as yet none has. My own feeling is that at least so far as science and technology policy analysis is concerned, we are now very much in a pre-paradigmatic situation in which a wide range of writers are searching for intellectual systems which show the promise of organising our thoughts in such a way that not only corresponds to reality but is internally consistent and provides a more coherent understanding of the world in which we live.

9.3.2 Policy and Theory

The second problem, closely related to the first, is concerned with the actual value of economic theory in the policy-making process.

A 'policy', defined at its simplest represents a decision to interfere with the socio-economic order so as to achieve a desired end. In turn the 'need' for policy exists because the existing pattern of socio-economic relations is perceived to be deficient in particular respects. These deficiencies define the 'problem' which the 'policy' is intended to eliminate. Defined in this way, policy is a function of its institutional context. At the level of the family, or household, for example, the 'policy' of limiting children's access to television may be taken to eliminate the perceived 'problem' that excessive viewing will produce passive and poorly socialised children. At the level of the firm the 'policy' of doubling the percentage of annual sales spent upon R & D may be taken because such action is felt to be the best way to eliminate the 'problem' of a declining market share, while at the national level the government may introduce a scheme of investment subsidies as a 'policy' to deal with the 'problem' of low rates of national investment.

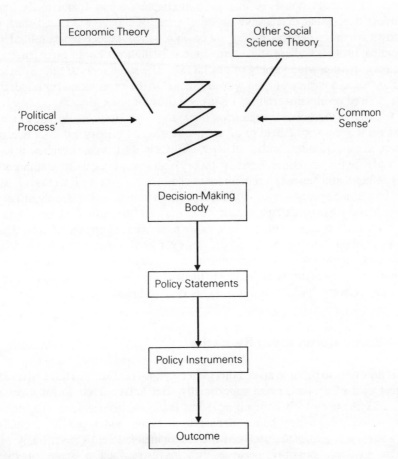

Figure 9.3   Theory and policy

At whatever institutional level we locate the analysis, it is clear that the link between the policy and the problem it is supposed to solve is *first* theory dependent, and *secondly* a function of perceptions and power. The 'theory' behind a government's decision to subsidise industrial investment is that subsidies actually bring about the desired results, namely increased rates of investment. The translation of such 'theory' into 'policy' requires also a *perception* on the part of decision-makers that the theory holds, and the *power* to implement the policy once the decision is taken. Very often the execution of an agreed policy requires the creation of an institution (or institutions) to implement it − like, for example, the Alvey Programme to develop and diffuse information technology throughout UK industry. Notice, however, that in general these 'enabling' theories are not often closely linked to the kinds of economic analysis discussed in chapters 3 and 4, nor to the more diffuse conceptual discussions in other parts of this text. Instead they are shown in more general policy statements which reflect the result of the political process and are at the same time a distillation of both experience and 'theory' from a wide variety of disciplines. The statements are then put into action using a variety of 'policy instruments' in the expectation (or hope) that the desired results materialise. Figure 9.3 illustrates the process.

Clearly if the policy in question does not work (as most do not to some extent) this cannot be held to be an invalidation of 'theory', if only because there are an infinite number of intervening circumstances which will have intruded in the meantime. Equally 'theory' can never hope to be unambiguously refuted, and hence can remain for ever as a set of accepted 'truths'. This is an important reason why many debates about social policy are doctrinal in nature and why, by extension as it were, derived 'theoretical' debates follow the same rather depressing pattern, as we have seen. I hope that this book has done enough to make the case that, however hard it may be, science policy analysts should not only be careful in their use of economic 'theory', they should be wary of *any* social science 'theory' since unlike the natural sciences the gap between 'policy' and 'theory' is very wide indeed.

9.4 Some Concluding Remarks

It is now time to bring to an end this rather complicated story. I have covered a great deal of ground, often superficially. But I have done so for a reason which I find personally compelling — and that is the need as I see it to open up the nature of science policy debate to a much wider public, including academic disciplines themselves which seem unable to engage seriously with these matters, possibly because they have reached a stage of over-specialisation reminiscent of Koestler's koala bear.

> Allow me to take you on a ride on the treacherous wings of analogy, starting with an excursion into genetics. Creativity . . . is a concept notoriously difficult to define; and it is sometimes useful to approach a difficult subject by way of contrast. The opposite of the creative individual is the pedant, the slave of habit, whose thinking and behaviour move in rigid grooves. His biological equivalent is the over-specialised animal. Take, for example, that charming and pathetic creature, the koala bear, which specialises in feeding on the leaves of a particular variety of eucalyptus tree and on nothing else; and which, in lieu of fingers, has hook-like claws, ideally suited for clinging to the bark of the tree — and for nothing else. Some of our departments of higher learning seem expressly designed for breeding koala bears.[26]

This may seem a harsh indictment, but I am afraid that there is more than an element of truth in it. Many of our social sciences have reached a stage of over-specialisation which precludes serious engagement with many important issues, including those associated with science policy. Because of this, students from the natural sciences and engineering are encouraged to treat social science with due respect but also with a healthy scepticism.

What is the way forward conceptually? I am now reasonably convinced that the ruling economics paradigm, with all its Cartesian and reductionist overtones, will have to be largely abandoned — at least in so far as science and technology policy analysis is concerned — and replaced with some version of the biological metaphor. I say this for three principal reasons. The first is that a biological analogy is clearly far more capable of handling the *systemic and dynamic* characteristics of technology as this is applied to economic production. Thus we have seen throughout this text numerous examples of 'technology behaving' in an organic fashion, subject to continuous change as contextual conditions and internal factors impinge upon it. Indeed, it is difficult to view technology in any other way. Secondly, *uncertainty* as we have seen, is an inherent quality of technological change and corresponds to what decision makers face in reality.

Of course, in all cases economic factors represent an important set of influences, but there are other influences of a non-economic character as well and these must also be included if the conceptual metaphor is to be at all realistic. In particular it must take account both of developments *within the firm* and of those *outside the firm*, in an integrated and coherent way. We have seen glimpses of this ocurring through recent writings in organisation theory,[27] but one of the most fruitful areas may well lie in the application of dynamic systems analysis as part of an attempt to develop a perspective of a 'non-reductionist' type which has general validity. The analogy here is explicitly biological.[28]

My final reason is concerned with *policy*. It should by now be abundantly clear that economic 'theory' has developed in ways which have little relevance to policy-making, and is therefore as a discipline in danger of becoming socially redundant. Surely, if the social sciences are to have any justification at all, this must lie in their capacity to inform us about how society 'works' and how it can be made to 'work better'. In so far as science and technology policy is concerned this very probably means a radically new approach, which has yet to be developed. Only when it does will we be in a position to understand this very complex area of social concern.

Bibliography

In addition to the generic texts outlined at the end of chapter 1, the following more specific sources are recommended. D. Collingridge, *The Social Control of Technology* (Oxford, Oxford University Press, 1980), J. Gershuny, *After Industrial Society* (London, Macmillan, 1978), C. Freeman and M. Jahoda (eds.), *World Futures: The Great Debate* (London, Martin Robertson, 1978), J. Gribbin, *Future Worlds* (London, Abacus, 1979) and K. L. R. Pavitt and W. Walker, 'Government Policies Towards Industrial Innovation', *Research Policy*, Vol. 5, No. 1, January 1976.

On technical change and unemployment, see A. Heertje, *Economics and Technical Change* (London, Weidenfeld and Nicolson, 1977), particularly chapter 2 where compensation theory is discussed; C. Freeman, J. Clark and L. Soete, *Unemployment and Technical Innovation* (London, Frances Pinter, 1982) — see also shortened version in their paper in *Futures*, Vol. 13, 1981; C. Freeman and L. Soete (eds.), *Technical Change and Full Employment* (Oxford, Basil Blackwell, 1985) and C. M. Cooper and J. Clark, *Employment, Economics and Technology* (Brighton, Wheatsheaf, 1982).

On the arms economy see M. Kaldor, *The Baroque Arsenal* (London, Deutsch, 1982). On energy policy see R. Williams, *The Nuclear Power Decisions* (London, Croom Helm, 1980), P. L. Cook and A. J. Surrey, *Energy Policy; Strategies for Uncertainty* (Oxford, Martin Robertson, 1977), and House of Commons Select Committee on Energy, *Energy Research, Development and Demonstration in the UK*, 9th Report, Session 1983/84, HC/585, July 1984. On Sizewell in particular see G. S. MacKerron, 'Sizewell: Good Value for Consumers' Money?', *Energy Policy*, Vol. 12, No. 3, September 1984, pp. 295–301. Also for a contrary view in the same edition of *Energy Policy*, see N. Evans, 'An Economic Evaluation of the Sizewell Decision', pp. 288–95. The Rothschild Debate is well summarised in Gummett, *Scientists in Whitehall*, chapters 5–7, and for a discussion of the application of Rothschild's ideas in a particular context, see M. Kogan and M. Henkel, *Government and Research* (London, Heinemann, 1983).

On the evaluation of basic science see J. Irvine and B. Martin, *Foresight in Science* (London, Frances Pinter, 1984). On the more general problem of the epistomological status of both economic analysis and of science policy studies there are no suitable texts of which I am aware which cover the whole ground. However, reference may be made to the following. B. R. Easlea, *Liberation and the Aims of Science* (London, Chatto and Windus, 1973), chapters 1–6; J. R. Ravetz, *Scientific Knowledge and its Social Problems* (Harmondsworth, Penguin, 1973), Parts I and II; Routh, *The Origin of Economic Ideas*, chapters 1 and 6; B. Ward, *What's Wrong with Economics?* (New York, Basic Books, London, Macmillan, 1972). Also see I. Lakatos and A. Musgrave (eds.), *Criticism and the Growth of Knowledge* (London, Cambridge University Press, 1972) especially papers by Kuhn, Popper, Lakatos and Feyerabend; B. Magee, *Popper* (Glasgow, William Collins, 1978).

Notes

1 Discussed in great detail by E. P. Thompson, *The Making of the English Working Class* (Harmondsworth, Penguin, 1968), chapters 6–9.

2 G. Routh, *Economics: An Alternative Text* (Oxford, Basil Blackwell, 1983), see pp. 115–21 for an elaboration of this point.

3 Cooper and Clark, *Employment, Economics and Technology*, p. 1.

4 See Heertje, *Economics and Technical Change*, chapter 2.

5 See, for example, Gershuny, *After Industrial Society*.

6 An alternative view put forward to me by William Walker is that established policy paradigms are often brought about and maintained by a small coterie of very senior people. Once this power base shifts, or is eroded in some way, the policy paradigm in question can change quite dramatically.

7 P. Baran and P. Sweezy, *Monopoly Capital* (Harmondsworth, Penguin, 1973).

8 Pavitt and Worboys, *Science and Technology in the Modern Industrial State*, pp. 23–33.

9 Kaldor, *The Baroque Arsenal*, pp. 17, 18.

10 This inquiry is only an advisory one and therefore there is no statutory obligation for the UK government to take any notice whatsoever of its findings.

11 MacKerron, *Sizewell*, p. 296.

12 MacKerron, *Sizewell*, p. 296.

13 MacKerron, *Sizewell*, p. 301.

14 Gummett, *Scientists in Whitehall*, p. 55.

15 *A Framework for Government Research and Development* (London, HMSO, Cmnd. 4814, 1971).

16 Gummett, *Scientists in Whitehall*, p. 197.

17 Gummett, *Scientists in Whitehall*, p. 202 *et seq.*

18 Gummett, *Scientists in Whitehall*, p. 150.

19 Kogan and Henkel, *Government and Research*.

20 See J. Irvine and B. Martin, 'Assessing Basic Research; Some Partial Indicators of Scientific Progress in Radio Astronomy', *Research Policy*, Vol. 12, No. 2, pp. 61–90.

21 E. F. Denison and W. K. Chung, *How Japan's Economy Grew so Fast* (Washington, DC, Brookings, 1976). See chapter 5. For the period 1961–71 the main growth determinants were 'Capital' (26.9%), 'Advances in Knowledge' (25.4%) and 'Economies of Scale' (20.5%).

22 Routh, *The Origin of Economic Ideas*, p. 76.

23 Popper's ideas are well summarised in Magee, *Popper*.

24 J. K. Galbraith, *Economics, Peace and Laughter* (Harmondsworth, Penguin, 1979), p. 31.

25 Galbraith, *Economics, Peace and Laughter*, pp. 34, 35 for an amusing discussion of this point.

26 A. Koestler, *Bricks to Babel* (London, Pan Books, Picador, 1982), p. 428.

27 A. G. Ramos, *The New Science of Organisation* (Toronto, University of Toronto Press, 1981), also N. M. Kay, *The Evolving Firm* (London, Macmillan, 1982).

28 See for example Koestler, *Bricks to Babel*, chapter 37.

SELECT BIBLIOGRAPHY

Abramovitz, M. (1966) 'Resources and Output in the US since 187O' *American Economic Review* Pap.Proc. Vol 46, pp.5−23.

Agarwala, A. and S. Singh (eds) (1971) *The Economics of Underdevelopment* London: Oxford UP.

Allen, G. C. (1981) 'Industrial Policy and Innovation in Japan' in C. Carter (ed) *Industrial Policy and Innovation* London: Heineman, pp.68−87.

Amin, S. (1973) *Neocolonialism in West Africa* Harmondsworth: Penguin.

——(1983) 'Expansion or Crisis of Capitalism?' in Third World Quarterly Vol 5. no 2 April.

Arkadie, B. van and C. Frank (1966) *Economic Accounting and Development Planning* London: Oxford UP.

Arrow, K. (1962) 'The Economic Implications of Learning-by-Doing' in *Review of Economic Studies* Vol 29. June, pp.155−173.

Atkinson, A. and J. Stiglitz (1969) 'A New View of Technological Change' *Economic Journal* Vol 79, pp.573−78.

Bacon, R. and W. Eltis (1983) *Britain's Economic Problem: Too Few Producers* 2nd edn. London: Macmillan.

Baldwin, R. E. (1966) *Economic Development and Growth* New York: John Wiley.

Baran, P. and E. Hobsbawm (1961) 'The Stages of Economic Growth' in *Kyklos* Vol. XIV, pp.234−42.

Baran, P. and P. Sweezy (1973) *Monopoly Capital* Harmondsworth: Penguin.

Barber, W. J. (1967) *A History of Economic Thought* Harmondsworth: Penguin.

Barnett, A., M. Bell and K. Hoffman (1982) *Rural Energy and the Third World* Oxford: Pergamon.

Baumol, W. J. and A. S. Blinder (1979) *Economics: Principles and Policy* Jovanovich: Harcourt-Brace.

Beckerman, W. (1980) *An Introduction to National Income Analysis* London: Weidenfield and Nicolson.

Bell, R. M. N. (1979) 'The Exploitation of Indigenous Knowledge, or the Indigenous Exploitation of Knowledge: Whose Use of What for What?' in *IDS Bulletin* Vol 10. No 2. University of Sussex.

——(1984) '"Learning' and the Accumulation of Industrial Technological Capacity in Developing Countries' in M. Fransman and K. King (eds) *Technological Capability in the Third World* London: Macmillan, pp.187−209.

et al (1984) 'Assessing the Performance of Infant Industries' *Journal of*

Bernstein, H. (ed) (1976) *Underdevelopment and Development* Harmondsworth: Penguin.

Bienefeld, M. (1981) 'Dependency and the New Industrialising Countries (NICs): Towards a Reappraisal' in D. Seers (ed) *Dependency Theory: A Critical Re-assessment* London: Frances Pinter, pp.79−96.

Biggs, S. (1982) 'Generating Agricultural Technology: Triticale for the Himalayan Hills' *Food Policy* Vol 7. February, pp.69−82.

Biggs, S. and E. Clay (1981) 'Sources of Innovation in Agricultural Technology' in *World Development* Vol 9. No 4.

—— (1983) 'Generation and Diffusion of Agricultural Technology' *Technology and Employment Programme* Geneva: ILO August.

Braverman, H. (1974) *Labor and Monopoly Capital* New York: Monthly Review Press.

Byerlee, D. and M. Collinson et al (1980) *Planning Technologies Appropriate to Farmers: Concepts and Procedures* CIMMYT Mexico.

Cardoso, F. H. (1972) 'Dependency and Development in Latin America' in *New Left Review* No 34. pp.83−95.

Carter, C. (ed) (1981) *Industrial Policy and Innovation* London: Heinemann.

Clark, N. G. (1975) 'The Multinational Company, the Transfer of Technology and Dependence' *Development and Change* Vol 6. No 1. June, pp.5−20.

—— (1980) 'The Economic Behaviour of Research Institutions in Developing Countries: Some Methodological Points' in *Social Studies of Science* Vol 10. No 1. pp.75−93.

—— (1982) 'Reply to Moravcsik' *Social Studies of Science* Vol 12. No 1. February pp.147−150.

—— and E. J. Clay (1984) 'The Operations Research Project at Indore (1974−80) − An Institutional Innovation in Rural Technology Transfer' mimeo (SPRU/IDS), University of Sussex, January.

Clay, E. and B. Schaffer (eds) (1984) *Room for Manoeuvre: An Explanation of Public Policy for Agriculture and Rural Development* London: Heineman.

Collingridge, D. (1980) *The Social Control of Technology* Oxford: Oxford UP.

Conway, G. R. (1984) *Rural Resource Conflicts in the UK and the Third World: Issues for Research Policy* Papers in Science, Technology and Public Policy No 6. Imperial College/SPRU/TCC.

Cook, P. L. and A. J. Surrey (1977) *Energy Policy: Strategies for Uncertainty* Oxford: Martin Robertson.

Cooper C M (1971) 'Science, Technology and Development' *Economic and Social Review* Vol 2. No 2. January, pp.165−89.

—— (1973) 'Choice of Techniques and Technological Change as Problems in Political Economy' in *International Social Science Journal* Vol XXV. No 3.

—— (ed) (1973) *Science, Technology and Development* London: Frank Cass.

—— and J. Clark (1982) *Employment, Economics and Technology* Brighton: Wheatsheaf.

—— and F. Sercovitch (1971) *The Channels and Mechanisms for the Transfer of Technology from Developed to Developing Countries* Geneva: UNCTAD, TD/8/AC.11/5 27th April.

Davies, S. (1979) *The Diffusion of Process Innovation* Cambridge: Cambridge UP.

Deirmentzoglou, A. (1983) *Technological and Structural Change in the Greek Textiles Industry* DPhil University of Sussex (SPRU).

Denison, E. (1962) 'United States Economic Growth' in *Journal of Business* Vol 35. April, pp.109–21.

―――and W. K. Chung (1976) *How Japan's Economy Grew so Fast* Washington DC: Brookings.

Dobb, M. (1976) *Studies in the Development of Capitalism* London: Macmillan.

Donaldson, P. (1978) *Worlds Apart: The Economic Gulf Between Nations* Harmondsworth: Penguin.

Dosi, G. (1982) 'Technological Paradigms and Technological Trajectories: a Suggested Interpretation of the Determinants and Directions of Technical Change' in *Research Policy* Vol 11. No 3 June, pp.147–62.

Easlea, B. R. (1973) *Liberation and the Aims of Science* London: Chatto and Windus.

Elkan, W. (1978) *An Introduction to Development Economics* Harmondsworth: Penguin.

Evans, N. (1984) 'An Economic Evaluation of the Sizewell Decision' *Energy Policy* Vol 12. No 3. September, pp.288–95.

Frank, A. G. (1967) *Capitalism and Underdevelopment in Latin America* New York: Monthly Review Press.

Fransman,M. (forthcoming) 'Conceptualising Technological Change in the Third World in the 1980s: An Interpretive Survey' in *Journal of Development Studies* July.

―――and K. King (eds) (1984) *Technological Capability in the Third World* London: Macmillan.

Freeman, C. (1965) 'Research and Development in Electronic Capital Goods' in *National Institute Economic Review* No 34. November, pp.40–97.

―――(1968) 'Chemical Process Plant: Innovation and the World Market' in *National Institute Economic Review* No 45. August, pp.29–57.

―――(1974) *The Economics of Industrial Innovation* Harmondsworth: Penguin. Also London: Frances Pinter (1982) considerably revised.

―――(1977) 'Economics of Research and Development' in I. Spiegel-Rosing and D. de Solla Price (eds) *Science, Technology and Society* London: Sage pp.223–76.

―――(1979) 'The Kondratiev Long Waves, Technical Change and Unemployment' in *Structural Determinants of Employment and Unemployment* Paris: OECD Vol 2. pp.181–96.

―――(1983) Article in the *Guardian* newspaper 30th August.

―――(ed) (1983) *Long Waves in the World Economy* London: Butterworth.

―――Clark, J. and L. Soete (1981) 'Long Waves, Inventions and Innovations' *Futures* August, pp.308–322.

―――(1982) *Unemployment and Technical Innovation* London: Frances Pinter.

―――and M. Jahoda (eds) (1978) *World Futures: The Great Debate* London: Martin Robertson.

―――and L. Soete (eds) (1985) *Technical Change and Full Employment* Oxford: Basil Blackwell.

Furtado, C. (1970) *The Economic Development of Latin America* Cambridge: Cambridge UP.

——(1971) *Development and Underdevelopment* Cambridge: Cambridge UP.

——(1983) *Accumulation and Development: The Logic of Industrial Civilisation* Oxford: Martin Robertson.

Galbraith, J. K. (1972) *Economics and the Public Purpose* London: Andre Deutsch.

——(1972) *The New Industrial State* Harmondsworth: Penguin.

——(1979) *Economics, Peace and Laughter* Harmondsworth: Penguin.

——(1979) *Money* Harmondsworth: Penguin.

Gelderen, J. van (1913) 'Springvleed: Beschauwingen over industriele ontwikkeling en prijsbeweging' in *Die Niewe Tijd* Vol 18. (Nos 4, 5 and 6) April-June.

Gerschenkron, A. (1965) *Economic Backwardness in Historical Perspective* London: Praeger.

Gershuny, J. (1978) *After Industrial Society* London: Macmillan.

Gibbons, M. and R. Johnston (1974) 'The Role of Science in Technological Innovation' in *Research Policy* Vol 3. No 3. pp.220–42.

Giersch, H. (ed) (1982) *Emerging Technologies: Consequences for Economic Growth and Structural Change* Tubingen: J C B Mohr (Paul Siebeck).

Godfrey, M. (ed) (1980) 'Is Dependency Dead?' in *IDS Bulletin*, University of Sussex Vol 12. No 1 December.

Gribbin, J. (1979) *Future Worlds* London: Abacus.

Griffin, K. (1974) 'The International Transmission of Inequality' in *World Development* Vol 2. No 3. March, pp.3–16.

——(1974) *The Political Economy of Agrarian Change* London: Macmillan.

——and J. Enos (1971) *Planning Development* London: Addison-Wesley.

Griliches, Z. (1957) 'Hybrid Corn: An Exploration in the Economics of Technological Change' in *Econometrica* Vol 25 October, pp.501–22.

——(1958) 'Research Costs and Social Returns: Hybrid Corn and Related Innovations' in *Journal of Political Economy* October, pp.419–31.

Guest, R. H. (1967) 'The Rationalisation of Management' in M. Kranzberg and C. W. Purcell (eds) *Technology in Western Civilisation* New York: Oxford UP.

Gummett, P. (1980) *Scientists in Whitehall* Manchester: Manchester UP.

HMSO (1971) *A Framework for Government Research and Development* London: Cmnd 4814.

Habakkuk, E. J. (1967) *American and British Technology in the Nineteenth Century* Cambridge: Cambridge UP.

Hagen, E. E. (1964) *On the Theory of Social Change: How Economic Growth Begins* London: Tavistock.

Harrod, R. (1939) 'An Essay in Dynamic Theory' in *Economic Journal* Vol 49. pp.14–33.

Hart, K. (1973) 'Informal Income Opportunities and Urban Employment in Ghana' in R. Jolly, E. de Kadt, H. Singer and F. Wilson (eds) *op cit* pp.66–74.

Heertje, A. (1977) *Economics and Technical Change* London: Weidenfeld and Nicolson.

Heilbroner, R. L. (1968) *The Making of Economic Society* 2nd edn Englewood Cliffs NJ: Prentice Hall.

——(1972) *The Worldly Philosophers* New York: Simon and Schuster.

Helleiner, G. K. (1972) *International Trade and Economic Development* Harmondsworth: Penguin.

——(1973) 'Manufactured Exports from Less Developed Countries and Multinational Firms' *Economic Journal* Vol 83. No 329. March, pp.21–47.

——(1975) 'The Role of Multinational Corporations in the Less Developed Countries' Trade in Technology' in *World Development* Vol 3. No 4. April, pp.161–89.

Hendry, D. F. and N. R. Ericsson (1983) 'Assertion without Empirical Basis: An Econometric Appraisal of Friedman and Schwartz' in Bank of England Panel of Academic Consultants, Panel Paper No 22. *Monetary Trends in the UK* October.

Hessen, B. (1931) 'The Social and Economic Roots of Newton's *Principia*' in N. Bukharin (ed) *Science at the Crossroads* London: Knight. Reprinted Cass (1971).

Hill, J. and H. Scannell (1983) *Due South* London: Pluto.

Hirschman, A. (1964) *The Strategy of Economic Development* New Haven: Yale University Press.

Hobday, M. (1985) 'The Impact of Microelectronic Change on Developing Countries: The Case of Brazilian Telecommunications' in *Development and Change* Vol 17. No 1. January.

Hobsbawm, E. J. (1969) *Industry and Empire* Harmondsworth: Penguin.

Hoffman, H. K. (1985) 'Microelectronics, International Competition and Development Strategies: The Unavoidable Issues' in *World Development* special issue March.

——and H. Rush (1985) *Microelectronics and Clothing: The Impact of Technical Change on a Global Industry* Geneva: ILO.

Hollander, S. (1973) *The Economics of Adam Smith* London: Heinemann.

House of Commons Select Committee on Energy (1984) *Energy Research, Development and Demonstration in the UK* 9th Report, Session 1983/84, HG585, July.

House of Lords/Select Committee on Science and Technology (1983) *Engineering Research and Development* London: HMSO.

Illich, I. (1975) *Tools for Conviviality* London: Fontana.

Irvine, J. and B. Martin (1983) 'Assessing Basic Research: Some Partial Indicators of Scientific Progress in Radio Astronomy' in *Research Policy* Vol 12. No 2. pp.61–90.

——(1984) *Foresight in Science: Picking the Winners* London: Frances Pinter.

——(1984) 'What Direction for Basic Scientific Research?' in M. Gibbons, P. Gummet and B. M. Udgaonkar (eds) *Science and Technology in the 1980s and Beyond* Harlow: Longman.

Jequier, N. (ed) (1976) *Appropriate Technology: Problems and Promises* Paris: Development Centre, OECD.

Jewkes, J.; D. Sawers and R. Stillerman (1969) *The Sources of Invention* rev. edn. London: Macmillan.

Jolly, R., E. de Kadt, H. Singer and F. Wilson (eds) (1973) *Third World Employment* Harmondsworth: Penguin.

Kaldor, M. (1982) *The Baroque Arsenal* London: Deutsch.
Kaplinsky, R. (1980) *Radical Change and Manufactured Export Growth Strategies* IDS University of Sussex (mimeo).
——(1982) *Computer-Aided Design: Electronics, Comparative Advantage and Development* London: Frances Pinter.
Kay, N. M. (1982) *The Evolving Firm* London: Macmillan.
Kennedy, C. and A. Thirlwall (1972) 'Technical Progress: A Survey' in *Economic Journal* Vol 82. March, pp.11–72.
Keynes, J. M. (1961) *The General Theory of Employment, Interest and Money* London: Macmillan.
Koestler, A. (1982) *Bricks to Babel* London: Pan Books, Picador.
Kogan, M. and M. Henkel (1983) *Government and Research* London: Heinemann.
Kondratiev, N. (1978) 'The Major Economic Cycles' reprinted in *Lloyds Bank Review* No 129.
Kuhn, T. S. (1970) *The Structure of Scientific Revolutions* 2nd edn London: Chicago UP.
Kuznets, S. (1963) 'Notes on the Take-Off' in W W Rostow (ed) *The Economics of Take-Off into Self-Sustained Growth* London: Macmillan.

Lakatos, I. (1972) 'Falsification and the Methodology of Scientific Research Programmes' in I. Lakatos and A. Musgrave (eds) *Criticism and the Growth of Knowledge* Cambridge: Cambridge UP pp.91–196.
——and A. Musgrave (eds) (1972) *Criticism and the Growth of Knowledge* London: Cambridge UP.
Lall, S. (1980) 'Developing Countries as Exporters of Industrial Technology' *Research Policy* Vol 9. No 1. January, pp.24–53.
Lancaster, K. J. (1966) 'New Approach to Consumer Theory' *Journal of Political Economy* Vol LXXIV. No 2. pp.132–57.
Landes, D. S. (1976) *The Unbound Prometheus* Cambridge: Cambridge UP.
Leonard, D. (1977) *Reaching the Peasant Farmers* Chicago: University of Chicago Press.
Leontieff, W. (1953) 'Domestic Production and Foreign Trade: The American Capital Position Re-examined' in *Proceedings of the American Philosophical Society* Vol 97.
Lipsey, R. G. (1979) *Positive Economics* 5th edn Weidenfeld and Nicolson.
Livingstone, I. (ed) (1981) *Development Economics and Policy* London: Allen and Unwin.

McClelland, D. C. (1961) *The Achieving Society* New York: Van Nostrand.
MacKerron, G. S. (1984) 'Sizewell: Good Value for Consumers' Money?' *Energy Policy* Vol 12. No 3. September, pp.295–301.
MacLeod, R. (1977) 'Changing Perspectives in the Social History of Science' in I. Spiegel Rosing and D. Price (eds) *Science, Technology and Society* London: Sage pp.149–96.

Magee, B. (1978) *Popper* Glasgow: William Collins.

Mansfield, E. (1961) 'Technical Change and the Rate of Imitation' *Econometrica* Vol 29. No 4. pp.741–66.

—— (1968) *The Economics of Technological Change* London: Longman.

—— (1979) *Micro-Economics Theory and Applications* 3rd edn London: Norton.

—— et al (1971) *Research and Innovation in the Modern Corporation* New York: Norton and London: Macmillan.

Mantoux, P. (1964) *The Industrial Revolution in the Eighteenth Century* New York: University Paperbacks.

Mathias, P. (ed) (1972) *Science and Society 1600–1900* Cambridge: Cambridge UP.

Maxwell, P. M. (1981) *Technology Policy and Firm Learning Effects in Less Developed Countries* DPhil Thesis University of Sussex (SPRU).

Meadows, D. H. and D. L. Meadows et al (1972) *The Limits to Growth* New York: Universe Books.

Mensch, G. (1979) *Stalemate in Technology: Innovations Overcome the Depression* New York: Ballinger.

Minasian, J. R. (1962) 'The Economics of Research and Development' in *The Rate and Direction of Inventive Activity* Princeton: Princeton UP.

Moravcsik, M. (1982) 'The Effectiveness of Research in Developing Countries' *Social Studies of Science* Vol 12. No 1. February, pp.144–46.

Mowery, D. C. and N. Rosenberg (1982) 'The Influence of Market Demand upon Innovation: A Critical Review of some recent Empirical Studies' in N. Rosenberg *Inside the Black Box op cit* pp.193–244.

Murray, R. (1972) 'Underdevelopment, International Firms and the International Division of Labour' in Society for International Development *Towards a New World Economy* Rotterdam UP pp.161–247.

Myint, H. (1971) *The Economics of Developing Countries* London: Hutchinson.

Myrdal, G. (1964) *Economic Theory and Underdeveloped Regions* London: Methuen.

Needham, J. (1954) *Science and Civilisation in China* Cambridge: Cambridge UP.

Nelkin, D. (1977) 'Technology and Public Policy' in Spiegel-Rosing and de Solla Price (eds) *op cit* pp.393–442.

Nelson, R. (1977) *The Moon and the Ghetto: An Essay on Public Policy Analysis* New York: W W Norton.

—— and S. Winter (1977) 'In Search of a Useful Theory of Innovation' in *Research Policy* Vol 6. No 1. January, pp.36–77.

—— (1982) *An Evolutionary Theory of Economic Change* Cambridge: Harvard UP.

Noble, D. (1977) *America by Design* New York: Oxford UP.

Norman, D. W. (1980) 'The Farming Systems Approach: Relevancy for the Small Farmer' *MSU Rural Development Paper* No 5. East Lancing: Department of Agricultural Economics, Michigan State University.

Nurske, R. (1953) *Problems of Capital Formation in Underdeveloped Countries* Oxford: Oxford UP.

OECD (1970) *The Measurement of Scientific and Technical Activities* Paris: OECD DAS/SPR/70.40 (mimeo).

——(1984) *Resources Devoted to R & D* Paris: OECD.

Ohlin, G. (1967) *Population Control and Economic Development* Paris: OECD Development Centre.

Palma, G. (1981) 'Dependency and Development: A Critical Overview' in D. Seers (ed) *Dependency Theory: A Critical Re-assessment* London: Frances Pinter pp.20−78.

Pavitt, K. (1982) 'R & D, Patenting and Innovative Activities: A Statistical Exploration' in *Research Policy* Vol 11. No 1. January, pp.33−52.

——(1983) *Patterns of Technical Change − Evidence, Theory and Policy Implications* Papers in Science, Technology and Public Policy, SPRU.

——(ed) (1980) *Technical Innovation and British Economic Performance* London: Macmillan.

——(forthcoming 1985) 'Sectoral Patterns of Technical Change: Towards a Taxonomy and a Theory' in *Research Policy*.

——and W. Walker (1976) 'Government Policies Towards Industrial Innovation' *Research Policy* Vol 5. No 1. January, pp.11−97.

——and M. Worboys (1977) *Science, Technology and the Modern Industrial State* London: Butterworth, SISCON.

Perez, C. (1983) 'Structural Change and Assimilation of New Technologies in the Economic and Social Systems' in *Futures* October, pp.357−75.

Phillips, A. (1971) *Technology and Market Structure* Lexington: Lexington Books.

Posner, M. (1961) 'International Trade and Technical Change' in *Oxford Economic Papers* Vol 13. No 3. pp.323−41.

Ramos, A. G. (1981) *The New Science of Organisation* Toronto: University of Toronto Press.

Ravetz, J. R. (1973) *Scientific Knowledge and its Social Problems* Harmondsworth: Penguin.

Robinson, J. (1983) *Economic Philosophy* Harmondsworth: Penguin.

——and J. Eatwell (1973) *An Introduction to Modern Economics* London: McGraw Hill.

Roche, M. (1966) 'Social Aspects of Science in a Developing Country' *Impact* UNESCO Vol XVI. No 1. pp.51−60.

Rosegger, G. (1980) *The Economics of Production and Innovation: An Industrial Perspective* Oxford: Pergamon Press.

Rosenberg, N. (ed) (1971) *The Economics of Technological Change* Harmondsworth: Penguin.

——(1976) *Perspectives on Technology* Cambridge: Cambridge UP.

——(1976) 'Science, Invention and Economic Growth' in N. Rosenberg *Perspectives on Technology* Cambridge: Cambridge UP.

——(1982) 'The Historiography of Technical Progress' in N. Rosenberg *Inside the Black Box op cit* Ch1 above pp.3−33.

——(1982) *Inside the Black Box: Technology and Economics* Cambridge: Cambridge UP.

Rosenbrock, H. (1977) 'The Future of Control' in *Automatica* Vol 13. pp.389−92.

Rosenstein-Rodan, P. (1951) 'Notes on the Theory of the Big Push' in H. S. Ellis and H. C. Wallich (eds) *Economic Development for Latin America*.

Rostow, W. W. (1966) *The Stages of Economic Growth* Cambridge: Cambridge UP.

Rothwell, R. and W. Zegveld (1984) *Reindustrialisation and Technology* Harlow: Longman.

Routh, G. (1977) *The Origin of Economic Ideas* London: Macmillan.

———(1984) *Economics: An Alternative Text* London: Macmillan.

Rothschild, Lord (1971) 'The Organisation and Management of Government R & D,' *Framework for Government Research and Development* London: HMSO, Cmnd 4814.

Russell, B. (1952) *The Impact of Science on Society* London: Allen and Unwin.

Sagasti, F. (1978) *Science and Technology for Development* Ottawa: IDRC/STPI/109e.

Sahlins, M. (1976) *Stone Age Economics* London: Tavistock.

Salter, W. E. G. (1966) *Productivity and Technical Change* 2nd edn Cambridge: Cambridge UP.

Scherer, F. (1982) 'Inter Industry Technology Flows in the United States' in *Research Policy* Vol 11. No 4. August, pp.227–46.

Schmookler, J. (1966) *Invention and Economic Growth* Cambridge: Harvard UP.

Schonberger, R. J. (1982) *Japanese Manufacturing Techniques* London: Collier Macmillan.

Schumacher, E. F. (1971) 'Industrialisation through Intermediate Technology' in R. Robinson (ed) *Developing the Third World: The Experience of the Sixties* London: Cambridge UP pp.85–93.

———(1973) *Small is Beautiful* London: Blond and Briggs.

Schumpeter, J. (1947) *Capitalism, Socialism and Democracy* 2nd edn New York: Harper and Row.

———(1961) *The Theory of Economic Development* New York: Oxford UP.

Seers, D. (1970) 'The Stages of Economic Growth of a Primary Producer in the Middle of the 20th Century' in R. I. Rhodes (ed) *Imperialism and Underdevelopment* New York: Monthly Review Press.

———(ed) (1981) *Dependency Theory: A Critical Re-assessment* London: Frances Pinter.

Sen, A. K. (ed) (1970) *Growth Economics* Harmondsworth: Penguin.

Sender, J. and S. Smith (1984) 'What's Right with the Berg Report and What's Left of its Critics?' in *IDS Discussion Paper* University of Sussex June.

Smith, A. (1961) *The Wealth of Nations* Edwin Cannon (ed) London: Methuen.

Smith, S. (1980) 'The Ideas of Samir Amin: Theory or Tautology' in *Journal of Development Studies* Vol 17.

———and J Sender (1983) 'A Reply to Samir Amin' in *Third World Quarterly* Vol 5. No 3. July, pp.650–6.

Soete, L. (forthcoming 1985) 'International Diffusion of Technology, Industrial Development and Technological Leapfrogging' in *World Development*.

———and S Wyatt (1983) 'The Use of Foreign Patenting as an Internationally Comparable Science and Technology Output Indicator' in *Scientometrics* Vol 5. No 1. pp.31–54.

Solow, R. (1957) 'Technical Change and the Aggregate Production Function' in *Review of Economics and Statistics*, Vol 39. August, pp.312–20.

Solla, Price D. de (1965) 'Is Technology Historically Independent of Science?' in *Technology and Culture* Vol VI. No 4. p.553.

Spiegel-Rosing, I. and D. Price (eds) (1977) *Science, Technology and Society* London: Sage.

Stead, H. (1974) *Statistics of Technological Innovation in Industry* Cat. No. 13–555, Statistics, Canada.

—— (1976) 'The Costs of Technological Innovation' in *Research Policy* Vol 5. No 1. pp.2–10.

Stewart, F. (1974) 'Technology and Employment in LDCs' in *World Development* Vol 2. No 3. March, pp.17–46.

—— (1977) *Technology and Development* London: Macmillan.

—— and J. James (eds) (1982) *The Economics of New Technology in Developing Countries* London: Frances Pinter.

Stewart, M. (1972) *Keynes and After* Harmondsworth: Penguin.

Stigler, G. J. (1961) 'Economic Problems in Measuring Changes in Productivity' in NBER *Output, Input and Productivity Measurement* Princeton: Princeton UP.

Sutcliffe, R. B. (1971) *Industry and Underdevelopment* London: Addison Wesley.

Tawney, R. H. (1961) *Religion and the Rise of Capitalism* Harmondsworth: Penguin.

Thompson, E. P. (1968) *The Making of the English Working Class* Harmondsworth: Penguin.

Trevithick, J. (1979) *Inflation* Harmondsworth: Penguin.

UNCTAD (1972) *Major Issues Arising from the Transfer of Technology to Developing Countries* Geneva: TD/B/AC.11/10 18th December.

UN National Science Board (1983) *Science Indicators, 1982* UN: Washington.

Vaitsos, C. (1974) *Intercountry Income Distribution and Transnational Enterprises* Oxford: Clarendon Press.

Walker, W. B. (1979) *Industrial Innovation and International Trading Performance* Greenwich: Jai Press.

Walsh, V. (1984) 'Invention and Innovation in the Chemicals Industry: Demand Pull or Discovery Push' in *Research Policy* Vol 13. No 4. August, pp.211–34.

Ward, B. (1972) *What's Wrong with Economics* New York: Basic Books; London: Macmillan.

Warren, B. (1980) *Imperialism, Pioneer of Capitalism* London: Verso.

Weber, M. (1930) *The Protestant Ethic and the Spirit of Capitalism* London: Allen and Unwin.

Weeks, J. (1973) 'Does Employment Matter?' in R. Jolly et al *op cit* pp.61–5.

Williams, R. (1980) *The Nuclear Power Decisions* London: Croom Helm.

—— (1983/84) 'British Technology Policy' *Government and Opposition* Winter pp.30–51.

World Bank (1981) *Accelerated Development in Sub-Saharan Africa: An Agenda for Action* Washington.

World Bank (1981) *World Bank Development Report* Washington DC: Oxford UP.

INDEX